FIND IT FAST . . . FIND IT EASILY

From *amortization* to *zone pricing*, this compact, on-target business dictionary was created specifically for those who need to know specialized business terms. General-use dictionaries do not include all of these phrases and abbreviations and do not provide the particular meanings related just to business.

Lightweight and portable, THE INSTANT BUSINESS DICTIONARY provides rapid access to important terms used daily in banking, real estate, commerce, corporate management, stock trading, sales, manufacturing, construction, transportation, taxes, public service agencies, and other business fields. It is an essential source book for every competitive student or business professional.

DON'T MISS THESE OTHER LAUREL INSTANT REFERENCE WORKS

INSTANT QUOTATION DICTIONARY

INSTANT SPELLING DICTIONARY

INSTANT SYNONYMS AND ANTONYMS

INSTANT ENGLISH HANDBOOK

Instant
Business
Dictionary

Compiled by
Lewis E. Davids, PH.D.
Hill Professor of Bank Management
University of Missouri

A LAUREL BOOK
Published by
Dell Publishing
a division of
Bantam Doubleday Dell Publishing Group, Inc.
666 Fifth Avenue
New York, New York 10103

ISBN: 0-440-20535-2

Reprinted by arrangement with Career Publishing, Inc.

Printed in the United States of America
Published simultaneously in Canada

August 1990

10 9 8 7 6 5 4 3 2 1

RAD

PURPOSE OF THIS BOOK

This dictionary is designed to clearly define special words or terms commonly used in business but which are not commonly defined in regular dictionaries.

To provide the definitions, many sources were consulted. Where a definition has been provided by an outside source, this fact is indicated by the use of a boldface number immediately following the definition. By referring to the numbered list of sources on page 332, the source or authority for the definition can readily be determined. The code number also is of help when a word or phrase has more than one meaning depending upon the field of business in which it is used. The code identifies the source and thus the field.

Where a term was not defined by an authoritative source or where it was not uniformly defined in various texts, the definitions were provided by the editor-author. Nonnumbered terms fall in this category.

Since the terms have been brought together from many sources, there is some variation in the approach and style of the various contributors. This in no way diminishes the use or value of the definitions. In only a very few cases, where trade names or institutional names have been used by the defining contributor, has the editor deemed it prudent to delete such designation.

A good number of the definitions have been "tested" by reference and review by professors of business administration and economics at several institutions of higher learning. However, it would be inappropriate to designate anyone but the editor as responsible for the selection of the terms included herein. In any study which covers a vast range of material such as this does, it is not only possible, but is probable, that some terms may have one meaning in one geographic area and a different connotation in another. This book should tend to reduce such a tendency and lead to greater conformity of meaning.

The editor is deeply grateful to the cooperating associations, companies, and individuals who have given permission to quote from their works and whose terms are included in this book.

Lewis E. Davids, PH.D.
Hill Professor, University of Missouri
Columbia, Missouri 65201

A

abandonment 1) The elimination from use of a fixed asset. **1**
2) The relinquishing of salvage to the insurers with a view to claiming the full amount of insurance. **57**
3) The relinquishment of a property right by voluntary surrender or neglect.

abatement Complete or partial cancellation of amounts levied or of charges made for services. See "levy." **29**

ability-to-pay concept Idea that those with more wealth or income should proportionally pay more than those with less wealth or income. The progressive tax on income is one example of this idea. A surgeon charging a rich patient much more for an identical operation than he charges a poor patient is another example.

abrasion The reduction of the weight of a coin. Under Gresham's Law there is the tendency for abrased coins to circulate more rapidly than unabrased coins.

abrogation The process of annulment by some authority such as the enactment of a law.

absolute advantage A condition in which an individual, country, district, or company can make or sell a product below the cost of another. See "comparative advantage."

abstinence theory Concept that presumes a postponement in the use of a good involves a cost that should be reimbursed by a payment such as interest.

abstract of title A brief statement of the legal evidences of real estate ownership. An abstract of title gives the history of a parcel of land, starting with the original grant and following through each transfer of title to the present titleholder. It also recites all mortgages outstanding on the property and any defects that would cause a cloud on the title. See "cloud on title." **33**

accelerated amortization 1) A writing off of the cost of a machine or facility in a shorter period of time than has been customary for the item. This technique reduces income taxes during the period and has been permitted by the federal government as an incentive to production of needed items.
2) Where payment date of the principal of a debt (such as a mortgage) is accelerated by special agreement.

7

acceleration clause A clause in a note, bond, or mortgage which provides that in the event of a default by the debtor the entire balance outstanding shall become due and payable.　**33**

acceleration premium Wage plan in which increased production by workers results in an increased rate of pay.

acceleration principle Economic concept that a stated change in the rate of consumption sales under certain circumstances will cause a greater proportionate change in purchases and production of capital goods.

acceptance 1) Agreeing to an offer made.
2) A time draft (bill of exchange) on the face of which the drawee has written the word "accepted," the date it is payable, usually the place where it is payable, and his signature. Thus an acceptance is an obligation which the drawee has agreed to pay at maturity. After accepting the draft, the drawee is known as the acceptor. See "bank acceptance" and "trade acceptance."　**25**

acceptance credit That type of credit which is the result of the substitution of the credit of a more widely known organization such as that of a bank for the credit of a lesser known firm or individual such as a bank's customer or a trade customer. The substitution comes when the bank or other firm "accepts" the commercial paper of its customer.

acceptance liability The total liability which the bank assumes when accepting negotiable instruments drawn upon it by its customers. A record of the instruments so accepted is usually maintained in account form for each customer in a separate ledger, termed the acceptance liability ledger.　**1**

acceptance supra protest The agreement by an individual or company, other than the debtor named in a protested note, to pay the note.

accession 1) The process whereby property which belongs to one person becomes the property of another by reason of its being added to or incorporated with the property of the latter.　**5**
2) Attainment to an office; elevation.

accessorial service A service rendered by a carrier in addition to a transportation service, such as assorting, packing, precooling, heating, storage, substitution of tonnage, etc.　**19**

accessory equipment Those industrial goods that do not become part of the physical product and which are exhausted only after repeated use, such as major installations, or installation equipment, and auxiliary accessories, or auxiliary equipment.　　**13**

accidental death benefit Provision for payment of an additional amount in the event death results from an accidental cause or means. See "double indemnity, health and accident" and "double indemnity, life."　　**42**

accidental means The unexpected or undesigned cause of an accident. The "means" which caused the mishap must be accidental in order to claim policy benefits.　　**43**

accommodation bill of lading A bill of lading issued by a common carrier prior to receipt of the goods for shipment.

accommodation endorsement When a person signs or endorses a note or draft solely for the purpose of inducing a bank to lend money to a borrower whose credit is not substantial enough to warrant a loan, such an endorsement is called an accommodation endorsement. The endorser, while being liable to repay the amount in full, ordinarily does not expect to do so. He derives no benefit from the transaction, but acts as a guarantor or surety for the borrower. Another form of accommodation endorsement is the practice among banks of endorsing the acceptances of other banks for a fee, in order to make them acceptable for purchase in the acceptance market.　　**1**

accommodation line An insurance company at times will accept from an agent or broker whose entire account is satisfactory, business which would ordinarily be rejected on a strict underwriting basis. Such business is known as an "accommodation line." Insurance that, by itself, would not be acceptable to an insurer, written as an accommodation where the possibility of securing other desirable business seems to justify it.　　**50, 51**

accommodation paper A note or similar obligation the payment of which is guaranteed by some party other than the one who receives the benefit. Thus, before advancing funds, a bank may require the endorsement of a director of known means upon the note of a corporation of doubtful strength.　　**25**

accord and satisfaction The settlement of a dispute by an executed agreement between the parties whereby the aggrieved party accepts something different from his original right or claim.

account A contract arrangement, written or unwritten, to purchase and take delivery, payment to be made later as arranged; also a record of a transaction. **59**

accountabilities Those items for which a person, firm, or corporation must render an account, although he or it may not be personally liable for them. For example, an official is responsible for the cash and other assets under his control and must account for them. Moreover, even if a trustee has disbursed all funds confided to his care and has relieved himself of liability, he is still obligated to account for them and the items are, therefore, accountabilities. **29**

account analysis The process of analyzing an account to determine activity, the size of the balance at given times, the cost of handling transactions on the account, the profit and loss on the account, etc. **34**

accountant An individual who is competent in accounting, systems, audits, balance sheets, profit and loss statements, and bookkeeping. Some accountants are Certified or Registered Public Accountants.

account balance The difference between the debit and the credit sides of an account. **16**

accounting The art of recording, classifying, and summarizing in a significant manner and in terms of money, transactions and events which are, in part at least, of a financial character, and interpreting the results thereof. **17**

accounting classifications Uniform system of accounts prescribed by some authority such as a governmental agency or recommended by a trade association or other authoritative group.

accounting period A time interval at the end of which an analysis is made of the information contained in the bookkeeping records. It is also the period of time covered by the profit and loss statement. It may be any length of time desired, but it is usually a month, three months, six months, or a year. **16**

account in trust An account opened by an individual to be held in trust and maintained for the benefit of another. In the absence of a legally constituted trust fund, withdrawals from the account are subject to the approval of the party establishing the account. An example is an educational fund established by an individual for the benefit of a minor. **1**

accounts payable A current liability representing the amount owed by an individual or a business to a creditor for merchandise or services purchased on open account or short-term credit. **1**

accounts receivable 1) Money owed by customers for merchandise sold to them on open account—that is, without the giving of a note or other evidence of debt.

2) Any amount owed to a business by a customer, any other individual, or another business on a current account.

accretion The increase or extension of the boundaries, or the acquisition of land by the gradual or imperceptible action of natural forces as by the washing up of sand or soil from the sea or a river, or by a gradual recession of the water from the usual watermark. **22**

accrual basis A method of keeping accounts that shows expenses incurred and income earned for a given fiscal period, even though such expenses and income have not been actually paid or received in cash. **16**

accrue 1) To be gained or obtained; to proceed, arise, or come from; such as, a profit or loss accrues from a commercial transaction.

2) As applied to a right, to come into existence as an enforceable claim; as, a cause of action has accrued when the right to sue has become vested and exercisable. **22**

accrued expense Expense incurred but not yet paid. **16**

accrued income Income earned but not yet collected. **16**
See "asset, accrued."

accrued interest Interest earned but not collected. **23**

accumulated dividend The amount of money due the equity holder which has not been paid.

accumulated earnings tax An additional tax imposed on corporations which allow earnings to accumulate instead of distributing them as dividends in order to avoid payment of tax in high brackets by individual stockholders. Every corporation may accumulate up to $100,000 over a period of years without risk of this special tax. That cumulative amount, plus whatever additional amount is necessary to be retained for the reasonable needs of the business, is allowed as a credit against the taxable income. Only the remainder of undistributed income can be subjected to the accumulated earnings tax.

accumulation 1) Percentage addition to policy benefits as a reward to the insured for continuous renewal. The opposite of the term "amortization." **5**

11

2) The purchase of a security or securities in such a way that securities are obtained without causing the price to materially increase. The purchase orders are frequently executed when the market is soft and on the down side. If the orders to purchase are expertly executed the price is not "run up" and additional accumulation may be made at relatively favorable prices.

3) The spread between the face amount of a bond and the discount price.

acid test The ratio between the quick assets and the current liabilities; an indication of the ability of a business to pay all of its current liabilities quickly in cash. It is also known as the "quick ratio." **16**

acknowledgment 1) A formal declaration made by a person before a competent officer, a notary public, or a court to the effect that he has executed an instrument. **33**

2) The certificate of such a declaration.

across-the-board A uniform action such as granting all employees a wage increase of the same amount per hour or the same percent of their wage per hour.

active trade balance Favorable balance of trade.

active trust A trust regarding which the trustee has some active duty to perform; opposed to bare, naked, or passive trust. **22**

act of God An accident or event that is the result of natural causes, without any human intervention or agency, that could not have been prevented by reasonable foresight or care, such as floods, lightning, earthquake, or storms. **50**

acts of bankruptcy Any act enumerated under Section 3 of the National Bankruptcy Act, the most common being the inability to pay debts as they mature of not less than $1,000 and voluntarily appearing in a bankruptcy court or by involuntary bankruptcy in which creditors who are unpaid petition the bankruptcy court.

actuarial assumptions Estimates of future experience with respect to the rates of mortality, disability, turnover, ages at retirement, rate of investment, income, and salary trends. Such estimates are generally determined from past experience, modified for possible changes in conditions which may affect the future experience. **32**

actuarial valuation A mathematical determination of the financial condition of a retirement plan. It includes the computation of the present monetary value of benefits payable to present members, and the present monetary value of future employer and employee contributions, giving effect to mortality among active and retired members and also to the rates of disability, retirement, withdrawal from service, salary, and interest. **32**

actuary A professional expert in pension and life insurance matters, particularly trained in mathematical, statistical, and accounting methods and procedures, and in insurance probabilities. **32**

addition An addition to a fixed asset already recorded in the property ledger (as distinguished from a newly acquired asset). Examples are additional floor space added to an existing building, and new attachments to a piece of equipment. **1**

additional extended coverage An endorsement for policies covering dwellings and similar property, extending the coverage to include insurance against direct loss caused by water damage from plumbing and heating systems, rupture or bursting of steam or hot water heating systems, vandalism and malicious mischief, vehicles owned or operated by the insured or by a tenant, glass breakage, ice, snow, and freezing, as well as fall of trees, and collapse. **5**

adjudication The decision of a competent court with regard to matters in dispute; to be distinguished from arbitration. **22**

adjustable currency See "elastic money."

adjusted trial balance A merger of the trial balance columns of the work sheet with the adjustment columns. The adjusted trial balance represents the trial balance that would be obtained if it were prepared immediately after the adjusting entries are posted. **16**

adjuster An individual who acts for the company or the insured in the settlement of claims. He leads to agreement about the amount of a loss and the company's liability. Adjusters may be salaried employees of adjusting organizations operated by insurance companies, individuals operating independently and engaged by the companies to adjust a particular loss, and special agents or staff adjusters employed by the company. The term "claim representative" is used interchangeably. Not to be confused with public adjusters who represent claimants only. **50, 52**

adjusting entries Those entries made in a journal at the end of

13

an accounting period to correct errors that have been found and to assign expenses and income to the correct time period by such devices as use of deferred charges and prepaid expenses.

ad litem For the purpose of the suit; for the duration of a suit.

administered price A price which is not the result of the full play of supply and demand but rather has been arrived at by some restraints such as monopoly, duopoly, oligopoly, or government action.

administration 1) Direction and evaluation by supervisory personnel including both administrative duties and administrative functions. **42**

2) The care and management of an estate by an executor, an administrator, a trustee, or a guardian. **30**

administrative expense Expenses chargeable to the managerial, general administrative and policy phases of a business in contrast to sales, manufacturing, or cost of goods expense.

administrative law As distinguished from common law or statute law, administrative law results from the regulations of a governmental body, either state or federal, which is responsible for carrying out statute law.

administrator A person or an institution appointed by a court to settle an estate when the decedent has left no will, when no executor has been named in the will if the decedent has left one, or when the named executor has died or is unwilling to serve. **25**

admiralty court A court having jurisdiction on maritime questions and offenses, including suits involving marine insurance contracts and general average adjustments. **52**

admission by investment Term meaning that a new partner is admitted into a partnership by contributing additional cash to the business, thereby increasing the assets and the proprietorship of the business. **16**

admission temporaire The free entry of dutiable goods for the purpose of processing the goods for export.

admitted company A company is termed "admitted" within a given state when licensed to do business in that state. An insurer of another state or country licensed under the insurance law of a state to do business in that state. **50, 51**

admitted to dealings Official approval by an exchange and the SEC to a security whereby it is "admitted to the list"; *i.e.,* the security has the privilege of being traded on the particular exchange to which it is admitted.

ad valorem Designates an assessment of taxes or duties against property or goods. Literally, "according to the value." Ad valorem duties are those estimated at a percentage of the value of the goods.

advance 1) A loan.

2) An increase in price.

3) A payment on account.

advance bill A bill of exchange drawn in advance of the shipment of goods.

adverse possession A possession inconsistent with the right of the true owner. **5**

advertising The practice of bringing to the public's notice the good qualities of something in order to induce the public to buy or invest in it. **38**

advertising agency A business which prepares advertising for its customers and performs other related services such as market research.

advertising media The means through which advertisements are conveyed to the consumers or users whom they are designed to influence. Magazines, newspapers, radio, television, and direct mail are all media.

affecting commerce The standard for determining National Labor Relations Board jurisdiction—a dispute must be one that "affects commerce."

affidavit A statement in writing sworn to before a person authorized by law to take oaths; it is made without cross-examination and in this respect differs from a deposition. **35**

affiliated company Under the Investment Company Act, a company in which there is any direct or indirect ownership of 5 percent or more of the outstanding voting securities. **3**

affinity Relationship by marriage; to be distinguished from consanguinity. **30**

afforestation Planting trees on land that has not recently been forest.

affreightment A bill of lading. A contract to transport goods by sea; either a charter party or a bill of lading. **51**

after-acquired clause That portion of a mortgage which states that any additional property which the mortgagor acquires after the mortgage is drawn will also be security for the loan.

15

age change In insurance, the date halfway between natural birth dates when the age of an individual, for the purpose of life insurance rating, changes to the next higher age, insurance age being the nearer birthday. Annuity age is commonly the last previous birthday. **58**

agency 1) The status or the relation between an agent and his principal.
2) A term used to describe certain types of accounts in trust institutions. The main distinguishing characteristic of an agency is that the title to the property does not pass to the trust institution but remains in the name of the owner of the property, who is known as the principal. See "agent." **30**

agency coupled with an interest An agency in which the agent has a legal interest in the subject matter of the agency. Such an agency is not terminated, as are other agencies, by the death of the principal but continues until the agent can realize upon his legal interest. **30**

agency shop A form of union security under which all employees, nonmembers as well as members of a union, pay union dues as a condition of employment. **12**

agent A person who is authorized to act for or represent another person (usually called the principal) in dealing with a third party. **31**

agents' qualification laws Laws which each state passes, setting up standards of specific knowledge and qualification that an agent must meet in order to be legally permitted to practice certain professions and occupations in that state. *i.e.,* brokers, agents, factors.

aggregate corporation An incorporated venture having more than one stockholder.

aggregate-of-intermediates clause A provision in Section 4 of the Interstate Commerce Act which prohibits a through rate higher than the sum of intermediate rates except as authorized by the Commission after investigation. **19**

aggregative economics See "macroeconomics."

aggressive portfolio A securities portfolio held primarily for appreciation rather than for defensive quality or yield possibility. **44**

aging accounts receivable The process of analyzing each customer's account to determine how old each unpaid charge is.

It is one basis for determining the estimate of bad debts expense. See "accounts receivable." **16**

agio A premium in the form of interest or some other valued differential. Full-bodied gold coins of two different nations might be identical in weight and fineness, yet not be traded at identical prices in the foreign exchange markets due to the market preference for one compared to the other. The differential is the agio.

agreed-amount clause Policy provision in which the holder agrees to carry a stated or determinable amount of insurance. An amount of insurance specified in the contract as being sufficient to nullify the effect of a coinsurance, average, or contribution clause of the contract. **51**

agricultural ladder Concept that farm laborers may advance by progressive steps into sharecroppers, then tenant farmers, and finally into owners and operators of farms.

agricultural paper Those acceptances, notes, and similar documents which have arisen out of agricultural, farming, or ranching transactions rather than trade, commerce, or industry.

agricultural parity See "parity."

agricultural revolution That period during the 19th and 20th centuries in which great strides were taken which resulted in higher yields as a result of application of the scientific method to farming. This included such factors as mechanization of farm implements, seed control, use of fertilizers, and irrigation.

airedale Slang expression for a fast-moving, slick-talking, sharply dressed, high-pressure salesman such as might be associated with a highly speculative firm.

air rights The rights vested by grant (fee simple, lease agreement, or other conveyance) of an estate in real property to build upon, occupy, or use, in the manner and degree permitted, all or any portion of space above the ground or any other stated elevation without vertical planes, the basis of which corresponds with the boundaries of the real estate described in the grant. **54**

aleatory contract The parties to a contract realize that the values given up by each party will not be equal. When such is the fact, it is an "aleatory contract."

alien company A company incorporated and existing under the laws of a foreign country.

all-commodity rate A freight rate, usually a carload rate, applying to a shipment regardless of the nature of the commodities included, subject to stated exceptions and conditions; also called all-freight rate.   **19**

allocation The crediting of a receipt in its entirety or the charging of a disbursement in its entirety to one account, as to the principal account or to the income account; to be distinguished from apportionment.   **30**

allonge A piece of paper attached to a negotiable instrument so that additional endorsements may be added.

allotment A share, part, or portion granted or distributed.   **38**

allowance for bad debts Same as "Reserve for Bad Debts"; an account for showing the estimated loss on uncollectible debts as an offset against the value shown for accounts receivable.   **16**

allowance for depreciation An account recording the accumulation of periodical credits made to reduce the value of fixed assets as a result of depreciation. See "depreciation."

allowed time That amount of time that employers permit their employees to have for such purposes as adjusting their machines, taking care of personal needs, etc., when the employees are on a piecework basis.

alloy That combination of base metal such as copper, zinc, or tin which is added to precious metals such as silver or gold to provide against abrasion.

alteration 1) A change or rearrangement in the structural parts of something.
2) Applied to a building or structure, alteration is a change or rearrangement in the structural parts or in the exit facilities; or an enlargement, whether by extending on a side or by increasing in height; including work, other than repairs, that would affect safety or a vital element of an elevator, plumbing, gas piping, wiring, ventilating or heating installation; the term "alter" in its various moods and tenses and its participial forms, refers to the making of an alteration.   **11**
3) Any change involving an erasure or rewriting in the date, amount, or payee of a check or other negotiable instrument. In accounting records, necessary alterations are best made by

18

crossing out the "old" figure, leaving it legible, and writing the correct one above or below the original.   **23**

amalgamation The uniting or combining of two or more businesses.   **44**

American Experience Table of Mortality A listing by age of the probable death rates among insurance risks.

American Federation of Labor and Congress of Industrial Organizations The national labor organization in the United States made up of national, international and local unions.

American Stock Exchange A leading securities exchange located in New York City. Formerly known as the Outdoor Market or New York Curb Exchange because it initially conducted operations outdoors at Wall and Hanover Streets. Moved indoors at 86 Trinity Place in 1921. Present name was adopted in 1953. It is the largest market for foreign securities in the United States.   **44**

amortization The gradual reduction of a debt by means of periodic payments sufficient to meet current interest and extinguish the debt at maturity. When the debt involves real property, often the periodic payments include a sum sufficient to pay taxes and insurance on the property. In connection with bond investment, the gradual extinguishment of a premium or a discount until the book value of the bond is equal to par value at maturity or at the earliest call date, as the case may be.   **34**

amortized mortgage A mortgage payable in installments, usually monthly, both as to principal and interest.   **35**

amortized value The investment value of a security determined by the process of amortization. This value is appropriate for use in connection with bonds which are fully secured and are not in default as to either principal or interest.   **42**

anarchism The abolishment of ownership of private property and of coercive government.

ancestor One who precedes another in the line of descent. At common law the term ancestor applied only to a person in the direct line of ascent (father, grandfather, or other forebear), but by statute it has been broadened to apply also to a person of collateral relationship (uncle or aunt, for example) from whom property has been acquired.   **30**

ancillary Subordinate or auxiliary; used in such terms as ancillary administration, ancillary administrator, and ancillary guardian.   **30**

annual report 1) The yearly report made by a company at the close of the fiscal year, stating the company's receipts and disbursements, assets and liabilities. Such a statement usually includes an account of the progress made by the company during the year.   **50**

2) The annual report, as of December 31, of an insurer to the state insurance department, showing assets and liabilities, receipts and disbursements, and other information.   **51**

annual return See "yield."

annual wage The rate of pay for one year's work including such agreed upon time off for vacation and/or sick leave.

annuitant The beneficiary of an annuity.   **22**

annuity A series of periodic payments for a fixed future period or for life, payable monthly, semiannually, annually, or at other specified intervals. It is frequently used to describe a part of the retirement allowance derived from the accumulated contributions made by the member, as distinguished from that part of the retirement allowance financed by employer's contributions which is called a "pension."   **32**

annuity, apportionable An annuity that provides for a pro rata fractional payment covering the period from the date of the last regular premium payment to the date of death.   **5**

annuity bond An investment, usually one not providing a maturity date.   **42**

annuity, cash refund A life annuity with an agreement that the insurer, on the death of the annuitant, will pay in a lump sum to a beneficiary any amount by which the consideration paid to the insurer exceeds the payments made to the annuitant.   **51**

annuity certain An annuity payable for a specified period of time, regardless of the time of death of the annuitant.   **32**

annuity, deferred An annuity under which payments will begin at some specified future date provided the specified beneficiary is alive at such date.   **32**

annuity, equity Term formerly used for variable annuities. The annuity is based on investments mostly in common stocks which are not guaranteed as to income or liquidation value but are expected or intended to provide a hedge against the impact of inflation on the purchasing power of the fixed annuities.   **5**

20

annuity, group A pension plan providing annuities at retirement to a group of persons under a master contract. It is usually issued to an employer for the benefit of employees. The individual members of the group hold certificates as evidence of their coverage. The most common type of group annuity provides for the purchase each year of a paid-up deferred annuity for each member, the total amount received by the member at retirement being the sum of these deferred annuities. Another type is the deposit administration plan. **53**

annuity, variable An annuity in which the insurance company agrees to pay an amount of money to the beneficiary. The amount will vary with the value of equities purchased as investments by the insurance companies. Most annuities are fixed as to the annual amount of payment but the variable annuity is not. Proponents of variable annuities believe that they provide a better hedge against inflation than the fixed annuities; however, variable annuities are not permitted to be sold in many states. See "annuity, equity." **5**

antagonistic cooperation The theory that holds that individuals work together and suppress their antagonisms because it is mutually advantageous.

antedated The insertion of a past date on a legal instrument. Some insurance policies are antedated so that the purchaser may come under the premium rates for one year younger individuals. Insurance is written on an attained age basis. By antedating a policy (and paying for the antedated period) a person may achieve savings over the life of the policy provided the antedated period is relatively short.

anticipated acceptance An acceptance which is paid prior to the stated terms of payment.

anticipation rate A discount or rebate for payment prior to the stated terms of payment.

anticipation, right of The privilege given the mortgagor, by a provision in the mortgage instruments, to pay all or any portion of the outstanding balance of the obligation prior to its due date without penalty. **33**

antidumping duty A tariff provision which penalizes attempts by an exporter to sell goods which have been priced at a lower rate in the recipient country than they sell for in the nation which has produced the goods.

anti-injunction law (Norris-LaGuardia Act) A federal statute restricting the use of injunctions by federal courts in labor disputes. Many state statutes have used this act as a model.

anti-racketeering act Federal statute forbidding robbery or extortion that affects interstate commerce.

anti-strikebreaking act (Byrnes Act) Federal law which prohibits interstate transportation of strikebreakers.

antitrust Opposed to trusts or large combinations of capital. **38**

any-quantity rate A rate applying on a weight basis but without regard to carload minimum weights, and applicable to any quantity of freight tendered. **19**

apportioned tax The distribution of a tax by the collecting unit among other governmental units.

apportionment clause A clause found in an insurance policy which distributes the insurance in proportion to the total coverage. Thus, you may have two $1,000 fire insurance policies on a building and one of them provides extended coverage against windstorm and the other does not. In the event of a $100 loss from a windstorm, you would only receive $50 or 50% of the loss. If both policies had provided this extended coverage, you would receive full payment, however, of the loss. **52**

appraisal 1) Evaluation of a specific piece of personal or real property, or the property of another as a whole.
2) The value placed on the property evaluated. **1**

appraisal clause A clause in an insurance policy which provides that the insured or the insurance company shall have the right to demand an appraisal to fix or determine the amount of damage in terms of money. This would also refer to loss as well as damage. **52**

appraisal surplus The excess of appraised values over book values. **54**

appraise Estimate the value. **38**

appraised value The values arrived at in an appraisal of property. **22**

appreciation The increase in the value of an asset in excess of its depreciable cost due to economic and other conditions, as distinguished from increases in value due to improvements or additions made to it. **1**

apprentice A worker serving a special training period in preparation to admission to full status as a skilled tradesman.

appropriation An authorized sum of money set aside, frequently in a separate fund, to pay certain known or anticipated costs of a given item or service. **1**

appurtenance Something belonging or attached to something else and passing as incident to the principal thing; as, a right-of-way (the appurtenance) over land (the principal thing). **30**

arbitrage The buying of stocks, bonds, or other securities in one market and selling in another. **22**

arbitration The hearing and determination of a controversy between parties by a person or persons chosen by the parties, or appointed under statutory authority, instead of hearing and determination by a judicial tribunal.

arbitration clause A provision in a contract requiring that disputes arising out of or relating to the collective bargaining agreement be finally determined by arbitration. **18**

arbitration of exchange The prices of bills of exchange payable in foreign currency vary in different financial centers in the world. Therefore, a person in country A may find it profitable to purchase a bill of exchange in country B for payment in country C. This is arbitration of exchange.

area agreement A collective-bargaining agreement covering a given physical or geographical region, its terms and conditions governing all companies which participate. **12**

area-wide bargaining Negotiation between a single union and the management of different companies in that skill or trade within a geographic area such as a state or section.

arithmetic mean A general or simple average obtained by adding the total value of the items and dividing that total by the number of items.

Armstrong Investigation A study in 1905 that was made in New York on practices of life insurance companies. As a result certain broad changes were enacted not only in New York but in many other states regulating such things as policy forms and provisions which were recommended by the committee. **5**

array A series of items arranged in a meaningful pattern. **41**

arrears Amounts past due and unpaid. A bond or preferred stock is "in arrears" when interest or dividends have fallen due but have not been paid. **3**

arrival notice A notice furnished to the consignee of the arrival of freight.

arson The willful and malicious burning of property; if someone deliberately sets fire to a property, that is arson. If an individual carries fire insurance the damage will be paid for under the terms of the policy just as though the fire had started accidentally; however, if it can be proved that the insured himself was the arsonist, that is, he started the fire himself or had someone do it for him for the purposes of collecting damages, the insurance is automatically voided.   **52**

articles of association A certificate similar to one of incorporation which is used by non-stock companies such as charitable, eleemosynary and mutual corporations. It sets forth the pertinent data on the organization and is filed with the appropriate governmental agencies upon approval and becomes part of the public record.

articles of copartnership The written agreement by which a partnership is formed.   **16**

articles of incorporation A certificate of incorporation which sets forth the pertinent data on a corporation. The certificate is filed with the appropriate governmental agencies upon approval and becomes part of the public record.

as is Goods which are sold "as is" have not the usual implied warranties and may be damaged or shopworn; for these reasons the prices are usually lowered from the regular prices.

asked price 1) That price at which a commodity or security is offered for sale either over the counter or on an exchange.
2) In the case of open-end shares, the price (including the selling charge or load) at which the buyer may purchase stock from the investment company. In the case of closed-end shares, the lowest price at which the stock is then offered for sale in the public market.   **3**

assay office A place designated for the testing of ore, commodities, and bullion as well as foreign coin.

assented securities Securities whose holders have agreed to some change in the terms or status of the securities.

assessable securities Securities such as common stock or classified A or B stock for which stockholders may be forced to pay an amount over the par value. Few securities since the Banking Acts of the 1930's have this liability. Prior to that time it was found in securities issued by national banks.

assessed valuation A valuation set upon real estate or other property by a government as a basis for levying taxes or for condemnation purposes.

24

assessment 1) A share of expenses.

2) The attempt to raise additional capital by making a levy on a security, the assumption being that without assessment for additional capital the corporation will experience difficulties but with additional capital the projected success of the corporation will more than compensate for the levy.

3) An appraisal or estimate.

assessment roll In the case of real property, the official list containing the legal description of each parcel of property and its assessed valuation. In the case of other property, the official list containing the name and address of each owner of such property and its assessed value. **29**

assessor The designated public official who makes the official estimate of value. **5**

asset Anything owned by a business or by an individual which has commercial or exchange value. Assets may consist of specific property or of claims against others, in contrast to obligations due to others (liabilities). **25**

asset, accrued Assets arising from revenues earned but not yet due, such as unbilled utility sales accrued since bills were last rendered to customers and accrued interest on investments. See "accrue." **29**

asset, capital Those assets which are not readily convertible into cash and in the ordinary course of business are not so converted, more often termed fixed assets. **15**

asset, current Those assets which are readily convertible into cash without substantial loss; included are cash, investments, notes and accounts receivable, and inventories. **15**

asset, dead Those assets which are not productive of income under normal operations. A standby machine tool or a high-cost facility that is not used except in emergencies is a dead asset during those periods it is not in use.

asset, deferred Assets which are not readily convertible into cash, or subject to current settlement. **19**

asset enter mains Any asset which is readily liquidatable and thus can be used to meet current claims.

asset, fixed Assets of a long-term character which are intended to continue to be held or used, such as land, buildings, machinery, furniture, and other equipment. The term does not indicate the immobility of an asset which is the distinctive characteristic of "fixture." See "asset, capital." **29**

asset, floating A quick asset such as cash, government bonds or prime listed securities.

asset, frozen Any asset which cannot be used by its owner because of legal action. The owner cannot use it, nor can he dispose of the asset until the process of the law has been completed and a decision passed down from the courts. **1**

asset, hypothecated Things pledged without transferring possession or title. **38**

asset, intangible Something to which a business enterprise attaches an arbitrary dollar value, not because it has real value in itself but because it helps to produce real values in a going business. Patents, trademarks, service marks, franchises, and goodwill are examples of intangible assets.

asset, liquid Those assets, generally current assets, which may be quickly turned into cash.

asset, nominal An asset whose value is inconsiderable, doubtful or difficult to evaluate such as judgments or claims in reorganization. Accounting conventions generally recommend that nominal assets be written down and carried at some token value. The customary amount is one dollar. This calls attention to the asset but also conservatively values it. Goodwill, copyrights and such assets may be considered at times to be nominal assets.

asset, quick Those current assets which can be immediately converted to cash; does not include inventories or other current assets that might take some time to convert to cash.

asset, tangible Those assets which are of a physical and material nature (perceptible to touch) as distinguished from intangible assets which are imperceptible to touch. Examples of tangible assets are: Cash, land, buildings, etc. **1**

asset value per share, net With regard to investment companies, this is the ratio of the current asset value of securities held in the portfolio minus all liabilities divided by the number of shares outstanding. This figure is computed at least once daily by investment companies and indicates investment progress. A load charge, or commission, is added to this net asset value per share to get the selling price of most mutual fund shares. **44**

asset, wasting Assets which are exhausted through use or lose their value through the passage of time, such as oil wells, mining claims, and patents. **22**

assigned account An account, such as an accounts receivable account, which has been assigned to a bank as security for a loan by the borrower. In theory, the bank actually takes possession of the account pledged, and when this account is paid by the borrower's customer, it should be paid directly to the bank to reduce the borrower's loan. In actual practice, and in order not to jeopardize the relationship between the borrower and his customer (whose account has been pledged), the bank will allow the account to be paid by the borrower in the normal manner, and rely upon the integrity of the borrower to apply this payment against the loan balance.   **1**

assigned risk A risk which insurance underwriters do not care to insure but which, because of state law or otherwise, must be insured. The insurance is, therefore, handled through a pool of insurers and assigned to companies in turn.   **50**

assignee One to whom property, or a limited interest, is transferred.   **42**

assignment The transfer of title to certain property, usually securities. The assignment form usually contains the wording, "sell, assign, and transfer unto."   **23**

assignor One who transfers property he possesses.   **42**

assimilation The successful distribution of new securities to the public by the underwriters of the issue and the members of their syndicate.

association agreement A collective-bargaining agreement applicable to all members of the employer association which has negotiated it.   **12**

assumed liability See "liability, contractual."

assumpsit An action to recover damages for a breach or nonperformance of a contract or promise, oral or in writing.   **35**

assumption of risk The common-law doctrine, since superseded by various states' Workmen's Compensation Laws, which held that employees by seeking employment in an occupation assumed the risk of injury in that activity.

assurance Same as insurance. Term widely used in England and Canada.   **42**

assured An interchangeable word that is the same in meaning as insured.   **52**

atomistic society A society made up mostly of small business units as compared with the large corporations and systems.

at sight A term used in the body of negotiable instruments indicating that payment is due upon presentation or demand.   **1**

attached account An account against which a court order has been issued, permitting disbursement of the attached balance only with the consent of the court. **23**

attachment 1) A legal process by which property is taken into custody or possession.

2) The instrument which issues from such a process. **33**

attestation clause The clause of a document containing the formal declaration of the act of witnessing; in the case of a will, the clause immediately following the signature of the testator and usually beginning, "signed, sealed, published, and declared by the said . . ." **22**

at the market An order "at the market" is executed at the current price. **55**

attorney-at-law A person who is legally qualified and authorized to represent and act for clients in legal proceedings; to be distinguished from an attorney-in-fact. **30**

attorney-in-fact A person who, as agent, is given written authorization by another person to transact business for his principal out of court; to be distinguished from an attorney-at-law. See "power of attorney." **30**

attractive nuisance A dangerous place, condition, or object which is particularly attractive to people, particularly children. In these cases the courts have frequently held that where "attractiveness" exists, the owner is under a duty to take steps to prevent injury to those that may be attracted, and the owner may be held liable for failure to do so.

auction A sale by verbal bids to the individual making the highest bid.

audit In general, an examination of accounting documents and of supporting evidence for the purpose of reaching an informed opinion concerning their propriety. An examination intended to serve as a basis for an expression of opinion regarding the fairness, consistency, and conformity with accepted accounting principles of statements prepared by a corporation or other entity for submission to the public or to other interested parties. **17**

audit function Periodic or continuous verification of a firm's assets and liabilities. This function is performed by an auditor. The auditor is responsible for the carrying out of this verification.

auditor An officer of a firm who is in charge of all audit functions. In some firms he is directly responsible to the board of directors.   **1**

auditor's certificate A statement signed by an auditor in which he states that he has examined the financial statements, the system of internal control, the accounting records, and supporting evidence in accordance with generally accepted auditing standards and in which he expresses his opinion, based on such examination, regarding the financial condition of a business firm or any of its enterprises, the results from operations, and any facts which he has investigated in his professional capacity. See "unqualified certificate."

audit trail An auditing concept that provides, in a step-by-step fashion, the history of an account by carrying in the account master file the date and serial number of the last previous transaction. This allows the auditor to trace back all transactions affecting the account.   **23**

austerity program An economic policy which reduces consumption and luxury expenditures.

Austrian School of Economics The economic doctrine developed around the concept of marginal utility by such economists as Von Mises, Von Hyack, and their followers.

autarchy Self-sufficiency in an economic sense.

authentication 1) The legal verification of a document, proving it genuine or true.
2) The signing, by the trustee, of a certificate on a bond for the purpose of identifying it as being issued under a certain indenture, thus validating the bond.   **30**

authority to purchase (letter of credit) This term is generally used in connection with Far Eastern trade. It is a substitute for a commercial letter of credit and permits the bank to which it is directed to purchase drafts drawn on an importer rather than on a bank. Drafts drawn under authority to purchase have to be marked with the "A/P" number and must conform to the conditions of the letter of authority to purchase. Drafts drawn under "A/P's" are usually confined to United States dollar transactions and branch or correspondent banks in the cities where such drafts originate.   **1**

authorized capital stock The total amount of stock that a corporation is permitted by its charter to issue.   **16**

authorized frequency The frequency assigned to a broadcasting station by the Federal Communications Commission and specified in the instrument of authorization.

authorized investment An investment that is authorized by a trust instrument; to be distinguished from a legal investment. **30**

authorized issue The amount of a security issue stipulated in a corporation's charter which can be changed only by amendment. **44**

authorized power The power assigned to a radio station by the Federal Communications Commission and specified in the instrument of authorization. The authorized power does not necessarily correspond to the power used by the Commission for purposes of its Master Frequency Record (MFR) and notification to the Bureau of the International Telecommunications Union. **63**

authorizer The individual in charge of the credit department designated to approve or disapprove requests for purchases to be charged to credit accounts.

automatic balance An economic concept of equilibrium. High prices will stimulate production and discourage purchases. Low prices stimulate purchases and discourage production. Thus, in the main area of economics, the price mechanism tends to automatically balance the various forces.

automatic check-off A deduction made by an employer from an employee's paycheck that goes into effect without any authorization by the employee, such as union dues sent directly to the union.

automatic cover Coverage provided in many forms of insurance usually for a specified period and limited amount, to cover increasing values, newly acquired and changing interests. **50**

automatic currency See "elastic money."

automatic premium loan A contractual agreement by an insurance company to utilize the cash value of the insurance policy to pay a past-due premium. This prevents a lapse in coverage. A feature in a life insurance policy providing that any premium not paid by the end of the grace period (usually 31 days) be automatically paid by a policy loan if there is sufficient cash value. **53**

automatic reinstatement clause A clause in an insurance policy which provides for the automatic reinstatement of the full face value of the policy after payment for a loss. See "reinstatement." **52**

automatic stabilizer See "built-in stabilizers."

automation Advanced mechanization or technical developments, including continuous-flow production processes controlled by electronics, electronic computing machines, and self-regulating machines which perform precise operations in sequence. **12**

autonomous investment The formation of new capital without regard for the cost of the investment in terms of interest rate or of national income. Most investments by public agencies are autonomous while most investments by private profit-seeking individuals or agencies would be induced.

autonomous tariff Import duties resulting from action by the legislative body and not from commercial treaties.

autonomous variable In statistics, a variable determined by factors in an area separate from the specific area being studied.

auxiliary equipment Accessory equipment necessary for the operation of something, such as a facility or plant. Example: Pumps, stokers, fans, etc.

availability date In banking, the date on which a check drawn on an out-of-town bank will be considered as having been converted into cash. **25**

avails The proceeds of a discounted note. The amount which a borrower receives on a note which is discounted.

average See "general average" and "particular average."

average clause 1) In insurance, a term loosely used to mean pro rata distribution or a coinsurance clause.

2) A clause providing that the insurer shall be liable in the event of loss for not more than that proportion of the loss which the amount of the insurance under the policy bears to a specified percentage of the actual cash value of the property insured. See "coinsurance clause" and "pro rata distribution clause." **50, 51, 52**

average daily balance In finance, the average amount of money that a depositor keeps on deposit, determined by adding the daily balances of his account for a given length of time and dividing the total by the number of days covered.

average distribution clause See "pro rata distribution clause."

average, mean See "arithmetic mean."

average, median The middle number or value of a series, or, if there is no middle number, the arithmetic average of the two middle numbers.

average, mode The value of the variable showing the greatest frequency in a series of numbers. That value or number which occurs most frequently in a series. It is characterized as being easy of determination when values in the series are repeated and, conversely, impossible of approximation when no values are repeated. **15**

average out To conclude a trade or commitment in the market without loss, or at a profit, by the process of averaging; *i.e.*, buying securities at different prices, but selling at a time when price is equal to or better than the average price of purchases. **44**

averages, stock Various ways of measuring the trend of securities prices on a stock exchange, the most popular of which is the Dow-Jones average of 30 industrial stocks. **2**

averaging up or down The practice of making purchases of the same security at different price levels, thereby arriving at a higher or a lower average cost than the first commitment. **40**

award A decision of an arbitrator; to be distinguished from a decree and a judgment. **30**

B

backdating 1) Predating the date of a document prior to the actual date it was drawn up or conceived (normally not legal or proper).

2) In insurance, establishing the policy issue date prior to date of application, usually to give the insured benefit of a premium rate for a younger age. Practice is limited to special conversion arrangements, or backdating of approximately one month. **42**

backhaul To haul a shipment back over a part of a route which it has traveled. **19**

backlog An accumulation of work or orders not completed.

back pay 1) Wages due for past services, often the difference between money already received and a higher amount resulting from a change in wage rates.

2) Under the National Labor Relations Act "back pay" is the

amount a discriminatorily discharged employee woul[...] earned if no discrimination had occurred, minus his ear[...] during the discrimination period.

backspread That less-than-normal price difference in an arbitrage transaction. If a spread of 5% between a currency, commodity or security is the general and long-standing difference in one market compared with another for such reasons as costs of insurance, telegrams, interest, etc., and the spread drops below 5%, it is termed "backspread."

backtracking Exercise of seniority rights to displace junior employees by longer-service workers when business conditions require temporary layoffs or the discontinuance of departments. **12**

bad delivery Security and commodity exchanges have specific regulations on delivery of certificates, titles, payment, etc. When delivery does not comply with these regulations, it constitutes "bad delivery."

bail The security given for the release of a prisoner from custody. **38**

bailee The person to whom goods are committed in trust. **38**

bailment The delivery of personal property by one person to another for some specific purpose, such as for use, repairs, or safekeeping, but without passing title to the property. The person delivering the property is known as the bailor; the person receiving it, the bailee. **22**

bailor One who delivers goods to another in trust for some particular purpose. **38**

balanced fund An investment company which at all times holds bonds and/or preferred stocks and cash in varying ratios to its holdings of common stocks, in order to maintain relatively greater stability of both capital and income. **3**

balance of payments In international finance, the difference between all visible and invisible trade payments made by a nation to foreign creditors and the visible and invisible items paid by foreign debtors during a stated period of time. Invisible items would include such payments of foreign exchange for insurance, shipping and immigrant remittances.

balance of trade In international finance, the relationship, expressed in monetary units between a nation's exports and imports. If the exports exceed the imports the term "favorable balance of trade" is used. If imports exceed the exports it is termed "unfavorable balance of trade." Annual figures are generally used.

balance sheet A detailed listing of assets, liabilities, and capital accounts (net worth) showing the financial condition of a company on a given date. The balance sheet of a bank is generally referred to as a statement of condition.　　25

balance-sheet accounts Accounts designated to show the assets, liabilities, and corporate surplus or deficit of the corporation.　　19

balances with domestic banks The total amounts that reporting member banks of the Federal Reserve System have on deposit in other commercial banks.

ballooning An outlawed practice of manipulation by which prices of stocks, groups of stocks, or the stock market would be forced to overinflated levels far beyond their intrinsic value.　　44

balloon loan A loan in which small periodic payments are made during the term of the loan. These sums are not sufficient to pay the full loan so that at the end of the period there is a need to refinance the loan since the last payment is a balloon or large amount that was not expected to be paid in full. Credit insurance of level term or decreasing term life may be written to cover the loan.

bank An organization, normally a corporation, chartered by the state or federal government, the principal functions of which are: To receive demand deposits and pay customers' checks drawn against them; to receive time deposits and pay interest thereon; to discount notes, make loans, and invest in government or other securities; to collect checks, drafts, notes, etc.; to issue drafts and cashier's checks; to certify depositors' checks; when authorized by a chartering government, it may act in a fiduciary or trustee capacity.

bankable bill A document that may easily be discounted at a bank.

bank acceptance A draft drawn on a bank and accepted by the bank.　　34

bank call The demand made upon a bank by a supervisory authority for a sworn statement of the bank's condition as of a certain date.　　25

bank charge plan Usually a copyrighted plan brought to a community by a bank or private organization under charter or franchise for providing a complete credit service including credit authorization, issuance of credit cards, and billing and collection of 30-day accounts for member stores. Most banks charge 5% or less of total credit sales for their service.

bank check A check drawn by a bank on itself and signed by an authorized officer. Savings banks do not usually draw such checks. Also called treasurer's check, officer's check, or cashier's check. **34**

bank clearing See "clearings."

bank credit The credit created by commercial banks through the media of loans and discounts—granted with or without collateral. The amount of credit so extended is controlled in part by the rediscount rates established by the Federal Reserve Board. **1**

bank debits The sum total of all debits (made up of sight drafts honored and checks and other instruments) drawn against deposited funds of individuals, partnerships, corporations and other legal entities during a given period of time—usually reported by banks daily. **1**

bank deposit The placing of money or other valuables in a bank for safekeeping.

bank discount The charge, generally expressed as a percent of the face amount of the commercial paper or personal note which is made by a bank, for payment of the paper or note before its maturity.

bank draft A check drawn by a bank against funds deposited to its account in another bank. **25**

bank-eligible issues Issues of United States Treasury obligations eligible for immediate purchase by commercial banks—mainly those due or callable within ten years. **40**

bank examiner A person who as the representative of a federal or state bank supervisory authority examines the banks under its jurisdiction with respect to their financial condition, management, and policies. **23**

bank exchanges Those items such as checks, notes, drafts, etc., which are collected through a clearinghouse system.

bank for cooperatives A financial institution created as part of the Farm Credit Administration to provide credit to farm cooperatives.

bank holiday Any day so designated by competent state authority or national authority. Most bank holidays are determined by state custom and may not be celebrated outside a state or region. About five holidays are observed in all states: New Year's, Washington's Birthday, 4th of July, Labor Day and Christmas. During emergencies some states and the national government have declared bank holidays for the purpose of preventing runs.

banking system The type, structure and method of operation of a nation's or state's banks.

bank note A noninterest-bearing promissory note of a bank issued for general circulation as money and payable to the bearer on demand. In the United States only the Federal Reserve Banks now issue bank notes. **25**

bank of discount Those banks, generally commercial banks, which will extend credit on acceptances, bills of exchange and notes.

bank of issue A bank that is legally permitted to issue money such as bank notes.

bank-post remittance Any bill of exchange of foreign origin which a bank has honored and pays through the use of the mail either by money order or by cash.

bank rate The interest rate charged by the bank on typical loans. Also the discount rate established by a central bank. This is the rate that the commercial bank must pay to discount or borrow from the central bank.

bank run A situation in which abnormally large withdrawals are made on a bank out of fear that the bank may close.

bankruptcy A state of conditions in which the financial position of an individual, corporation or other legal entity is such as to cause them to be actually or legally bankrupt. Such condition is commonly referred to as a condition of insolvency. **1**

bank statement A monthly statement of account which a bank renders to each of its depositors. It shows in detail the amounts deposited, the checks paid by the bank, and the balance on hand at the end of the month. **16**

bargaining agent Union recognized or designated as the exclusive representative of employees in a bargaining unit.

bargaining rights 1) Rights of workers to negotiate through chosen representatives concerning terms and conditions of employment.

2) The right of the union designated by a majority of the

workers in an appropriate bargaining unit to represent the
group in collective bargaining.   **12**

bargaining unit The employee group that, in the light of all factors of related skill and interest, is the appropriate unit for
collective bargaining.   **12**

barometers Those business indexes which are used to evaluate
the condition of a market or economy. Industrial production,
total employment, freight car loadings, etc., are among some
of the statistical series which are considered to be barometers.

barometer stock A security which moves in the same direction
as the market and for this reason is considered to be representative of the market. USX Corporation is an example of a
barometer stock.

barter The exchange, without the use of money, of one item or
service for another.

base coins Minor coins made of copper, nickel, zinc, or alumi-
num as distinguished from gold and silver.

base pay Wages paid, exclusive of overtime, premiums and bonuses.

base period Many statistical series choose a "base period" or
normal period which is given the weight or value of 100. As
the time series are computed the current data are related to
the base. If the measurement in the base period, for example,
was 200 units and current measurement is 300 units, one
could express the base as 100 and current as 150. By reducing
the data to a percentage of the base period, complex data may
be more easily evaluated.

base rate The straight-time rate of pay, excluding premiums,
incentive bonuses, etc.   **12**

basic crops Those agricultural commodities designated by the
Congress as such. Currently corn, cotton, peanuts, rice, tobacco and wheat are considered as being basic crops. As such,
they are under price support programs.

basic yield A concept similar to pure interest; that is, the annual
rate of return in percent on a risk-free investment such as a
long-term United States Government bond. Even in this illustration there is some risk including the effect of inflation on
purchasing power of the future income from the bond.

basing point A technique for quoting prices of products. The
buyer figures his delivered cost from the geographic point used

as the base even though the product is not necessarily shipped from there.

basis point A measure for small differences in yields; 100 basis points equaling 1%. For example, there is a 20 basis point spread (difference) between bonds quoted at yields of 1.30% and 1.10%.　　**40**

batch A group of deposits, or a group of other items, which are proved in one operation. Also termed block.　　**25**

batch proof A system for proving deposits, usually performed in the following sequence: Deposits are assembled in groups of various sizes; deposit tickets are sorted into one group; checks are sorted into several classifications, as clearings, transit, bookkeeping, etc.; cash release tickets are sorted according to tellers; deposit tickets, checks, and cash release tickets are listed on a "batch" or "block" sheet in their respective columns; the total of the deposits and other credits should equal the recapitulation of the checks and other debits.　　**1**

bear Someone who believes the stock market will decline. See "bull."　　**2**

bear clique An informal group of people who combine their attempts to depress security or commodity prices by the practice of short selling.　　**44**

bearer The individual who has physical possession of a negotiable instrument which is payable to the bearer.

bearer form In a form payable to bearer, the security having no registered owner.　　**40**

bear market A period of generally declining market prices.　　**40**

bear position Means a "short position" or the prevailing market position of a pessimist; *i.e.,* one who has sold securities short in hopes that the market will turn downward, at which point securities will be bought at a lower price to give a net profit.　　**44**

bear raiding A prohibited, as well as impossible, form of manipulation in which a group of bear operators conduct an intense short selling campaign to depress the price of a security or group of securities; thereby frightening other security holders into selling or forcing liquidation of inadequate margin accounts. Once the prices have been driven down, the bear raiders can close out their short contracts (buy the security at a lower price than they received in the sale of it) at a profit.　　**44**

belt line A short railroad operating within and/or around a city. **19**

bench marks Identification symbols on stone, metal, or other durable matter permanently fixed in the ground from which differences of elevation are measured as in tidal observation or topographical surveys. **5**

beneficiary One who receives benefits, profits, or advantages. **38**

benefit of selection The advantage afforded an insurance company through careful selection of insurance risks and therefore is desirable; as, for example, risks that have fully guarded their machinery are more desirable for workmen's compensation insurance than those that have not. **5**

benefits-received tax principle Concept that a person or company should be taxed in the same proportion to the benefits he receives from the tax agency. The use of a gasoline tax to build better roads for the motorists is an illustration of this principle.

bequeath To give personal property by will; to be distinguished from devise. **22**

bequest A gift of personal property by will; a legacy. **22**

best bid The highest price anyone is willing to pay for something offered for sale. This bid is the relevant one in establishing the market for a stock. **44**

betterment An improvement in a property which is considered to add to the investment or capital cost as distinguished from repairs or replacements where the original character or cost is unchanged. **54**

bid A price offered subject, unless otherwise stated, to immediate acceptance for a specific amount of a commodity or a stock.

bid-and-asked price The price at which an owner offers to sell (asked) and the price at which someone has agreed to buy (bid). Usually used in reference to stocks and bonds but may apply to any property in which there is an active trade.

bidding up The act of successively raising the price bid for a security or commodity to higher levels for fear of failing to have an order executed before an advance is under way. **44**

bid price In the case of open-end shares, the price at which the holder may redeem his shares; in most cases it is the current net asset value per share. In the case of closed-end shares, the highest price then offered for stock in the public market.   **3**

Big Board The New York Stock Exchange.

bill 1) A note or bill of exchange.

2) A document showing the amount that is due a creditor which is given or sent to a debtor.

3) A bill of sale, a way bill, a due bill, or paper money such as a ten dollar bill.

bill broker An individual or firm which acts as a middleman and sells commercial paper to financial institutions. The bill broker was much more active and important during the 19th century than he is today.

bill discounted A promissory note or bill of exchange from which the bank deducts, in advance, its fee or interest for lending the money (usually to the holder or endorser).   **1**

bill of credit A written instrument in which the drawer requests the firm or individual addressed to advance credit to the bearer or named firm or individual at the risk of the drawer.

bill of exchange An unconditional order in writing, addressed by one person to another, signed by the person issuing it, which requires the person to whom it is addressed to pay a specified sum of money to the order of a third person. Used interchangeably with "draft."   **23**

bill of lading A document issued by a railroad or other carrier. It acknowledges the receipt of specified goods for transportation to a certain place, it sets forth the contract between the shipper and the carrier, and it provides for proper delivery of the goods.   **25**

bill of material A prescheduled list of materials and component assemblies required for a given work assignment or job.   **29**

bill of sale A formal legal document which conveys title to, or right or interest in, specific personal property from the seller to the buyer.   **1**

bills payable 1) A comprehensive term that includes the sum total of notes and trade acceptances which a business owes to trade creditors and which the business must pay at their maturity.

2) The sum of money which a member bank has borrowed, on its own collateral note, from the Federal Reserve Bank.   **1**

bills receivable A comprehensive term that includes the total of all notes and trade acceptances given by customers, usually in payment of merchandise, which the debtors must pay at maturity. **1**

bimetallism The "free" or unlimited coinage of two metals, generally of gold and silver. The coins have full legal tender value and an established relationship or ratio of value such as sixteen ounces of silver of a standard fineness or purity to one ounce of gold of a standard fineness or purity.

binder 1) A temporary agreement which obligates the several parties of the contract. In insurance, the insurance company is obligated to pay if the loss insured against occurs before the policy is written.

2) A preliminary agreement to provide immediate insurance until a policy can be written, either by an agent or by a company. It should contain a definite time limit, should be in writing, and clearly designate the company in which the risk is bound, the amount and the perils insured against, as well as the type of insurance.

3) A temporary insurance contract pending execution of the policy contract. Except for specified differences, the terms of the binder are by implication those of the contract which is intended to replace it. **50, 51, 52**

bird dog 1) To search for facts which will aid in analyzing a company's status and future prospects.

2) A tout; *i.e.,* one who is paid to solicit business for a high-pressure salesman, or spread fraudulent information. **44**

birthrate The number of births per year per thousand population in a stated geographic area.

Black Friday September 24, 1869, when the attempt to corner the gold market was broken. The excesses resulted in a business panic and depression. Since then a number of sharp drops in the securities markets have occurred on Friday and the term has been carried forward to indicate a sharp drop approaching panic proportions.

blacklist 1) A list of persons considered to be undesirable and to be avoided such as bad credit risks.

2) List of union members circulated among employers to advise them of the union activities of job applicants.

3) List of contractors who have violated Federal Government Walsh-Healey Act specifications. **12**

black market A place where illegal transactions take place. Gen-

41

erally these violations involve rationing, price, or exchange controls.

blank bill A bill of exchange with no payee designated.

blank endorsement The endorsement or signature of an individual or company on an instrument such as a check or note making it payable to the bearer and thus negotiable without restrictions.

blanket injunctions Injunctions prohibiting, in the future, acts or violations that have not actually been committed in the case presently before the court. **12**

blanket mortgage A mortgage that takes in or "covers" all the assets or property of the debtor.

blanket policy A broad type of insurance coverage, commonly used in fire and burglary insurance. **38**

blanket rate An insurance rate applied to more than one property or subject of insurance. **5**

blind pool A speculative device at times used in the securities markets in which a group of speculators let one of their members handle the operation or management of their obligated funds. The pool's membership, other than the one selected member, is generally not revealed to the public. The pool operates for a stated period of time or until a specific goal has been reached. See "bobtail pool."

block A large number of shares of stocks or large number of bonds. See "batch." **1**

blockage 1) Placing an account subject to United States Treasury control because of enemy or suspected enemy interest.
2) A discount from the established market for which a large block of stock of a single corporation would have to be sold if the entire holding were placed on the market at a given date (a term used in connection with federal estate tax). **22**

blocked account Any account in a bank the handling of which is closely circumscribed by government regulations. The term in this country is used to designate any account whose administration is subject to United States Treasury license because of enemy or suspected enemy interest. **22**

blocked currency A device used by some nations to discriminate against certain types of holders of the claims against a nation. It is generally used to try to control foreign exchange rates and the balance of payments as well as trade movement. Blocked currencies are quoted at discounts from the unblocked or regular currency of a nation. At times the blocked currency may be used only in certain regulated ways and may involve the need for special permits from the monetary authorities.

block limits The maximum amount of insurance that an insurance company will write in any one city block. This reduces the risk of large losses in case of a fire that burns the entire block. **5**

block policy A policy covering all the property of the insured (usually a merchant) against most perils, including transportation. It may also cover property of others held by the insured on consignment, goods sold but not delivered, goods left for repairs, or goods otherwise held. It usually covers both on and off the insured's premises.

blue chip 1) Something of exceptionally high quality or value. 2) Common stock in a company known nationally for the quality and wide acceptance of its products or services and for its ability to make money and pay dividends in good times and bad. Usually such stocks are relatively high-priced and offer relatively low yields. **2**

blue-collar workers Workers employed in a plant or in production, as distinguished from white-collar workers employed in an office. **12**

blue list A composite list published five days a week by The Blue List Publishing Company, New York City, showing current municipal bond offerings by banks and municipal bond houses all over the country. **40**

blue-sky laws A popular name for laws various states have enacted to protect the public against securities frauds. These laws pertain to the punishment of persons who sell illegal stocks, and they provide jurisdiction over investment companies. The term is believed to have originated when a judge ruled that a particular stock had about the same value as a patch of blue sky.

board lot A round lot. The regular unit of trade for the designated exchange. The board or round lot on the New York Stock Exchange is generally 100 shares of stock or $1,000 par value for a bond unless an exception is made.

board of directors Those individuals elected by the stockholders of a corporation to manage the business. An inside board has directors who are also active in the day-to-day operation of the firm while an outside board is made up of individuals who do not make active day-to-day decisions in the business but are rather concerned with policy and broad general direction.

Board of Governors of the Federal Reserve System A board of seven members (located at Washington) which supervises, coordinates, and controls the operations of the twelve Federal Reserve Banks and branches. The Board has regulatory powers with respect to member banks.   **25**

board of managers A term given in some states to the board of trustees of a mutual savings bank.   **34**

board of trade A chamber of commerce or a produce exchange.

board of trustees The body in an institution which manages and administrates the organization, establishes the policies under which it is to be operated, appoints the officers, etc.

bobtail pool A group of speculators who act independently of each other but with a common goal and agreement in mind. The commitments made by each member are his own responsibility. See "blind pool."

bodily injury Injury to the body of a person. The term is usually specifically defined in an insurance policy, and these individual definitions have variations.   **5**

boiler-room operation A dubious operation involving the sale of very speculative and frequently valueless securities through the use of high-pressure phone techniques and misleading literature. The appeal of quick profit and rapid price change is used to stimulate the unsophisticated to purchase the security without making a proper investigation as to the merits of the security.

bond 1) An interest-bearing certificate of debt, usually issued in series by which the issuer (a government or corporation) obligates itself to pay the principal amount and interest at a specified time, usually five years or more after date of issue. Bonds may be distinguished from promissory notes or other evidences of debt because of their formal execution under seal and certification by a bank or trust company that they are authorized by the board of directors of a corporation or other governing body. Corporate bonds are usually secured by a lien against certain specified property. Bonds may be issued in "bearer" form or "registered."   **1**

2) An obligation of an insurance company to protect the insured against financial loss caused by the acts or omissions of another person or persons known as the principal. A fidelity

44

bond on employees would reimburse the insured up to the limits of the policy for the loss caused by dishonesty of the covered employee. Originally it meant any obligation under seal.

3) In a noninsurance sense, a bond is a debt instrument consisting of a promise to pay and usually issued on the security of a mortgage or a deed of trust or on the credit of the issuer. **52, 54**

bond, adjustment The term used for income bonds that have been issued out of a reorganization. See "bond, income."

bond, assumed Bonds which originally were the obligation of one corporation but which for some reason such as a subsidiary relationship have been assumed as obligations as well by another corporation. Most assumed bonds are found in the area of railway divisional bonds in which the parent company has assumed the interests and principal obligation of the original debtor, which is a division of a system.

bond, bearer Bonds whose proceeds (principal and interest) are payable to the bearer, that is, to whoever has physical possession. Since there is no identification, such bonds always have attached coupons, which are cut and presented to collect the interest. **40**

bond, bid A guarantee that a contractor will enter into a contract on which he has bid if it is awarded to him and furnish a contract bond as required by the terms of the contract. **51**

bond, blanket A broad fidelity bond covering all employees of a firm and in the case of financial institutions including insurance against enumerated hazards.

bond, callable Bonds which the issuing corporation or body may redeem before their maturity. Generally some premium is paid by the issuing corporation to the holder of the bond should it be called. Interest stops when a bond is called.

bond, collateral trust An issue of bonds for which collateral has been pledged to guarantee repayment of the principal. This type of bond usually arises out of intercompany transactions where the parent company will issue bonds with securities of a subsidiary as the underlying collateral. Railroads often do this type of financing. **23**

bond, consolidated A debt instrument issued to take the place of two or more previously issued bonds. This may be done to simplify a debt structure or to take advantage of a lower prevailing interest rate.

bond, continued A debt instrument that does not have to be redeemed at maturity but can continue to earn interest. The Series E bonds have been "continued." Extended bonds.

bond, contract A guarantee of the faithful performance of a construction contract and the payment of all labor and material bills incident thereto. In those situations where two bonds are required, one to cover performance and the other to cover payment of labor and material, the former is known as a performance bond and the latter as a payment bond. **50**

bond, convertible Bonds having the special provision for being converted into stock at a certain time and at a specified price. **22**

bond, coupon Bonds to which are attached coupons representing the interest payments. As the interest becomes due, the coupons are clipped and presented for payment. **22**

bond, debenture Bonds which represent a company's funded debt backed only by its credit and not secured by a pledge or mortgage of property. **55**

bond, deferred A debt instrument in which a due payment has been postponed until some future time.

bond, definitive This term applies to any bond issued in final form. It is used particularly with reference to permanent bonds for which temporary bonds or interim certificates were issued. **23**

bonded warehouse A warehouse owned by persons approved by the United States Treasury Department and under bond or guarantee for the strict observance of the revenue laws; utilized for storing goods until duties are paid or goods are otherwise properly released. **19**

bond, extended Continued bonds; bonds which have matured without the debtor paying the principal but which the debtor agrees to extend or continue to pay at some future date.

bond, external Bonds issued by a country or business for purchase outside that country. These bonds are frequently denominated in the currency of the purchaser. At times the option is given the purchaser to elect in which currency he wishes to receive payment of interest and principal. See "bond, internal."

bond, fidelity A bond covering the risk of loss due to larceny, embezzlement, or culpable negligence and the faithful discharge of an employee's duties. **1**

bond, foreign Foreign bonds may take even more forms than domestic bonds. Some domestic issues of a nation become foreign bonds by being moved from their country of origin. Foreign bonds which are deliberately sold abroad are external bonds; those that are payable in dollars are called foreign dollar bonds. Some foreign bonds are payable in more than one currency at the option of the holder and some are tied to price indexes as to value of principal. Foreign bonds that have defaulted may be assented or stamped. Those still in default are sold flat. They may be obligations of nations, states, municipalities or of foreign corporations.

bond, funding Bonds issued to retire outstanding floating debt and to eliminate deficits. **29**

bond, government Obligations of the United States Government regarded as the highest grade issues in existence. Obligations of governments other than the United States are generally designated as foreign government bonds. **2**

bond, guaranteed Bond on which the principal or income or both are guaranteed by another corporation or parent company in case of default by the issuing corporation. **23**

bondholder One who owns bonds and therefore is a creditor of the issuer. **34**

bond, income An obligation upon which interest is payable to the extent earned in each year except that interest not earned and unpaid may be either fully or partially cumulative according to the terms of the contract. The income bond may be or may not be secured by the pledge of either real or personal property. **19**

bond, indemnity A written instrument under seal by which the signer, usually together with his surety or bondsman, guarantees to protect another against loss. An indemnity bond in which the obligation assumed by the surety is not a fixed amount is known as an open penalty form of indemnity bond. **30**

bond indenture A contract describing the interest and maturity date and other important terms under which bonds are issued. **44**

bond, indeterminate A callable bond which has no established maturity date. The call feature generally is not effective until some stated period has elapsed.

bond, interchangeable A bond in either coupon or registered form which may be converted to the other form or back to its original form at the option of the holder. There may be some service charge for such conversion.

bond, interim The temporary paper certificate, generally printed and not engraved, to be exchanged for the definitive and engraved certificate. The engraving is for the purposes of preventing forgery and alteration.

bond, internal A bond issued by a country payable in its own currency; to be distinguished from an external bond which is a bond issued by one country and sold in another country and payable in the currency of that other country. **22**

bond, joint and several A debt instrument in which the holder may look to payment from more than one party up to the full face amount of the security. These securities are mostly associated with railroad financing for such facilities as terminals used by more than one railroad. The users of the terminal agree to be responsible for the payment in the event the others default. The holder may only collect the face amount once, but he may collect from all or only one of the obligors.

bond, junior Bonds which are not senior; that is, are secondary or subordinate to another issue which in the event of liquidation would have a prior claim to the junior bonds. See "bond, senior," "senior interest," or "senior securities."

bond, legal Bonds that state or federal law prescribe as suitable and legal investments for fiduciary institutions. In a number of states a "legal list" states by name and issue those investments that a fiduciary or trustee may purchase and hold for the beneficiary.

bond, mortgage A bond secured by a mortgage on a property. The value of the property may or may not equal the value of the so-called mortgage bonds issued against it. See "bond, debenture." **2**

bond, open-end A mortgage bond of an issue which does not have a limitation on the number or amounts of bonds which may be issued under the mortgage though some relationship may be required to the number and amount of bonds to the value of the property mortgaged.

bond, passive A bond which does not bear any interest. Such bonds may be issued as a result of reorganization or where normal economic forces are subordinated to some charitable or eleemosynary purpose.

bond power A signed instrument in the form of a power of attorney by which the owner of registered bonds authorizes another party to sell and transfer the bonds. **34**

bond, registered A bond which is registered on the books of the issuing company in the name of the owner. It can be transferred only when endorsed by the registered owner. See "bond, bearer" and "bond, coupon." **2**

bond, revenue Bonds the principal of and interest on which are to be paid solely from earnings; usually those of a municipally owned utility or other public service enterprise the revenues and possibly the properties of which are pledged for this purpose. **29**

bond, second mortgage A bond which is issued on property which already has a first mortgage outstanding on it.

bond, senior Bonds which have first or prior claim to the assets of the debtor in the event of liquidation.

bond, serial An issue of bonds in which a certain proportion of the bonds are retired at regular intervals. Serial bonds are issued where the security depreciates through use of obsolescence, and they usually provide that the bonds outstanding shall not exceed the value of the security. **83**

bond, sinking fund A bond which has as one of its features the requirement that the debtor provides and maintains a sinking fund to provide for the ultimate repayment and retirement of the bond.

bond, surety A bond or guarantee usually given by a bonding company to answer for the debt, default, or miscarriage of another. The surety (company) binds itself to pay if the obligor shall default in his obligation. **22**

bond, temporary A bond which is the same as the definitive bond except that it is printed rather than engraved. Since some exchanges require engraving to prevent counterfeiting on listed securities, the temporary bond may be issued until the engraved definitive bond is ready. At that time they will be exchanged.

Bond, United States Savings A nonnegotiable bond issued in different series such as E, F, and G, the most commonly issued being the series EE. Such bonds are issued in small, odd units such as $18.75 with a maturity value of $25 or $37.50 with a maturity value of $50. The typical period such bonds were originally issued for was 10 years, but, because of changed interest rates, the maturity has been altered rather than the redemption amount.

bonus Anything, although generally money, which is given without legal obligation by an individual or firm in addition to that which is required for some action.

bonus stock A sweetening device used to encourage the sale of another class of securities. For example, the issuing of a share or shares of a common stock for each unit of purchase of a preferred stock. The bonus stock may be given to the ultimate purchaser, the salesman, or the underwriter of the issue.

book credit Those items shown on the ledger accounts which represent obligations of firms and individuals which are not secured by notes or other security. Also described as book accounts or open book accounts.

book crowd Those traders in inactive bonds on the New York Stock Exchange. Sometimes the term "cabinet crowd" is used in the same sense since the information on the inactive bonds is kept in cabinets.

bookkeeper A person who records all the business affairs of a business in an orderly manner.   **16**

bookkeeping The art, practice, or labor involved in the systematic recording of the transactions affecting a business. Single Entry is the system using only one entry per transaction. Double Entry is the system using two entries for every transaction, one on the debit and one on the credit side of the ledger.

bookkeeping cycle The entire bookkeeping process applicable to a fiscal period (journalizing, posting, preparing a trial balance, preparing financial statements, etc.).   **16**

book of final entry A book to which information is transferred from a book of original entry. The ledger is a book of final entry.   **16**

book of original entry A book in which transactions are recorded completely, one after another, in the order in which they occur. The journal is a book of original entry.   **16**

books (close) The date the transfer agent closes the transfer books of a corporation and checks the stockholder list to determine those eligible to vote or receive dividends.   **44**

books (open) The date the transfer agent opens a corporation's transfer books to resume the normal business of transferring stocks after they had been closed to check the stockholder list. **44**

book value 1) The price at which assets are carried on a financial statement.

2) The value of each share of common or capital stock based on the values at which the assets of a corporation are carried on its balance sheet. It is obtained by deducting from total assets all liabilities of the corporation and dividing the remainder by the number of shares outstanding. **22**

boom A period of rapidly rising prices, characterized by substantial excess of demand for goods and services, full employment, sharply increasing demand for and supply of luxury items, inflation, rising interest rates, abnormal commercial and industrial plant expansion, and profitable use of marginal (and even submarginal) agents of production, and a carefree attitude by a substantial part of the public. **15**

boondoggle An uneconomic utilization of labor or tools of production. Wasteful.

boot Any material (note, cash, boat, or mortgage) other than the qualifying real property being exchanged. These items are included or "thrown in to boot."

bordereau 1) A memorandum containing detailed information concerning documents that accompany it.

2) An economical procedure of reporting business to the home office employed in handling the business from some branch offices. Also it is used extensively in passing reinsurance from one company to another under a reinsurance agreement. **50**

borrowed reserves Discounts and advances from Federal Reserve Banks; mainly advances secured by United States Government securities or eligible paper. **56**

borrowed stocks Stocks that brokers borrow for the purpose of providing delivery on short sales made for their clients.

Boston bookkeeping or ledger A single-entry bookkeeping system. A progressive ledger.

bottom dropped out of Refers to the market condition of a security when it declines so abruptly and suddenly that it appears the price may drop to zero. **44**

bottom out A condition in which something with a variable value such as the national economy, a security, or a business condition, after reaching a low point or phase, has started to rise or improve.

bounty A subsidy or bonus paid to encourage some action.

bourgeoisie (French) Broadly, the middle class as distinguished from peasants, manual or unskilled workers, and the well-to-do.

bourse A stock exchange in Europe.

boycott Refusal to buy from or sell to a certain company. To stop buying or using certain products. **38**

branch banking Any bank which maintains complete banking facilities in offices away from its main office, or head office, may be considered as carrying on branch banking business. The separated units are called branches or offices and are permitted among the various classes of banks in the several states under certain conditions. Generally speaking, national banks are allowed to have branches in a state under the same conditions granted to a state-chartered bank. That is, if a state bank is permitted to have statewide branches, then the same privilege is afforded national banks. **1**

brand A design, mark, symbol or other device which distinguishes one line or type of goods from those of a competitor.

brand name 1) Special name registered to prevent copying. **38** 2) An expression that has come into use to refer to a well-established, quality product.

Brannan Plan A proposal for a federal subsidy to be paid to farmers of covered crops which would be sold in a free market. The difference between the free price and complicated index of prices for a base period would determine the subsidy.

brassage The charge made by the government mint for coining bullion which is the cost to the government for that service. If a charge is greater than the cost it is known as seigniorage.

brazen law of wages Also known as the iron law of wages or the subsistence law of wages. This discarded theory held that wages would only equal an amount which would provide bare subsistence.

breach of contract Breaking an agreement; refusing to do one's part in the agreement. **38**

breach of promise Violation of one's plighted word, especially of a promise to marry. **35**

breach of trust Violation of a duty which a trustee owes to a beneficiary. **30**

break even To have neither a profit nor a loss at the termination of a transaction but to have just covered the costs incurred. **44**

break-even point Where the income from the business just equals the cost of doing business leaving neither a profit nor a loss. **38**

break in the market An unusually sharp drop in the price for a product.

break-in-time Period during which group earnings under a group incentive system are adjusted to allow for new members of the group. **12**

breakout The market action of a security or a market average in penetrating either above an apparent resistance level (supply) or below an apparent support level (accumulation). **44**

breakup price or value The liquidating price or value of a firm.

broad market A situation permitting the sale and purchase of a large number and types of securities or commodities.

broken lot An odd lot. Generally, less than one hundred shares of a stock or less than the usual unit of measurement or unit of sale of any item.

broker A middleman who brings together buyers and sellers of the same product, service, commodity, or security and executes the orders, charging a commission for this service. In contrast to a principal or a dealer, the broker does not own or take a position in the item being sold.

brokerage 1) The business of a broker.
2) The fee or commission paid by a client to a broker for the execution of his order. **44**

brokerage account A client's account which is managed by the broker on behalf of and subject to the client's order. **44**

broker-agent One who is licensed to act both as broker and as agent. While generally one is either a broker or an agent, some individuals maintain two offices, one as a broker and the other as an agent. **51**

broker's loan Loans made to stock brokers and secured by stock exchange collateral. Statistics on this type of loan are tabulated by the Federal Reserve Banks and others as a guide to the investing public. **1**

brotherhood Term frequently appearing in the titles of labor unions, particularly the older craft groups to show unity and common bond.

bubble A speculative situation in which the capitalization of the future value of the activity is so high that there is little probability of the venture making a reasonable profit on such high valuations. When this is recognized the bubble bursts and prices fall. The most famous bubbles include the Mississippi Bubble, the East India Bubble, and the Tulip Bubble.

bucket shop An illegal stock-brokerage operation now almost extinct. The bucket shop operator accepted a client's money without actually ever buying or selling securities as the client ordered. Instead he held the money and gambled that the customer was wrong. The customer's loss was the bucket shop's gain. When too many customers were right, the bucket shop closed its doors and opened a new office. 2

buck the trend To go contrary to "the crowd"; for example, selling short in an advancing market or buying long in a declining market. 44

budget 1) An estimate of the income and expenditures for a future period of time, usually one year.
2) A systematic estimate or plan for a future fiscal period of a business.
3) A limited allotment or appropriation for a specific purpose, such as an advertising budget.

budgetary accounts Those accounts necessary to reflect budget operations and conditions, such as estimated revenues, appropriations, and encumbrances, as distinguished from proprietary accounts. See "proprietary accounts." 29

budgetary control A plan to control all operations in order to secure maximum profit from a minimum capital investment. This is accomplished by setting standards against which actual performance can be measured. An efficient budgetary control program not only detects inefficiencies but also definitely fixes responsibility upon the proper person or persons. 28

budget, cash A summary of anticipated receipts and disbursements for a forthcoming period. It is generally used in forecasting cash requirements to meet future bond redemptions, dividends, plant expansions, etc. 28

buffer-stock plan As a stabilizing device to help reduce cyclical fluctuations, a federal agency buys certain commodities at a minimum price and sells them at a higher price. The prices would be determined by normal costs of production and normal price fluctuations.

building and loan association See "savings and loan association."

building loan A mortgage loan which is made to finance the construction of a building. It is advanced in stages as the construction work progresses. See "construction loan." **34**

built-in stabilizers Those business and government practices, policies, customs and laws which tend to automatically moderate fluctuations in business or economy. Unemployment insurance, social security, and progressive income taxes illustrate such stabilizers.

bulk-line costs Those costs in any industry at which over 80% of the goods are produced. On the basis of such bulk-line costs, price fixing or stabilization programs can be established.

bull One who believes the market will rise. See "bear." **2**

bull clique An informal group of people or interests that conduct a "bull campaign," *i.e.,* attempt to push prices upward. **44**

bullion Precious metals such as platinum, gold, or silver which are cast in ingots or bars and considered merely as metal. **5**

bull market A period of generally increasing market prices. **40**

bull pool A form of manipulation now prohibited which consisted of a formally organized fund contributed by financial interests who desired prices to advance. A pool manager was selected and an agreement entered upon which stipulated the division of profits or losses and that none of the members should make individual transactions in the particular security being manipulated. **44**

bull position Refers to the prevailing status of market optimists, or bulls. If most of the market is on the buying side, *i.e.,* leading securities are being acquired by institutions and individual investors, this is said to be a strong bull position. **44**

bumping Exercise of seniority rights to displace junior employees by longer-service workers when business conditions require temporary layoffs or the discontinuance of departments. **12**

bunco game Any of a number of methods of swindling.

burden of proof The duty of proving a position taken in a court of law. Failure in the performance of that duty calls for judgment against the person on whom the duty rests. Thus, the burden of proof that a certain paper writing is not the valid will of the testator is upon the person who contests the will.

bureau An office for giving out information. **38**

business agent Person employed by an individual or a group to represent them and to protect their interests. An example would be a business agent appointed by a local union or several locals to conduct union activities and negotiate with employers.

business atmosphere The political setting and degree of public acceptance in which economic activity is carried on. **59**

business barometer 1) A composite of weighted index numbers used to estimate the level of business.

2) A single index of a business activity which is considered to be reflective of business activity such as total employment.

business cycles Broad swings up and down in the state of business.

business insurance trust A trust of life insurance policy contracts created in connection with a business enterprise. The term is applied both to a trust created for the liquidation of business interests and to a trust created for credit purposes or otherwise for the benefit of a business enterprise. **30**

businessman's risk The justifiable risk taken in a business or securities venture based on the assumption that a businessman is situated to handle the risk emotionally and financially. **44**

business risk There are a number of different risks which are involved in granting credit. These include insurable risks, moral risks, and the risk from acts of God such as floods and earthquakes. One major risk, the business risk, involves the ability of a businessman to operate his business in an efficient and profitable manner.

business trust See "Massachusetts trust."

business unionism American union philosophy of improving the condition of the worker within the framework of the free enterprise system.

buy and put away An old Wall Street maxim that claims a successful stock market practice is to buy stocks then put them away and forget about them. This, of course, is not always true because all securities will not advance in price as hoped. However, in an inflationary period this might be a successful practice for most stocks. **44**

buyers' market A period of a lessening demand; prices are on a downward trend thus giving the buyer an advantage over the seller.

buyer's monopoly A market situation characterized by many sellers and one buyer.

buyers' strike A situation in which the buyers of a product stop their purchases. This may be because the price is simply too high, or it may be caused by a concerted attempt by organizers to exert pressure on the sellers to force price reductions.

buyer's surplus An economic concept to recognize that many buyers would pay more for a product than the seller has asked. The difference between what the buyer pays and what he would pay if he had to is known as the buyer's surplus.

buying on balance That situation in which a broker's orders to buy exceed the orders he has to sell. In a market the sales equal the purchases, but for a brokerage firm they need not equal each other.

buying on margin Many items are bought without the purchaser paying immediately the whole price. Examples of buying on margin include purchase of a home with a mortgage or of a security with a partial payment and borrowing the difference from a broker or bank. Margin refers to the proportion of down payment that is made by the purchaser. The Board of Governors of the Federal Reserve Board has the right to establish margin requirements for the purchase of listed securities. This is a selective credit control.

buying on scale A method used in purchasing securities in which the broker is instructed to buy a given number of shares at given intervals of a price decline. Since the buyer does not know how low the price will drop, by buying on scale as the price drops his average cost per share also drops.

buy-sell agreement An agreement wherein owners of a business arrange to transfer their respective ownership interests upon the death of one, or upon some other event, so as to provide continued control of the business or some other desired end.   **22**

bylaws Regulations, ordinances, or rules enacted by an organization for its own government and in accordance with which its affairs are to be conducted.

by-product A substance that is produced as an incident of a major product. In meat packing certain glands are used to make medicine. The major product is meat; the by-product, in this illustration, is medicine.

Byrnes Act Federal law which prohibits interstate transportation of strikebreakers.　　　　　　　　　　　　　　　12

C

cable rate A term used in foreign exchange to refer to the rates quoted for a cable transfer of foreign exchange. The cable rate is higher than the check, demand, 30-, 60-, or 90-day bill of exchange rate.

cable transfer The transfer of funds in a foreign country through instructions sent by cable.　　　　　　　　　　　25

cadastre An inventory of the appraised value of real estate which is used for the purposes of apportioning taxes in the district.

call To demand payment immediately or at a specified date.　　59

callable Redeemable at option of issuer. Applied to a bond or preferred stock that is subject to redemption, usually on or after a specified date or dates, under designated terms and at a stated price or scale of prices.　　　　　　　　　　　40

call-back pay Wages for a minimum number of hours sometimes guaranteed workers called back to work outside of their scheduled working hours.　　　　　　　　　　　12

call-in pay Wages to which an employee is entitled under a union contract or by custom when required to report and there is not a full day's work available.　　　　　　　13

call loan A loan made on a day-to-day basis, callable on twenty-four hours' notice. Typically, loans made to members of the New York Stock Exchange to facilitate the exchange of securities.　　　　　　　　　　　25

call money Money loaned by banks to brokers which is subject to call (demand payment) at the discretion of the lender.

call-money market Those financial institutions which are active in providing call money. Today brokers individually arrange with the big banks for their day-to-day needs to finance margin purchases.

call pay The reimbursement paid to an employee who upon reporting for work as scheduled is not assigned to a job or work

58

call price The price at which a corporation or other obligor is permitted to redeem securities containing call provisions. To compensate for this privilege, a price above par is usually paid. **22**

call purchase A technique for purchasing commodities in which the seller has some option of pricing in the future within a stated range of the present price.

call report Banking authorities such as the Comptroller of the Currency, Federal Reserve Banks, Federal Deposit Insurance Corporation and State Superintendent of Banking call a minimum of three times and sometimes four times a year for the banks under their supervision to provide statements of condition as of the call date. The actual date is not released prior to the "call" so that banks may not engage in "window dressing" activities.

cambism or cambistry The technique of engaging in foreign exchange.

cambist A specialist in foreign exchange or a publication tabulating rates of foreign exchange and associated regulations.

Cambridge School of Economics See "neoclassical school of economics."

cameralism See "kameralism."

cancellation Rendering null and void. This may be done by use of rubber stamps which are used to print the word canceled or a perforation device to cut similar words on a document. In some cases the instrument is burned or cremated.

cannibalization To completely dismantle a vehicle or unit, salvaging usable parts and discarding worn-out items as unserviceable material. **39**

canvasser 1) One who solicits, inspects, or examines for a specific purpose or program.
2) A salesman who is primarily engaged in making sales direct to ultimate consumers in their homes. **13**

capacity factor The ratio of the average load on a machine, plant or system for a given period of time (commonly one year) to the capacity of the machine or equipment. This factor is based on nameplate capacity except when otherwise qualified. **21**

capital 1) Savings or accumulated wealth put to economic use such as invested in business, banking, production, etc. **59**

2) In an accounting sense, the excess of assets over liabilities.

3) In a corporation, it is the sum of the various capital stock accounts, surplus, and undivided profits; hence capital is synonymous with net worth.

4) The ownership interest in a business.

5) In finance, the total tangible assets of a firm.

capital account 1) An account maintained in the name of the owner, or owners, of a business and which indicates his or their equity in that business—usually at the close of the last accounting period.

2) Accounts which show what has been invested in an enterprise.

capital budget The formal estimate of anticipated sales and purchases of capital items as compared with ordinary income receipts and expenditures.

capital charges Sums required to satisfy interest upon and amortization of monies invested in an enterprise.

capital consumption allowances A measure of the plant and equipment worn-out, damaged or rendered obsolete during a given period of time.

capital costs Cost of improvements which extend the useful life of property and/or add to value. Not deductible for tax purposes in the year incurred but depreciable over their useful lives.

capital expenditures Expenditures for the original cost of fixed assets and expenditures that increase the value for fixed assets.

capital formation The creation of capital through savings. In this sense capital is not money or securities or land but a productive good such as machinery which may be purchased with the money savings.

capital gains (and losses) The difference between purchase price and selling price in the sale of assets. The computation is used primarily in tax computations.

capital gains tax rates The tax charged against any gains or profits earned in the transactions of assets. Net profits resulting from sale or exchange of securities held for more than six months are subject to federal taxation at the taxpayer's regular rate with a maximum effective rate of 28 percent.

capital goods Commodities such as raw materials, which are used to produce other goods, either consumer goods or other capital goods.

capital investments A collective term representing the amounts invested in capital, fixed assets, or in long-term securities as contrasted with those funds invested in current assets or short-term securities. Generally speaking, capital investments include all funds invested in assets which, during the normal course of business, are not expected to be realized upon during the ensuing fiscal period. **1**

capitalism The free-enterprise system founded upon private property right, freedom of choice of occupation, limited governmental regulation for the preservation of order, and conviction that the price system permits the best incentive through profit, thus economic growth.

capitalization Total amount of the various securities issued by a corporation. Capitalization may include bonds, debentures, preferred and common stock. Bonds and debentures are usually carried on the books of the issuing company in terms of their par or face value. Preferred and common shares may be carried in terms of par or stated value. Stated value may be an arbitrary figure decided upon by the directors or may represent the amount received by the company from the sale of the securities at the time of issuance. See "par." **2**

capitalization rate 1) The relationship of income to capital investment or value, expressed as a percentage.
2) The (percentage) rate at which an anticipated future income stream is discounted to present worth, *i.e.*, market value. **15**

capitalize 1) To convert into money which may be used in production.
2) To apply something to the purposes of business.
3) To include in the investment account expenditures for purchase or construction of property, or for organization.
4) To issue securities to represent such investment.
5) To divide income by a rate of interest to obtain principal. **19**

capitalized value The asset value (principal) of a given number of income dollars determined on the basis of an assumed rate of return. For example, the capitalized value of a $500 perpetual income at a rate of 5% is $10,000 (obtained by dividing $500 by .05). **40**

capitalized-value standard See "earning-capacity standard."

capital levy A tax on capital as contrasted to income. The tax is on the total appraised or reported valuation as contrasted with a capital gains tax which is only on the appreciated value of the capital.

capital loan A loan which cannot be repaid without disposing of capital assets, in contrast to a loan, for example, to purchase merchandise, the sale of which will provide funds to repay the loan.   **25**

capital movement The liquidation of capital investment in one area and the reinvestment in another area.

capital rating Many mercantile agencies divide their evaluation of a credit risk into two phases, one being an estimation of the net worth of a business which is called the capital rating and the second phase which refers to the payment record of the subject as to his practice of discounting, paying on time or of being slow.

capital requirements 1) The total monetary investment essential to the establishment and operation of an enterprise.

2) The appraised investment in plant facilities and normal working capital. It may or may not include appraised cost of business rights such as patents, contracts and charters.   **54**

capital stock That evidence of ownership in a corporation, in the form of stock certificates, issued in exchange for money or property or out of accumulated earnings. Stock which takes precedence in the distribution of earnings and assets is known as preferred stock. Stock which enjoys no such precedence is generally called common stock, or sometimes capital stock.   **60**

capital-stock subscribed In bookkeeping, a temporary capital account that contains a record of capital stock subscribed for but not issued because the subscriptions have not been fully paid.   **16**

capital structure The distribution of a corporation's capital among its several component parts, such as stock, bonds, and surplus.   **34**

capital surplus Paid-in surplus, donated surplus and revaluation surplus; that is, surplus other than earned surplus. Surplus not arising from profits of operation but from such sources as sale of capital stock at premium, profit on dealings in a corporation's own stock, donated stock, appraisal valuations, and surplus shown by the accounts at the time of organization. **54**

capital turnover A term commonly used by the credit department of a lending institution which represents the number of times the outstanding capital has "turned over" in relation to the net sales for a given period of time, frequently a year. **1**

capitation tax A poll or head tax.

care of securities The action of an investor after buying and paying for a security. Safekeeping practices include registering the security in his own name, using only registered mail when transferring the certificate, endorsing the back of the certificate only when necessary, keeping a separate and identical record such as the transfer agent keeps, and leaving the certificate with either a bank or securities firm. **44**

carloadings The number of railroad freight cars loaded during a stated time period. Formerly this was regarded as a good index of business activity, but inroads of trucking and air freight have caused the figures to have a downward bias.

car-mile Movement of a unit of car equipment a distance of one mile. **19**

carrier's lien Right of carrier to retain property which it has transported, as security for the collection of charges. **19**

carrying broker A broker who is supplying funds for a customer who is trading on margin.

carrying charges 1) Generally, expenses incident to the continued ownership or use of property, as taxes on real property.
2) Specifically, charges made for carrying a debtor, as interest charged on a margin account with a broker. **22**

carrying value The value of a fixed asset remaining after its accumulated depreciation reserve has been deducted from its original depreciable cost. **29**

carry-overs and carry-backs There are two kinds of carry-overs and carry-backs available to corporations for federal income tax purposes: Net operating loss, and unused excess profits credit. The net operating loss carry-over or carry-back is the excess of the deductions allowed under the income tax law over the statutory gross income, with certain exceptions, additions and limitations. The excess profits credit carry-over or carry-back is the excess of the excess profits credit over the excess profits net income. It is to be understood that an operating deficit will not necessarily produce a carry-over or a carry-back for income tax purposes. **19**

cartel Syndicate, combine, or trust generally formed to regulate prices and output in some field. **38**

cash 1) A term associated with any business transaction involving the handling of currency (paper money) and specie (metal coins).

2) In the broader sense, the term "cash" as used in banks includes any item which the bank will immediately credit for deposit or make payment in currency or specie. **23**

cash-and-carry wholesaler 1) a merchant middleman who sells to retailers and other merchants and/or to industrial, institutional, and commercial users but who does not sell in significant amounts to ultimate consumers. In the basic materials, semifinished goods, and tool and machinery trades, merchants of this type are commonly known as "dealers," "distributors," or "supply houses."

2) A wholesaler who does business with the understanding that the customer pays for the goods upon purchase, and takes the goods with him.

cash audit An audit of cash transactions for a stated period, for the purpose of determining that all cash received has been recorded, that all disbursements have been properly authorized and vouched, and that the balance of cash is either on hand or on deposit. A cash audit can be limited from a complete inquiry into all cash transactions (a complete cash audit) to one involving only some of them (a limited cash audit). Such an audit establishes the accountability of the persons responsible for cash. **29**

cash basis The system of accounting under which revenues are accounted for only when received in cash, and expenditures are accounted for only when paid. **29**

cashbook A book of original entry in which the cash receipts journal and the cash payments journal are brought together to form one book. **16**

cash credit The British custom of permitting check overdrafts to an amount which is called the cash credit.

cash discount A deduction that the seller offers to allow on the amount of an invoice to encourage prompt payment by the purchaser by a certain date.

cash dividend Declared dividends that are payable in cash. In

64

this case, cash would include checks as distinguished from a stock or commodity dividend. **1**

cash flow 1) The sources and uses of a company's cash funds over a designated period. In the preparation of a cash-flow statement, both income and balance sheet items are traced in order to highlight the financial progress of a company.
2) Disposition of funds received by a revenue bond project. **40**

cashier One who is usually charged with the custody of receiving and paying out money in a bank or trading establishment and whose signature is necessary on many official documents.

cashier's check A check signed by a cashier or other authorized officer of a bank drawn by the bank on itself. **31**

cash items Items (commonly checks and coupons) which a bank accepts for immediate credit to depositors' accounts. **25**

cash market The spot market as contrasted with the futures market.

cash on delivery Abbreviated COD. That transaction which requires the buyer to pay cash upon receipt of the goods.

cash position The percentage of cash to total net assets indicates relative cash positions. It includes cash and United States Government securities, and is the net amount after deducting current liabilities. **3**

cash reserve 1) An amount of cash, or very liquid securities quickly convertible to cash, kept in reserve for special purposes or to protect against sudden emergency need. **59**
2) Those legal requirements for banks to maintain legal reserves. Banks that are members of the Federal Reserve System keep their cash reserves on deposit with their district Federal Reserve Bank and are permitted to count some of their till cash also as part of their legal reserves. The cash reserves of state nonmember banks are determined by the individual state law.

cash sale One in which cash is received for the full amount at the time of the sale. **16**

cash surrender value The amount which an insurance company will pay the insured on the cancellation of a policy. **85**

casual worker A temporary employee who does not acquire any seniority rights or fringe benefits. He is typically hired because of an unanticipated increase in activity or unforeseen development which is not expected to continue for a long period of time.

catastrophe hazard The hazard of loss by reason of a simultaneous peril to which all insured in a group or a large number of insureds are subject. 5

cats and dogs (Securities) Stocks and bonds of dubious value. Lenders such as banks will not accept such securities as collateral for loans.

causa mortis See "gift causa mortis."

caveat emptor A Latin phrase for: Let the buyer beware.

caveator An interested party who gives notice to some officer not to do a certain act until the party is heard in opposition, as the caveator of a will offered for probate. 22

caveat venditor A Latin phrase for: Let the seller beware.

cease-and-desist order Order issued by a court or government agency directing a business, employer, or union to end an unfair or illegal practice or policy.

cede 1) To buy reinsurance.
2) To effect reinsurance. See "reinsurance." 50, 51

ceiling prices Maximum prices under some system of price controls.

central bank A bank which deals chiefly with other banks in holding the banking reserves of its county or district and normally government agencies or government-related agencies and operates in the broad public interest. In the United States, central banking functions are carried on by the twelve regional Federal Reserve Banks under the supervision of the Board of Governors of the Federal Reserve System. In many other countries there is but a single institution that functions as a central bank, *e.g.*, Bank of England. 8

central merchandising Use of a central office to buy and distribute goods to individual stores belonging to a chain store system. The manager of the branch store has little to do with the decisions of the central office.

central reserve city bank A member bank in New York City or Chicago. At one time, St. Louis also was a central reserve city. Banks in these money centers frequently held the legal reserves of state banks and for this reason were considered unique. In recent years this special treatment, especially in the form of reserve requirements, has declined.

certificate A written or printed statement or declaration of truth that can be used to prove a fact (birth certificate, school certificate, ownership, etc.).

certificate of accounts That document and statement which is issued by a certified public accountant which states the accountant's evaluation of the books of accounts of a firm which he has audited or from which he has prepared statements.

certificate of beneficial interest A legal instrument which is issued to owners of a business. The document describes the owner's equity and is commonly used in voting trusts.

certificate of claim A contingent promise of the Federal Housing Administration to reimburse an insured mortgagee for certain costs incurred during foreclosure of an insured mortgage provided the proceeds from the sale of the property acquired are sufficient to cover those costs.   **33**

certificate of convenience and necessity A certificate issued by a governmental agency to an applicant granting right to operate in the carriage of persons or goods for hire such as required under the Interstate Commerce Act—Part II Motor Carriers; Part III Water Carriers; Part IV Freight Forwarders.   **19**

certificate of deposit Evidence of an investment with an association or bank. Has no stockholders' liability and carries no voting rights. Resembles an investment certificate.   **31**

certificate of incorporation The franchise or charter issued by the state to the original petitioners of an approved corporation. Such franchise or charter constitutes the authority granted by the state for the organization to transact business as a corporation.   **1**

certificate of indebtedness A short-term negotiable promissory note issued by a government or a corporation to show and evidence a floating indebtedness.

certificate of insurance 1) A statement of insurance coverage taking the place of the policy as evidence of insurance and often transferring the right to collect claims to the holder of the certificate.

2) A document evidencing the fact that an insurance policy has been written and includes a statement of the coverage of the policy in general terms. It is frequently found where there are group plans. Thus a master policy is issued to the company, and certificates of insurance are given to the individuals covered by the terms of the policy.   **51, 52**

3) In group insurance, a statement issued to a member of the

group certifying that an insurance contract has been written and containing a summary of the terms applicable to that member.

4) In insurance other than marine or group, a statement that a specified insured and risk are covered to a specified extent, but ordinarily without responsibility on the part of the insurer to notify the certificate holder of termination of the insurance.

certificate of necessity A certificate issued by a federal authority certifying that certain emergency facilities are necessary in the interest of national welfare, which permits the accelerated amortization of all or a part of the cost of the facilities for income tax purposes.

certificate of origin A certificate issued by the proper authorities which accompanies the documents attached to a draft covering the shipment of goods. The certificate usually specifies the origin of material or labor used in the production of such merchandise.   1

certificate of protest That document which a notary public prepares when a dishonored negotiable instrument is again presented but not paid. The certificate is legal evidence that presentation has been made and refused.

certificate of public convenience and necessity A license granted to a private enterprise such as a public utility by the state. This allows government to protect existing franchises from injurious competition.

certification 1) The act of testifying to the truth or validity of something through a written statement.

2) Formal finding by the National Labor Relations Board that a union has been duly selected by a majority of the employees in a bargaining unit and is therefore the exclusive bargaining agent for all employees in the unit.

3) The processing of checks in which the bank guarantees the signature of the drawer and that the drawer has that amount in his account. The amount of the certification is deducted from the drawer's account and held until the certified check is presented for payment.

certified check A depositor's check across the face of which an authorized official of the bank has stamped the word "certified," the bank's name, and signed his own name. By its certification, the bank guarantees that sufficient funds have been set aside from the depositor's account to pay the check when payment is demanded. **23**

certified mail First-class mail for which proof of delivery is secured, usually by the receiver or addressee signing a statement to this fact.

certified public accountant An accountant to whom a state has given a certificate showing that he has met prescribed requirements designed to insure competence on the part of the public practitioner in accounting and that he is permitted to use the designation Certified Public Accountant, commonly abbreviated as C.P.A. **29**

certiorari A proceeding to review in a competent court the action of an inferior tribunal, board, or officer exercising judicial functions, when such action is alleged to be without jurisdiction or otherwise illegal. **5**

certiorari, writ of The method used to direct inferior courts, officers, boards or tribunals to certify to the superior court the record of their proceedings for inspection and review. **15**

cession 1) A yielding of property or a right to another.
2) Reinsurance, or the amount ceded as reinsurance. **42**

cestui que trust A person for whose benefit a trust is created; a beneficiary. **22**

cestui que vie 1) A person whose lifetime measures the duration of an estate.
2) The person on whose life insurance is written. The applicant for the insurance is properly called the insured whether the applicant be the person whose life is insured or not.
3) Where the beneficiary applies for a policy and retains all the incidences of ownership. The person (other than the beneficiary) on whose life the policy is issued is not a party to the contract and has no rights in it.

ceteris paribus (Latin) All other things being equal.

chain banking A term used to refer to an arrangement by which control of a number of banks is exercised through entire or majority ownership of stock by a group of individuals who take an active part in formulating the policies of the banks in the group. See "group banking." **25**

chain of title The succession of conveyances from some accepted starting point whereby the present holder of real property derives his title. **54**

chain stores A number of retail stores under the same ownership, under a central management selling the same merchandise, and following a uniform policy.

chain-store tax A tax especially designed to aid small independent stores by levying a sharply progressive tax on chain stores with more than a minimum number of branches. The tax is paid at the time application is made for a license to start the operation of the store.

chain, voluntary Two or more voluntary groups operating under a common name.   **24**

chamber of commerce An organization of businessmen designed to advance the interests of its members. Three levels are noted: The Chamber of Commerce of the United States is at the national level, the state level, and the city or town level.

channel of distribution The path by which goods move from the producer to the consumer.

chapel Union members of printers' local who are all employed by one firm.

charge 1) The setting or stating of a price for a good or service.
2) To set down the amount that is due from someone.
3) A price.

charge account A means of making sales on credit to retail customers.   **38**

charge-off The act of writing off an account to its present value. This may be to zero or some amount lower than the amount the account is being carried at prior to the writing down or off. It is the result of the recognition of the change in value of an asset. Thus, an account receivable which has proven not to be collectible may be charged off.

charitable bequest A gift of personal property to a charity by will. See "charity."   **30**

charitable devise A gift of real property to a charity by will.   **30**

charitable trust A trust created for the benefit of a community, ordinarily without a definite beneficiary; as, a trust for educational purposes. The same as a public trust; opposed to a private trust.   **30**

charity An agency, institution, or organization in existence and operation for the benefit of an indefinite number of persons and conducted for educational, religious, scientific, medical, or other beneficent purposes.   **22**

charter 1) The grant of rights from a state to a business corporation such as the right to incorporate and transact business.

2) It also means the renting or leasing of a ship.   **5**

chartered accountant A member of an Institute of Chartered Accountants in the British Empire. Admission to such institutes is dependent upon serving a period of apprenticeship and passing an entrance examination.   **29**

charter party A written document stating the terms of agreement between the individual or company chartering a ship and the owner of the vessel.   **5**

charts 1) Any tabular lists of instructions or facts, oftentimes plotted on graph paper.
2) Records of price changes in a stock or market average kept on graph paper with the associated volume of transactions. Analysts utilize these in trying to determine future market action and the resulting actions they should take.

chattel Every species of property, movable or immovable, which is less than a life estate in land.   **5**

chattel mortgage A legal document in which personal property (chattels) is made security for payment of a debt but is left in the hands of the debtor so long as payments are kept up as contracted.   **59**

chattel, personal An article of personal property, as distinguished from an interest in real property.   **30**

chattel, real Any item of property which is connected or concerned or annexed with or to real estate.   **54**

cheap money The economic condition characterized by low interest rates and high price level. Inflationary.

check 1) A restraint or hindrance.
2) A mark used to note that an item has been attended to.
3) A written order on a bank for the payment of money to a stated person or to bearer on demand out of funds which the drawer of the check has in his account in the bank.

check currency Demand deposits created by a bank loan and subject to withdrawal by check as contrasted with paper money or coin.

checkoff A system by which union dues and other assessments are deducted from the employees' pay checks by the employer, either automatically or on specific authorization from the workers.   **12**

check rate The demand rate or most common rate used in foreign exchange quotation which generally is lower than a cable rate but higher than the time bill rate.

check-routing system A device to facilitate the handling and routing of transit items through banks that remit at par all over the United States.   1

check the market In the over-the-counter stock and securities market, this refers to asking for price quotations from several firms to determine the best quotes and the depth of the market. When used to refer to any stock, it is for the purpose of finding out if the market for the stock has changed since the last time it was sold or quoted.   44

cheque The designation of a check in Canada and other foreign countries. See "check."   1

Chicago Board of Trade The largest grain exchange in the world where spot or futures contracts are made in a large range of agricultural products.

child labor Under the 1938 Fair Labor Standards Act it is the gainful employment of individuals under sixteen years of age in nonexcepted activities such as on a farm during vacation from school. In some hazardous activities the age is raised to eighteen.

chose in action A right to personal property which has not been reduced to possession or enjoyment but which is recoverable in an action at law; for example, a patent right, a copyright, a royalty right, a right growing out of a contract or out of damage to person or to property, or a right under a life insurance policy. While the right itself is the chose in action, the evidence of the right, such as the life insurance policy, sometimes is referred to as if it were the chose in action. To be distinguished from a chose in possession.   22

chose in possession Any article of tangible personal property in actual, rightful possession, such as a watch, an automobile or a piece of furniture; to be distinguished from a chose in action.   30

churning 1) Continuous buying and selling of securities which does not move the market very much in either direction.

2) An illegal practice referring to a broker's frequent attempts to buy and sell securities for his clients in order to generate commissions.   44

circular letter of credit A document, usually issued by a bank, that is not addressed to any specific bank or agency. The bank agrees to accept drafts upon it if they are within the terms of the letter.

circulating capital As contrasted with fixed capital which is relatively permanent, circulating capital is used synonymously with working capital.

circulating medium 1) Money.

2) An item of exchange which is generally accepted without endorsement.

circulation 1) Distribution or wide transmission of something.

2) The number of copies of a publication such as a newspaper or magazine which are sold or distributed. Paid circulation is the actual amount of a distribution that is paid for while total circulation may include unpaid or controlled copies.

3) The amount of money outside the Federal Reserve Banks and the Treasury of the United States.

circulation statement The monthly report of the Treasury of the United States which gives the amount of money outstanding, and the amount of currency which is held by the Federal Reserve Banks and the United States Treasury.

city central A union council formed to correlate activities of union locals in a community. **12**

civil authority clause Provision in a fire policy which provides that the insured is protected against damages which may be caused by firemen, policemen, or other civil authorities in their efforts to check fire. **52**

civil corporation An artificial being, created by law for the purpose of engaging in the business purposes stated in its charter which is granted by the state.

civil law The legal system prevailing in the European, Asiatic, Central American, and South American countries which inherited their legal systems from Rome; in other words, in practically all except the English-speaking countries. Compare common law. **30**

claim 1) A right to demand as due a title to any debt.

2) To demand, assert as true.

claim against estate 1) A demand made upon the estate to do or to forbear some act as a matter of duty. A common example would be the claim submitted by a creditor for a debt owed him by the decedent at the time of his death.

2) A title.

class gift A gift to members of the same class; as, for example, the class consisting of the children of the same parents. **22**

classical economic school The line of thought started by Adam

Smith and continued by John Stuart Mill, Thomas Malthus, David Ricardo and Jean Baptiste Say. The idea of the Economic Man, an individual that is rational and will act in his own materialistic self-interest, is the basis upon which many of the principles of the school are founded.

classification 1) A systematic method of arranging or designating.

2) An individual class or group, as insurance underwriting classifications, or stock classifications.

classified stock Equity security divided into groups such as Class A and Class B. The difference between the two classes will be determined by the provisions of the charter and by-laws. Typically the difference between A and B classes of stock is the right of voting.

classified tax A tax in which different tax rates are assigned to each class of property. Thus a luxurious property may be taxed at a higher rate than a simple property.

class price The higher price which may be charged an uninformed buyer. Tourists' purchases in foreign or strange places not infrequently fall in the category of being class priced.

class rate In insurance, the premium rate applicable to a specified class of risk. See "minimum rate."   50, 51

class struggle The communistic doctrine that the propertyless class will overthrow the capitalistic class.

class system A stagger system for the election of members of a board of directors. Each group or "class" has a term of more than one year. Only one class would be voted upon for election in any one year. This permits a perpetuation of control and makes it difficult to unseat the existing management or administration of a corporation.

Clayton Act Federal statute passed in 1914 as an amendment to the Sherman Antitrust Act. Notable for its declaration that human labor is not "a commodity or article of commerce" and for its privileging of certain labor activities.   12

clean bill of exchange A bill of exchange which has no other documents attached to it such as a bill of lading.

clean bill of lading A bill of lading which has not been changed or modified by such limitation clauses as may be added by a carrier such as "shipper's load and count."

clean draft A sight or time draft which has no other documents attached to it. This is to be distinguished from "documentary draft." See "draft" and "documentary draft." **1**

clean letter of credit A letter of credit which does not require such documents as bills of lading as a condition of acceptance by a bank. Such letters are issued only to prime risks.

clear This term has three meanings in banking circles: The clearing of a check is the collection and final payment of it through a clearinghouse; the clearing of active securities through a stock exchange clearinghouse; a legal term meaning "free from encumbrances," such as "clear title" referring to title of property or goods. In transportation, the term refers to the certification given by customs that a vessel may depart since it has complied with the customs requirements. **1**

clearance papers The certificate issued to the vessel's captain which shows that customs requirements have been met.

clearing Domestic clearing (clearing within a country) is the off-setting of bank counterclaims and the settlement of balances; it may be either local or nationwide. This is carried on at a clearinghouse. International clearing is the settlement of balances between countries through the medium of foreign exchange.

clearing agreement Accord between participating nations whereby buyers of foreign goods or services pay for them with their own domestic currency. Periodically the central banks of the agreeing nations will balance at the previously agreed upon rates of exchange.

clearinghouse A place where representatives of banks meet each day at an agreed time to exchange checks, drafts, and similar items drawn on each other and to settle the resulting balances. **25**

clearings The incoming cash letters of items which must be proved, sorted, returned if necessary, and for which settlement must be made. **23**

clique A gentlemen's agreement by a number of individuals to manipulate stock by such techniques as matched orders and short or wash sales. There is no formal organization but rather reliance on concerted action. The action of a clique is today illegal.

clock overtime Overtime paid because more than the contract-specified "regular rate" hours are worked in the day or week even though the statutory maximum regular rate hours are not exceeded. **12**

closed accounts Those accounts which have had no balance remaining for a period of time, and have been reported to management as no longer subject to activity.

closed contract of insurance An insurance contract under which rates and policy provisions cannot be changed. Fraternal insurance companies are not permitted to write this type of insurance. **5**

closed corporation A corporation whose shares are not held by the general public but rather by a small group such as members of a family or the management of a company. The term "close corporation" means the same but is used less frequently.

closed-end investment company A management investment company which has raised its capital by means of a public offering, over a limited period of time, of a fixed amount of common stock (and which may also have raised capital by the issuance of senior securities). The stock of a closed-end investment company is bought and sold on securities exchanges or over-the-counter markets, as are the securities of business corporations. **14**

closed-end investment trust An investment fund which allows only the original prescribed number of shares to be distributed. **22**

closed mortgage A corporate trust indenture under which bonds have been authenticated and delivered (as an original issue) to the extent authorized under the indenture. Compare open-end mortgage. **30**

closed shop A form of union security in which the employer obligates himself to hire and retain in employ only union members. **12**

closed trade The consummation of a transaction by selling a security which had been purchased long previously, or covering a short sale, *i.e.,* buying a security previously sold short. **44**

closed union A union which unreasonably withholds union membership. **12**

closely held Stock which is not likely to come onto the market in the immediate future, especially that stock held by a family or another company for long-term investment purposes. **44**

closing a mortgage loan The consummation of a loan transaction in which all appropriate papers are signed and delivered to the lender, the making of the mortgage becomes a completed transaction, and the proceeds of the mortgage loan are disbursed by the lender to the borrower or upon the borrower's order. **33**

closing charges The expenses or costs incurred in the sale, transfer, or pledging of property, such as recording fees and title-examination fees, which must be provided for and distributed among the parties upon the consummation of the transaction. **33**

closing entries In accounting, those journal entries which are used to balance and close the nominal accounts into summary accounts which in turn are transferred into the income statement or profit and loss statement and balance sheet.

cloud on title A defect in the owner's title to property arising from a written instrument or judgment or from an order of court purporting to create an interest in or lien upon the property, and therefore impairing the marketability of the owner's title though the interest or lien may be shown by evidence to be invalid. **30**

codicil An amendment or supplement to a will. It must be executed with all the formalities of the will itself. **30**

cognovit note A form of note (legal evidence of indebtedness) which is both a promissory note and chattel mortgage. The borrower, within the wording of the instrument, waives his right of action to the chattel property in case of his default in any payments agreed to in the transaction. The holder is entitled to enter judgment without a trial.

coin A piece of metal stamped and issued by the authority of the government for use as money. **38**

coinage The minting of coins from strips of metal. The coins are used as money.

coinsurance 1) Insurance held jointly with another or others. **15**
2) A system of insurance in which the insured is obligated to maintain coverage on a risk at a stipulated percentage of the property's full value, or in the event of loss suffer a penalty in proportion to the deficiency.

coinsurance clause Provision in policy which details the terms of coinsurance. **52**

77

collateral Security pledged to insure an agreement or pledge, such as for the payment of a loan. **38**

collateral heir An individual who is not a brother, sister, aunt, uncle, niece or nephew of a deceased person and thus not in a direct line of descent.

collateral loan A loan which is secured by the pledge of specific property, the borrower depositing with the lender either the property itself or a document bearing evidence of title to the property. **25**

collateral note A promissory note which is secured by the pledge of specific property. **25**

collateral security Real or personal property which is put up or pledged for a loan as to be distinguished from a co-endorsement.

collateral surety Commercial paper, such as stocks or bonds, which is placed with the lender as security for the payment of a loan. **16**

collateral value That estimate of value of the thing put up as security for a loan which is made by the lender. In the case of securities and traded commodities, the lender may be further restricted in his valuation by regulations of an appropriate body such as the exchange or Federal Reserve Board.

collection charges Those fees charged for collecting drafts, notes, coupons and accounts receivable. Since most banks are on a "par" collection system for checks there is no direct charge from such banks. However, in some rural areas there still are "non-par banks"; these banks do charge a fee for paying checks that are not directly presented to them.

collection item (As distinguished from a cash item.) In banking, an item which is received for collection and credit to a depositor's account after final payment. Collection items are usually subject to special instructions regarding delivery of documents when attached, protested, etc., and in most banks are subject to a special fee for handling which is called a collection charge. **23**

collection period Obtained by dividing annual net sales made on credit terms by 365 days to obtain average daily credit sales, then dividing the average daily credit sales into notes and accounts receivable, including any discounted. **61**

collection ratio The ratio of receivables (accounts, notes, and interest) to net sales and it indicates the efficiency of a business in collecting its accounts with customers. **16**

collective bargaining The process of negotiating a union contract or settling grievances in line with the grievance procedure provided in an existing contract, with union representatives on one side, and management representatives on the other.

collective ownership Possession of a good in common with no particular part or proportion assigned to anyone. A public building or road is owned by the taxpayers of the district or subdivision; however, no one taxpayer can identify or claim any particular part.

collectivism A governmental system that operates with most decisions being reached by the centralized government. Communism is an example of a government using the collectivism system.

collector of customs The individual in charge of a port of entry and responsible for the collection of import duties.

Collector of Internal Revenue The Director in charge of a district office of the Internal Revenue Service of the United States Treasury Department.

collusion A secret agreement between two or more persons to defraud a third party of his rights, to injure him, to deceive a court, or to obtain an unlawful object.

color of title An appearance of title founded upon a written instrument which, if valid, would convey title. **5**

comaker A person who signs the note of another as an additional maker for the purpose of strengthening the credit of the principal maker. **25**

combination The merger of two or more companies for the purpose of controlling and lessening competition or to achieve economies.

combination in restraint of trade Any agreement or understanding between individuals or companies with the objective of restricting competition in the sale, production, or the distribution of a good or service.

combination plan In insurance, a retirement plan which combines two or more of the established methods of funding, such as a combination of group annuities for current service benefits and individual annuities for prior service benefits, or a life insurance program with a self-administered retirement plan. **32**

combination rate A through rate made by combining two or more rates.

combined entry (compound entry) One that contains more than two bookkeeping elements. Such an entry may consist of two or more debits and one credit, or one debit and two or more credits. It may also consist of several debits and several credits. **16**

commerce Trade, communication, etc., between the states and between nations; the basis for Congressional labor legislation through exercise of its "commerce power." **12**

commerce power The power of Congress under the Federal Constitution to regulate domestic trade between the states. **12**

commercial bank A banking corporation which accepts demand deposits subject to check and makes short-term loans to business enterprises, regardless of the scope of its other services. **25**

commercial bar That bar, or brick of precious metal such as gold or silver, which is designed for use in the arts and industry area as distinguished from one designed for monetary use.

commercial bill Those bills of exchange which have resulted from a commercial business transaction as compared to the noncommercial bills such as a banker's bill. In theory, a commercial bill, if discounted, would provide a desirable expansion of the money supply while a bill arising out of, say, a financial speculation, would generally be undesirable and inflationary, if rediscounted.

commercial credit That credit used by manufacturers, retailers, wholesalers, jobbers, and commission agents for the production and distribution of goods. It is distinguished from investment, agricultural, bank, and personal credit.

commercial credit company A finance or credit company. One which buys and sells installment contracts and open book accounts which are obtained from retailers and wholesalers. At times they also engage in factoring.

commercial credit documents A general expression for those papers and documents such as bills of lading and warehouse receipts which accompany an extension of commercial credit.

commercial discounts That discount which is given to encourage prompt payment of a commercial account.

commercial draft A written order signed by one person or firm requesting another person or firm to pay a stated sum of money to a third party. **16**

commercial letter of credit An instrument by which a bank lends its credit to a customer to enable him to finance the purchase of goods. Addressed to the seller, it authorizes him to draw drafts on the bank under the terms stated in the letter. **25**

commercial loan A short-term loan made by a bank to a business enterprise for use in the production, manufacture, or distribution of goods or in the financing of related services. **25**

commercial paper This term applies to notes, drafts, bills of exchange, and other negotiable paper originating from commercial transactions (the transfer and movement of goods). These are usually notes or acceptances with a definite maturity date which are received by a business enterprise in payment for goods sold or services rendered.

commercial paper house Those principals and dealers who buy commercial paper at one rate and attempt to sell it at another. Note brokers.

commercial policy 1) An administrative plan of action on the part of government, business, or some other organization to stimulate or retard sale, production or distribution of a good or service.
2) An accident or health insurance policy sold to persons in less hazardous occupations such as sales, teaching, clerical, business administration, etc.

commercial treaty The agreement between two or more nations which enumerates the rights and responsibilities of individuals and companies doing business between the two nations.

commission 1) A percentage of the principal or of the income (or of both) which a fiduciary receives as compensation for its services; to be distinguished from allowance, charge, and fee. **30**
2) Formal, written authority granting certain privileges or powers, or commanding the performance of certain duties or acts.

commission broker An agent who executes the public's orders for the purchase or sale of securities or commodities, for which he receives a percentage of the transaction as his compensation. See "dealer."

commission house A brokerage firm, in securities or commodities or both, that buys and sells for its customers for a commission of the transaction.

commission merchant A business that is established for the purpose of selling goods as the consignee for producers, merchants, and manufacturers.   **16**

committee 1) Persons appointed to deal with or take charge of some matter.

2) One (or a group) appointed by court to manage the estate of a mentally incompetent person. In most states he is known as a guardian.

Committee for Economic Development A group of business executives who engage in and sponsor economic research and publish their findings.

commodity Economic goods such as raw or semi-processed materials which may be quoted either on a cash or immediate delivery basis or on a futures basis. Such commodities are frequently quoted in the financial or business sections of newspapers and have agreed upon standards of quality or type.

commodity agreement Contract between producers to control marketing or production of the covered commodity for the purpose of preventing price decline.

Commodity Credit Corporation A corporation formed by the government of the United States for the purpose of providing the facility for the United States Department of Agriculture's programs of agricultural price support and related activities such as storage, transportation, sale, loans and purchase.

commodity dollar A nonrealized economic concept which would stabilize the value of money by removing the metallic base and freeze the value of the dollar to an index of commodity prices.

commodity exchange An association of member traders in agricultural products which have standards of quality. The typical exchange deals primarily in futures which provide the opportunity of hedging. Spot or actual commodity transactions may also take place on some exchanges but the proportionate volume is much smaller than the futures contracts.

Commodity Exchange Act The 1936 Act which created the Commodity Exchange Commission which regulates trading in the contract markets and has other broad powers to prevent fraud and manipulation in covered commodities and to establish limits in trading for the purpose of preventing excessive speculation.

Commodity Exchange Authority The unit within the United States Department of Agriculture which enforces the Commodity Exchange Act of 1936.

Commodity Exchange Commission The Secretary of Agriculture, the Secretary of Commerce, and the Attorney General are designated by the Commodity Exchange Act of 1936 as the Commodity Exchange Commission.

commodity paper Any note, draft or other document with accompanying warehouse receipts or bills of lading for commodities. In the event of default, the lender may sell the commodities up to the value of the loan and the expense of collection.

commodity rate That interest rate charged by banks on notes, bills of exchange, drafts and similar documents issued on staple commodities.

commodity standard An occasionally proposed monetary system which would substitute a commodity or commodities for the precious metal or other base of a currency.

commodity theory of money A proposed explanation of the value of money which holds that money is valued by the value of its base such as gold or silver. While it is recognized that there is a relationship between the base and the value of money, it is further recognized that other factors also have a deep influence on the value of money.

common capital stock Represents the funds invested by the residual owners whose claims to income and assets are subordinated to all other claims. See "common stock."   **21**

common carrier A business engaged in transportation on a hire basis. It is required by the terms of its charter to charge uniform rates and within the limits of its facilities to serve all comers.

common disaster Sudden and extraordinary misfortune which brings about the simultaneous or near-simultaneous death of two or more associated persons.   **22**

common-disaster clause In insurance, a clause that provides for an alternative beneficiary in event both the insured and the original beneficiary die at the same time in an accident.   **5**

common law An unwritten system of laws which has grown out of custom and traditional usage. It originated in England and its form of development was different from that of Roman (civil) law. Compare civil law. **30**

common-law defenses 1) Defense pleas which are based on common law, rather than civil law.

2) Pleas which would defeat an insured workman's suit against his employer (and which are still effective in the absence of Workmen's Compensation or Employer's Liability legislation). They are: Contributory negligence on employee's part, injury caused by fellow servant, assumption of risk by the employee in the course of his work. **50**

common-law trust See "Massachusetts trust."

Common Market A group of West European countries who have negotiated to build a common tariff wall against outside interests while gradually disintegrating tariffs among themselves. **44**

common stock A security representing ownership of a corporation's assets. The right of common stock to dividends and assets ranks after the requirements of bonds, debentures and preferred stocks. Normally, increases in asset values and earnings beyond the fixed claims of bonds and preferred stocks rebound to the benefit of the common stock. Similarly, common stocks are affected first by decreases in asset values and earnings. Generally, shares of common stock have voting rights. **3**

common-stock dividends Dividends declared on common stock during the year whether or not they were paid during the year. Unless otherwise qualified, it is the amount of such dividends charged to retained income (earned surplus) and includes those payable in cash or stock. **21**

common-trust fund A fund maintained by a bank or a trust company exclusively for collective investment and reinvestment of money contributed to the fund by the bank or trust company in its capacity as trustee, executor, administrator, or guardian and in conformity with the rules and regulations of the Board of Governors of the Federal Reserve System pertaining to the collective investment of trust funds by national banks as well as with the statutes and regulations (if any) of the several states. **30**

communism A political and economic theory calling for the complete abolition of all private property and complete control by the community of all matters including labor, religion, politics and social relations. As an emotionally charged word, communism must be interpreted within the context of its use.

community property Property in which a husband and wife have each an undivided one-half interest by reason of their marital status; recognized in all civil-law countries and in certain states of the Southwest and Pacific Coast area of the United States. **22**

community trust A charitable trust which receives and administers gifts for the public benefit of a community or locality.

commuted value Present value of future payments due or receivable, computed on the basis of a given rate of interest. **42**

company An association of persons, whether incorporated or not, for the purpose of carrying on some business. **5**

company store A store maintained by an employer which sometimes advances supplies to workers on a scrip payment basis. **12**

company town A community which, including residences and premises occupied by the workers, is owned by the employer. **12**

company union An unaffiliated union whose membership is limited to the employees of a single company. **12**

comparative advantage Situation in which an individual, firm, locality or nation can produce a good or service cheaper than another.

comparative statement The income, expense, profit and loss, balance sheet or other financial statements of the same concern for two or more consecutive years that are analyzed to determine the increase or decrease in their component items, frequently for credit purposes. **1**

comparative statistics The analysis of conditions of equilibrium as a result of changing one variable.

compensated dollar A monetary unit in which the gold content would be changed from time to time to keep the purchasing power level with some commodity index.

compensating balance The amount of a commercial loan which the banker requires his borrower to keep with the bank.

compensation Something given or received as an equivalent for services, debt, loss, suffering; indemnity. **38**

compensatory duty An import duty of an amount sufficient to balance a domestic excise tax, or a foreign producer's governmental subsidy.

compensatory fiscal policy Functional financial policy. A Keynesian concept. When economic conditions are poor the government should spend a great deal, sufficient to take up the slack in business. The spendings should be deficit financed. When economic conditions are above normal the government should reduce spendings and operate with a surplus.

competency A fitness or sufficiency to undertake something, such as to enter into a contract. For example, in insurance, the company must have the charter and permission of the state to write business. The other party to the insurance contract must have the mental faculties to be able to contract. **5**

complaint The allegation of damages or accusation of crime, with an offer to prove the truth and fact of same.

complete audit An audit in which an examination is made of the system of internal control and of the details of all of the books of account, including subsidiary records and supporting documents, as to legality, mathematical accuracy, complete accountability, and application of accepted accounting principles. One of the main features of a complete audit is that the auditor is not expected to make any qualifications in his report except such as are imposed by lack of information, that is, physical inability to get the facts. See "limited audit." **29**

complex trust A trust in which the trustee is not required to distribute income currently, or distribute amounts other than income, or make a charitable contribution. **22**

composite demand The complete schedule of demand for a good or service.

composite supply The complete supply schedule for a good or service or function.

composition settlement The acceptance by a creditor of an amount smaller than that which he is legally entitled to from a debtor. In doing this he waives his right to the full amount.

compound duty A specific tariff duty in addition to an ad valorem duty.

compound entry See "combined entry."

compound interest Interest upon principal plus accrued interest. **23**

comptroller In large firms this office is often held by a vice president with the title "Vice President and Comptroller." The duties of a comptroller generally embrace the audit functions of the firm and the establishment of control over all systems in use in operations. The comptroller also is one of the key officers in the future planning of the firm's operations.   1

Comptroller of the Currency An appointed official who is responsible for the chartering, supervision, and liquidation of national banks. His office is located in the Treasury Department.   25

Comptroller's Call The Comptroller of the Currency may "call" upon all national banks to submit a complete financial report of their activities at any given date. Reports must, according to law, be submitted at his call at least three times a year. These "called reports" must also be published in all local newspapers in the town nearest to the bank.   1

concession 1) A deviation from higher regular terms or previous conditions.

2) The right to use property for a stated purpose or purposes.

conciliation Attempt by third party, a conciliator, to aid the settling of a labor dispute by hearing both sides and offering advice and nonbinding suggestions.   12

condemnation The legal taking of private property for the public use and interest. The taking of such property must be through the exercise of due process of law.   54

condemnation, excess An expression used to describe the taking of more property or property rights than the condemning authority actually needs for the project involved.   15

conditional endorsement An endorsement of a negotiable instrument which states and imposes conditions upon the transferee. The instrument may still be negotiated within the terms of the condition but the individual who has made the conditional endorsement has the right to the proceeds of the instrument should the conditions not be fulfilled.

conditional gift A gift of property by will which is subject to some condition specified in the will or in the trust instrument; opposed to an absolute gift.   30

conditional sale A sale in which the transfer of title to property (real or personal) is dependent upon the performance of a stipulated condition.   33

conditional sales contract An installment contract which stipulates that title to the property referred to in the contract shall not pass to the purchaser until the price is fully paid in cash.   16

condition precedent A qualification or restriction which must happen or be performed before the contract or estate dependent upon it can arise or vest. **22**

condition subsequent A condition, by the failure or nonperformance of which an estate already vested is defeated. **22**

condominium The common ownership of a piece of property by one or more individuals, each of whom owns an absolute undivided interest in the property, or a portion of it. It is an interest which has all of the characteristics associated with free ownership, such as alienability, mortgageability, divisability and inheritability. **64**

confession of judgment An admission by a party to whom an act or liability is imputed. **35**

confidence man An individual who cheats and defrauds. A swindler.

confirmed letter of credit A foreign bank wishing to issue a letter of credit to a local concern may request a local bank in the city in which the beneficiary is located to confirm this credit to the beneficiary. The purpose of this confirmation is to lend the prestige and responsibility of the local bank to the transaction because the status of the foreign bank may be unknown to the beneficiary. The confirming bank assumes responsibility for the payment of all drafts drawn under the credit and usually charges a fee for doing so. **1**

confiscation The governmental seizure of private property without compensation for the action.

conflict of laws That branch of the law which is concerned with the legal principles applicable in a situation wherein the law of two or more jurisdictions is claimed to be applicable by the parties to the controversy and the laws of the two or more jurisdictions are in conflict with one another.

conglomerate The term used to describe a corporate consolidation in which one company acquires another in a different industry. **48**

Congress of Industrial Organizations See "American Federation of Labor and Congress of Industrial Organizations."

consanguinity Blood relationship; to be distinguished from affinity. **30**

consent decree The settlement of equity cases whereby the defendant agrees to stop certain actions that caused the case to be brought. This agreement is expressed as a judicial decree and the legal suit is dropped.

conservator The appointed official charged with the protection of the interests in an estate. He may protect the creditors of a bank or a declared incompetent as well as see that certain laws that are in the public interest are enforced.

consideration Something of value given by one party to another in exchange for the promise or act of such other party. **22**

consignee The person to whom articles are shipped. **19**

consignment The act of an individual or company of delivery or transfer of goods to an agent to be cared for or sold. **5**

consignor The owner of goods sent to a consignee. **16**

consolidated The results obtained when the accounts of a parent company and its subsidiary companies are combined to reflect the financial position and results of operations of the group as if operated as a single entity. Such a consolidation involves proper intercompany eliminations and minority interest adjustments. **21**

consolidated balance sheet A balance sheet showing the financial condition of a corporation and its subsidiaries. See "balance sheet." **2**

consolidated mortgage A mortgage on several separate units of property which are covered by the consolidated mortgage.

consolidation See "merger."

consols Originally referred to a three percent bond issue of Great Britain which had no stated maturity. Since the consols have no maturity and bear a fixed rate of interest the price they sell at may be converted into a yield rate which in turn approaches what economists refer to as "pure" interest. See "pure interest."

conspicuous consumption Term used by Veblen to refer to the use of goods or services for purposes of impressing others rather than normal and useful consumption.

constant, annual The percentage which, when applied directly to the face value of a debt or capital value of an asset, develops the annual amount of money necessary to pay a specified net interest rate on the reducing balance and to liquidate the debt or value of the asset in a certain period of time. This is the percentage equivalent of the level payment mortgage plan or the annuity factors developed in the Inwood tables, whereby the annual payment (or return) is applied first to interest on the reducing balance of the debt, or value of the asset, with the remainder applied to principal reduction. **15**

constant cost Costs of production may be fixed or variable. The fixed or constant costs are those that do not change with changes in production. The variable costs of production do change with the volume of production. If reference is made to unit costs of production then many of the fixed costs of total production will become variable unit costs.

construction loan Funds extended on the security of real estate for the purpose of constructing improvements on the property and usually advanced during the period of construction. **33**

constructive discharge A form of discrimination that forces a worker to "quit." **12**

constructive eviction The act whereby the owner does not provide the tenant with such comfort or peace as the tenant desires so that the tenant will, therefore, voluntarily break the lease.

constructive mileage An arbitrary mileage allowed to a transportation line in dividing joint rates, etc., on a mileage prorate (not the actual mileage). Also arbitrary mileage allowed train and engine employees for mileage paid for and not run. **19**

constructive trust A trust imposed by a court of equity as a means of doing justice, without regard to the intention of the parties, in a situation in which a person who holds title to property is under a duty to convey it to another person; to be distinguished from an express trust and a resulting trust. **30**

consul A nation's foreign service officer located in a foreign country who represents his nation's tourists, businessmen and other traveling nationals.

consular invoice An invoice covering a shipment of goods certified (usually in triplicate) by the consul of the country for which the merchandise is destined. This invoice is used by customs officials of the country of entry to verify the value, quantity, and nature of the merchandise imported. **1**

consult account A trust in which the trustee is required by the instrument to consult a designated party before taking action; to be distinguished from consent trust. **22**

consumer credit Credit extended by a bank to borrowers (usually individuals) for personal use and for the purchase of consumer goods and services. Repayable in regular equal installments. Loans may be secured or unsecured, depending upon pertinent factors. **23**

consumer goods Commodities whose ultimate use is to contribute directly to the satisfaction of human wants or desires—such as shoes and food—as distinguished from producers' or capital goods. **33**

consumer price index A measure of the average change in prices of goods and services purchased by city wage earner and clerical worker families. The index represents the total cost of a selected "market basket" of goods and services expressed as a percentage of the average cost of the same "market basket" in a selected period.

consumers' cooperative An association of ultimate consumers organized to purchase goods and services primarily for use by or resale to the membership. **13**

consumer sovereignty The idea that the consumer determines what products are made and sold since if the consumer does not buy the product the merchant will not reorder from the manufacturer who in turn will discontinue producing the good. Tied to it is the idea of the price system and private profit as well as a reasonable balance between demand and supply.

consumer surplus That difference in price or utility which results in the consumer obtaining goods or services at a price below that which he would be willing to pay.

consumption The use of a good or service to satisfy a desire.

consumption function When plotted on a chart, it is a schedule which shows the proportion of expenditures for consumption as they are related to the disposable income of the individual or group.

contemplation of death Act of considering and acting upon the possibility of death. In estate taxes, transfers near the date of death are commonly considered transfers in contemplation of death and as such taxable in the estate even though they would be excludable had the decedent lived a greater number of years. **22**

contestable clause In insurance, that section of the contract that states conditions under which the policy may be contested or voided. Such factors as fraud or material misstatement would be grounds for invoking this clause. **5**

contest of a will An attempt by legal process to prevent the probate of a will or the distribution of property according to the will. **30**

contingency reserve A reserve created to cover the deficiency that might arise in departments where an original appropriation proves to be inadequate to cover the necessary expenditures. In some instances, the law prohibits the creation of such a reserve. **29**

contingent beneficiary The beneficiary whose interest is conditioned upon a future occurrence which may or may not take place. Unless or until the condition takes place, the interest is only contingent. **22**

contingent duty In international trade, a countervailing duty levied on an importation to offset a subsidy or similar export aid granted by the exporting nation.

contingent fund An amount of money set aside to take care of the expenses of emergencies. These emergencies may not be predictable, but the fund should be able to permit the company to continue to operate in the event the contingencies develop.

contingent interest A future interest in real or personal property that is dependent upon the fulfillment of a stated condition. Thus, the interest may never come into existence. To be distinguished from vested interest. **22**

contingent order An order to buy or sell a security at a certain price dependent upon the execution of a prior order. **44**

contingent remainder A future interest in property that is dependent upon the fulfillment of a stated condition before the termination of a prior estate; to be distinguished from a vested remainder. **30**

continuing account An open-book account which is periodically settled by the debtor but, since purchases are continually being made, is not closed out.

continuing agreement That phase of a regular borrower's loan agreement with his bank which simplifies his borrowing since the borrower does not have to make a loan application and sign a note every time he borrows. Once the continuing agreement is signed the borrower may borrow within the terms of the contract on a continuing basis.

continuing guaranty A form given to a bank by a person to guarantee repayment of a loan to another party. This guaranty promises payment by the guarantor in the event of default by the borrower and is so worded that it may apply to a current loan or to one made at a later date. The guaranty may or may not pledge collateral as security for the loan. **1**

continuity of coverage In insurance, a clause attached or contained in a fidelity bond which takes the place of another bond and agrees to pay the losses that would be recoverable under the first bond except that the discovery period has expired. This would be in a case where losses have been caused by a dishonest employee and have not been discovered, though they had occurred at various times stretching over a period of time, that time being a period under which several bonds had been insured. This may involve a chain of several bonds, each one superseding a prior obligation. Those losses will be covered if the chain of bonds is unbroken and each has included continuity of coverage clause. **52**

continuous audit An audit in which the detailed work is performed either continuously or at short, regular intervals throughout the fiscal period, usually at the shortest intervals (*e.g.*, weekly or monthly) at which subsidiary records are closed and made available for audit in controllable form. Such "continuous" work leads up to the completion of the audit upon the closing of the accounting records at the end of the fiscal year. **29**

continuous market The market for a security or commodity which is so broad that normal amounts may usually be sold with little difficulty and small price variation.

contra balances In bookkeeping, balances in accounts that are the opposite of the normal balances of such accounts (as an account payable with a debit balance). **16**

contract An agreement between two or more parties to do or not to do some lawful thing for a lawful consideration. **38**

contract carrier A motor carrier transporting goods for one or more concerns under contract specifically designed to cover type of service, special equipment, etc. **19**

contract clause That portion of the United States Constitution which prohibits any state from impairing the rights and obligations of legal contracts.

contract for deed An agreement by a seller to deliver the deed to the property when certain conditions have been fulfilled, such as the completion of certain payments and provision of insurance. It has similar features to a mortgage. **5**

contract labor Workers who have signed an agreement to only work for a stated employer. Such an agreement is not legal in the United States.

contract market Any commodity exchange which may engage in the business of futures contracts and is approved by the Secretary of Agriculture subject to the Commodity Exchange Administration supervision.

contract of adhesion The insurance contract is a contract of adhesion since there is no bargaining basis between the insurance company and the insured. **5**

contract of sale A written document whereby an owner agrees to convey title to a property when the purchaser has completed paying for the property under the terms of the contract. **31**

contractor A person who contracts to perform work or to supply materials under specified conditions. **33**

contract rent That amount agreed upon between a tenant and owner for the use of real estate for a stated period of time. This contract rent may be higher or lower than the theoretical economic rent which is the difference between the productivity of the land and marginal land.

contractual plan By common usage, an investment-accumulation plan with a stated paying-in period and provision for regular investments at monthly or quarterly dates. Substantially synonymous with prepaid charge plan. **3**

contribution Something given such as money, time, etc. **38**

contribution clause See "coinsurance clause" and "average clause." Both clauses are similar in effect. **50, 51, 52**

contributory pension A retirement system in which the employer and the employee both make payments for the benefit of the employee. The system may in addition be vested, that is, subject to tenure; the employee, upon termination of employment, may take his and his employer's contribution with him. A nonvested pension would not have the employer's contribution go with the employee until actual retirement.

control 1) Power or authority to manage or administrate.

2) Maintaining records and preparing reports to meet corporate legal and tax requirements and measure the results of the company operations; providing accounting services structured for use by managers in planning and controlling the business. **20**

controlled account 1) A discretionary account.

2) A trading account in securities or commodities in which the principal does not necessarily instruct his broker to buy or

sell but rather gives a power of attorney for his broker to exercise his own discretion.

3) An account which a salesman is able to take with him in the event he changes firms.

controlled economy The administration of the means of production and consumption by a large amount of government planning and controls with only nominal use of the price system, the objective being to direct and guide the economy.

controlled inflation That economic situation in which the monetary and fiscal authorities of a nation deliberately create inflationary conditions, generally through increasing the supply of money. The objective is to pull the economy out of a recession or period of deflation into prosperity. By such controls as the authorities have over the money supply they are able to reduce the increase in inflation as they approach their goal.

controlling account In bookkeeping, an account, usually kept in the general ledger, which receives the aggregate of the debit and of the credit postings to a number of identical, similar, or related accounts called subsidiary accounts so that its balance equals the aggregate of the balance in these accounts. See "general ledger" and "subsidiary account." **29**

controlling company A parent company that controls other companies through several devices. Some of them are: Through stock ownership, through interlocking boards of directors, by use of a holding company, through leases, patents, copyrights and common management.

controlling interest In a legal sense slightly over fifty percent of the voting stock will control any corporation, and thus constitute a controlling interest. However, in a de facto sense, many corporations may be controlled by a much smaller percentage of voting stock if the rest of the stock is widely dispersed and not active in voting.

convenience goods Those consumer goods which are of low price which consumers wish to purchase with little effort and for which they generally do not "shop."

conventional loan A non-Federal Housing Administration or Veterans Administration loan on property whose principal usually is not extinguished by periodic payments if it is a nonamortized conventional loan. **5**

conventional mortgage loan A mortgage loan made directly to the borrower without government insurance or guaranty. **33**

conventional tariff A tariff established by a commercial treaty between nations.

convention values Values at which the Commissioner of Insurance permits certain securities to be carried on insurance companies' books. Also known as "commissioner's values." The values are used during very abnormal business conditions, such as in periods of panic and severe depression.　　　**5**

conversion 1) The exchange of personal or real property of one nature for that of another nature.

2) The exchange of one type of security for another, as for example, the exchange of bonds for stock.

3) The exchanging of a charter granted by the state for a federal charter, etc.

4) The appropriation of, dealing with, or using the property of another without right or consent as though it were one's own.　　　**1**

conversion price That amount or rate at which a holder of a convertible bond may exchange it for the stock of the same corporation. This price may be fixed or determinable.

convertible Subject to exchanging for something else; as, stock convertible to bonds, or bonds to stock, or an asset convertible to cash.　　　**59**

convertible money Any money which may be exchanged at par for the standard or legal money.

conveyance 1) The transfer of ownership of property.

2) The instrument by which title to property is transferred.　　　**33**

cooling-off period A period of time (usually 30 to 90 days) during which a union is barred from striking, or an employer from locking out his employees. The period may be required by law or be a part of a labor agreement.

cooperative A type of business enterprise that is owned by its customers.　　　**16**

cooperative bank The name which is used in several New England states for a savings and loan association.　　　**31**

cooperative marketing The process by which groups composed of producers, middlemen, consumers, or combinations of them act collectively in buying or selling or both.　　　**13**

copartnership (or **partnership**) A company of partners, as distinguished from a proprietorship or a corporation.　　　**35**

copyright The exclusive legal right of writers, composers, playwrights and artists to publish and dispose of their works for a period of time. In the United States this term is author's lifetime plus fifty years.

corner Buying of a stock or commodity on a scale large enough to give the buyer, or buying group, control over the price. A person who must buy that stock or commodity, for example one who is short, is forced to do business at an arbitrarily high price with those who engineered the corner. See "short." **2**

corner influence In real estate, the effect of street intersection upon adjacent property. The cause of a different value for real estate adjacent to a corner as compared with property away from the corner. **54**

corn-hog ratio That relationship between the selling price of corn and the selling price of hogs. The farmer knowing how many pounds a hog will gain from eating one bushel of corn is able to decide whether it is more profitable to sell the corn or to feed it to his hogs and sell the hogs.

corporate agent Trust companies act as agents for corporations, governments, and municipalities for various transactions. In each case, a fee is charged for the particular service rendered. **1**

corporate depositary A trust institution serving as the depositary of funds or other property. See "depositary" and "depository." **30**

corporate fiduciary A trust institution serving in fiduciary capacity, such as executor, administrator, trustee, or guardian. **30**

corporate resolution A document given to a bank by a corporation defining the authority vested in each of its officers who may sign and otherwise conduct the business of the corporation with the bank. Corporate resolutions usually are given with or without borrowing powers. These powers are granted by the board of directors of the firm. **1**

corporate shell A company that exists without fixed assets aside from cash but may have a stock exchange listing. **44**

corporate stock The equity shares of a corporation. These shares may be common, preferred or classified. The term corporate stock is also used occasionally to refer to bonds of some municipalities.

corporate surety 1) Insurance provided by a surety company as compared to surety provided by an individual.

2) The writing of bonds by a corporation as obligor.

corporate trust A trust created by a corporation, typical of which is a trust to secure a bond issue.   30

corporation A form of business organization that may have many owners with each owner liable only for the amount of his investment in the business. It is an artificial person created by state or federal law. As defined by the Supreme Court of the United States, a corporation is "an artificial being, invisible, intangible, and existing only in contemplation of law."   16

corporation finance That area of business which is concerned with providing the funds needed by a business. This would include the technique of organizing and raising the initial capital of the corporation, the provision of working capital through proper cash-flow practices, the emergency steps needed in the event of insolvency or bankruptcy, as well as those techniques such as dividend policies which will permit a corporation to obtain needed capital for expansion.

corporation income tax A progressive tax levied on earnings of corporations and Massachusetts trusts by either the federal or state government.

corporation sole A one-man corporation, the authority, duties and powers of which are attached to and go with the office and not the natural person who for the time being holds the office.   30

correspondent bank One which carries a deposit balance for a bank located in another city or engages in an exchange of services with that bank.   25

correspondent firm A brokerage firm that maintains a mutually advantageous business and financial association with another brokerage firm. This quite often occurs between one firm located in a city where there is an exchange and another out-of-town firm which has business executed and cleared by the member firm.   44

cost The amount, measured in money, of cash expended or other property transferred, capital stock issued, services performed, or a liability incurred, in consideration of goods or services received or to be received.   17

cost accounting That method of accounting which provides for the assembling and recording of all the elements of cost incurred to accomplish a purpose, to carry on an activity, or operation, or to complete a unit of work or a specific job. **29**

cost, book The cost of acquisition shown in the general ledger of an individual partnership or corporation which generally includes direct and indirect costs, financing costs, and all development costs, except preliminary operating losses. **15**

cost, center A purely arbitrary division or unit of a plant set up for costing purposes only. It may be a man at a bench, a machine or group of machines, a department, a floor, or an entire building. **28**

cost, direct Costs computed and identified directly with a specific product, job or function. It usually refers to identifiable costs of raw materials, labor, overhead, etc.

cost, expired Costs which are not applicable to the production of future revenues and, for that reason, are treated as deductions from current revenues or are charged against retained earnings. Examples are costs of products or other assets sold or disposed of and current expenses. **17**

cost, indirect A cost not particularly identifiable with a specific product, job or function.

cost-of-goods sold A firm's production cost or inventory value of the products the company sells, which appear in the profit and loss statement.

cost of living A misnomer frequently applied to an index developed by the Bureau of Labor Statistics, Department of Labor. The proper designation is consumer price index. It shows the relationship of wages to the cost of commodities. See "consumer price index."

cost-of-living adjustment The device found in some union contracts which provides that the employer shall adjust his hourly wage rate up or down in sympathetic relationship to some index such as the consumer price index so that the covered employees will maintain the same purchasing power.

cost-of-merchandise sold In accounting, the result obtained by subtracting the ending merchandise inventory from the sum of the beginning merchandise inventory and the net purchases for the month. **16**

cost-of-production theory of value Concept developed by Ricardo that holds that the value of a good or service is determined by not only the labor-time value but also includes the capital-time value.

cost-of-service taxation principle The theory that taxpayers should pay taxes at the same rate that the government provides services for them. A school tax would only be paid by parents of those attending school and then only for the cost of the child to the school.

cost of subsistence Theory of wages which holds that over a period of time workers are only paid an amount which will permit them to exist with their family dependents.

cost plus contracts An agreement by which the buyer pays the seller or producer his costs of the product and also a percentage of the costs in addition for his profits. Contracts for production of devices of unknown costs such as a space vehicle may take this form. Where costs are better known, it is probable that a fixed price contract will be used.

cost unit A term used in cost accounting to designate the unit of product or service whose cost is computed. These units are selected for the purpose of comparing the actual cost with a standard cost or with actual costs of units produced under different circumstances or at different places and times. See "unit cost" and "work unit." **29**

cosurety One of a number who jointly insure a particular bond. One of two or more sureties on the same bond. **51**

Council of Economic Advisers That group of economists brought together as a result of the Employment Act of 1946 to serve as advisers to the President of the United States in such roles as preparation of the annual report to Congress.

counsel Legal advice; also a lawyer or lawyers engaged to give such advice or to conduct a case in court. **5**

counter check A form of check provided by a bank for the convenience of the depositor. A counter check can be cashed only by the drawer personally. **25**

counterfeit money Money illegally manufactured in imitation of genuine money (currency or coins). **25**

counterpart fund The amount of domestic currency a nation sets aside as an offset adjustment for loans or gifts from abroad.

countersign To sign what has already been signed in order to verify the authenticity of an instrument. **25**

countervailing duty See "contingent duty."

countervailing power Economic theory which holds that when one side of an economic situation obtains an advantage then, in turn, the other side tends to obtain a balancing power.

100

country bank The American Bankers' Association, for the purpose of making studies of bank operations, considers banks whose total assets are $7,500,000 or less as being, generally speaking, "country banks." In a geographic sense, a country bank is any bank not classified as being a Reserve City Bank. **1**

county agent The man or woman jointly employed by the Department of Agriculture of the United States, county government and state agricultural school (land grant college) to bring to farm families improved farm practices and agricultural research.

coupon One of a series of promissory notes of consecutive maturities attached to a bond or other debt certificate and intended to be detached and presented on their respective due dates for payment of interest. **25**

coupon policy An insurance policy also called guaranteed investment policy. A type of policy sold by some nonparticipating companies as a competitive offering. Typically it is a 20-payment life policy with attached coupons. Each coupon is redeemable in cash at the end of each policy year. Since the coupon is guaranteed, it has a selling feature over dividends. **5**

Court of Claims That federal court which handles all claims against the United States which arise out of any contract with the Government, regulation of the President or act of Congress as well as claims directed to it by the Senate or House of Representatives.

court of equity Courts applying a system of jurisprudence more flexible than that of the common law in order to work justice where the common law, by reason of its rigidity, fails to recognize a right or is unable to enforce it. **22**

court trust A trust coming under the immediate supervision of the court, such as a trust by order of court or, in some states, a trust under will. **30**

covenant A promise, incorporated in a trust indenture or other formal instrument, to perform certain acts or to refrain from the performance of certain acts. **22**

cover 1) In securities transactions, shorts are said to cover when they buy back the contracts they had previously sold, thereby liquidating their position. **9**
2) An insurance contract. **51**

3) The backing for some instrument; such as, the bond has a cover of gold or securities.

coverage 1) Frequently used interchangeably with the word "protection" or "insurance." The extent of the insurance afforded under an insurance contract. **50**

2) The extent of membership under a retirement plan. The term is frequently applied to the types of employees included under a plan. The guarantee against specific losses provided under the terms of a policy of insurance. **32**

3) As used in credit analysis, coverage is the amount of one item in a financial statement in relationship to another item. Thus, if accounts payable is shown as $1,000 and cash as $2,000, the coverage of cash is two times.

cover note Written statement by an insurance agent informing insured that coverage is in effect; used in lieu of a binder but differing in that the binder is prepared by the insurance company while the cover note is prepared by the broker or agent. **5**

craft union A labor organization, the membership in which is restricted to individuals possessing or working a specific skill or trade.

credit 1) Used in general sense means act of allowing person or persons immediate use of goods or services with payment deferred until an agreed future date.

2) Used in bookkeeping sense means an entry on ledger signifying cash payment, merchandise returned, or an allowance. Opposite of "debit." **26**

credit agency Those companies which make a business of providing credit and collection information. See "mercantile agency."

credit bureau Place where information about payment records of individuals and firms and all other relevant data are assembled. Information released to members and nonmembers on request. Credit bureaus can be merchant-owned, that is, ownership held by local merchants and others, or can be privately owned. **26**

credit controls Those restraints which are imposed by authoritative bodies. The Federal Reserve Board controls credit in several ways: Reserve requirements for member banks; open-market operations; rediscount rates; margin requirements. In addition, in periods of national emergency, other regulating devices are used to regulate credit such as the fiscal operation of the United States Treasury, gold sterilization and action by the American Bankers' Association.

credit currency Any currency which does not have full convertibility into standard money. Fiduciary money.

credit instruments Any document, contract or paper which may be used to obtain credit. This would include paper money not redeemable in standard money, checks, notes, drafts, bills of exchange, traveler's checks, letters of credit, coupons, money orders, and cashier's checks. The above are debt credit instruments. In addition, such things as preferred and common stock certificates may be classified as equity credit instruments.

credit interchange Information on credit may be interchanged in two ways: Direct—in which two creditors exchange their credit experience for mutual benefit—and by use of a central clearing bureau in which accounts of certain categories, such as 30-day past-due accounts are listed and sent to the bureau which in turn collates the data for its members.

credit line The maximum amount of credit a financial institution or trade firm will extend to a customer. The customer may in many cases be unaware of the trade credit line.

credit memorandum A special business form that is issued by the seller to the buyer and that contains a record of the credit which the seller has granted for returns, allowances, overcharges, and similar items.   **16**

credit money Fiduciary money which is not fully backed by precious metals.

creditor One to whom money or its equivalent is owed.   **31**

creditor nation A country which on a net basis is owed more by foreigners than it owes to them. Such a nation would tend to have a "favorable" balance of trade.

credit rating The appraisal of one's credit standing, ability and willingness to pay obligations.   **59**

credit union A cooperative financial society organized within and limited to a specific group of people. Any group of people with common interests is eligible to form a credit union. Each union is self-managed and is intended to provide a convenient system of saving money and of lending funds to members in need at lawful rates of interest. It functions under either state or federal law and supervision.   **34**

crisis A phase found in some business cycles in which a turning point is recognized but not fully materialized. Thus, after a period of prosperity and increases in security prices, the failure of a big brokerage firm or bank may result in a crisis. Should additional adverse factors develop, the crisis could precipitate a panic.

critical materials Those commodities determined by the agency enforcing the Strategic and Critical Materials Stockpiling Act of 1946 to be essential to national defense and which are in short supply below anticipated national emergency needs.

crop year The commodity term referring to the period from the harvest of a crop to the next year. Harvest dates vary for different crops. **44**

crossed trades A manipulative device prohibited on both the securities exchanges and the commodity exchanges in which a broker or two brokers offset an order to buy with an offer to sell and do not execute the orders on the exchange. This prevents the trade from being recorded and may mean that one of the parties to the cross did not obtain the price which would have been obtained on the exchange.

cross elasticity The influence that a change in the price of one item or product will have on the quantity taken or purchases of a product that has a use as a substitute for the original product.

crossing The function performed by a broker in handling both sides of a transaction, *i.e.,* buying a security from one customer and simultaneously selling the same to another customer. This is legal, but a broker-member of a stock exchange must first publicly offer the security for sale at a price higher than his bid; then if no buyer appears, he may consummate the transaction with himself. **44**

cross-picketing When two rival unions picket the same business each contending they are representatives of the striking employees.

cross-purchase agreement Plan of partnership insurance that has each partner individually buying and maintaining enough insurance on the life or lives of other partners to fund the purchase of the others' equity. **5**

cross rate The calculation of the rate of exchange of two foreign currencies by using the rate of exchange of each currency in a third nation's currency. If A currency is quoted at ten pesos to a United States dollar and B currency is quoted at five rupees to a dollar, we can derive a cross rate of two pesos to a rupee.

cum dividends With dividends; corporate stock may be termed ex-dividend which means that the buyer is not entitled to a declared dividend, or cum-dividend which means that the buyer is entitled to the declared dividend.

cum rights With rights; corporate stock which still has the privilege of buying a stated amount of stock to be newly issued. Generally, the new stock is of a different class.

cumulative An arrangement whereby a dividend or interest which, if not paid when due or received when due, is added to that which is to be paid in the future. **22**

cumulative dividend See "accumulated dividend."

cumulative voting A method of voting for corporate directors which enables the shareholder to multiply the number of his shares by the number of directorships being voted on and cast the total for one director or a selected group of directors. **2**

curator An individual or a trust institution appointed by a court to care for the property or person (or both) of a minor or an incompetent. In some states a curator is essentially the same as a temporary administrator or a temporary guardian. **30**

curb exchange Former name of the American Stock Exchange, second largest exchange in the country. The term comes from the market's origin on the streets of downtown New York. **2**

currency Technically, any form of money which serves as circulating medium and includes both paper money and metallic money (coins). In banking terminology, however, the term generally refers to paper money only. **23**

current debt See "liabilities, current."

current ratio The ratio of current assets to current liabilities, indicating the ability of a business to pay its current liabilities in cash as they fall due. **16**

current yield The expression as a percentage of the annual income to the investment, *e.g.*, annual income is five dollars and investment is one hundred dollars then current yield is five percent. See "return."

curtail schedule A list of the amounts by which the principal of an obligation is to be reduced by partial payments and of the dates when these payments are to become due. **33**

curtesy The widower's common-law right in certain states in his deceased wife's real estate. This right has been amended materially by statutory provisions in most states.   **5**

custodian One whose duty it is to hold, safeguard, and account for property committed to his care.   **22**

custody account An agency account concerning which the main duties of the custodian (agent) are to safekeep and preserve the property and perform ministerial acts with respect to the property as directed by the principal. The agent has no investment or management responsibilities. To be distinguished from a managing agency account and a safekeeping account.   **30**

customer's man See "registered representative."

customhouse That place designated for the payment of import duties in the United States and for the payment of import and export duties in many other nations.

customs broker The licensed individual who for a fee handles the necessary papers and steps in obtaining clearance of goods through the customs.

customs duty A tax levied on goods imported into the United States. In some nations it may also refer to the tax on goods exported from that country.

Customs Union Tariff Union—The treaty between two or more nations to reduce or do away with customs duties between themselves and to adopt a similar policy of tariff regulations with nations not a party to the customs union.

cutback The reduction in the volume of work or workers because of a decline in orders or sales or source of supply.

cutthroat competition Severe but independent endeavoring by two or more firms for the business patronage by the offer of very advantageous terms to the buyer. These terms may actually cause the failure of one or more of the competitors because of low-profit margin.

cybernetics The field of technology involved in the comparative study of the control and intracommunication of information, handling machines and nervous systems of animals and man in order to understand and improve communication.   **41**

cyclical fluctuation See "business cycle."

cyclical stocks Stocks which move directly with the general business cycle, *i.e.,* advancing when business improves and declining when business slackens.   **44**

cyclical theory A theory reflected in the stock market which claims that there are identifiable, regular cycles in which the volume of trade rises or falls. The Major Cycle in which business and commodity prices move up or down, alternatingly, spans about 30 years. The Minor Cycle, and best known one, spans about 8–11 years within the trend of the Major Cycle. The Short-Term Cycle of approximately 2 years is a sharper fluctuation within the Minor Cycle. **44**

cyclical unemployment Unemployment which has been caused by the drop in business-activity level.

cy pres doctrine Cy pres means "as nearly as may be." The doctrine, applied in English and Scots law and in some of the states of the United States, that where a testator or settlor makes a gift to or for a charitable object that cannot be carried out to the letter, the court will direct that the gift will be made as nearly as possible, in its judgment, in conformity with the intention of the donor. **22**

D

damages The estimated compensation paid for a specified injury, loss, or wrong sustained. **54**

date of acceptance The date on which a time draft is honored, or accepted. **16**

date of payment of dividends The date on which declared dividends are payable. **16**

daylight trading Effecting a purchase and sale of a commodity or a security during the same day so that one does not hold a "position" in the item traded overnight or longer. Scalpers generally engage in "daylight trading" and probably more is done in commodities than in securities.

day loan This is a loan made for one day only for the convenience of stock brokers. The loan is granted for the purchase of securities. When the securities are delivered, they are pledged as collateral to secure a regular call loan. **1**

day order An order to buy or sell stock at a specified price which expires on the day the order is given unless executed. An investor may also specify a longer time or good until canceled. See "limit order" and "good until canceled." **2**

days of grace The reasonable length of time allowed, without suffering a loss or penalty, for postponed payment or for the presentment for payment of certain financial documents.   **1**

deadbeat Term commonly used in credit work (but not recommended) describing a person or persons who are undesirable credit risks.   **26**

dead rent That portion of the payment for the use of a quarry or mine which is a stated amount per year. The remainder, a royalty payment, will vary depending upon the amount of mineral removed.

dead stock Merchandise that can't be sold.   **38**

dead time Time during which production employees wait for materials or for machinery adjustments and for which pay is sometimes provided.   **12**

dealer A person or firm that transacts business as a principal rather than as an agent. See "principal."   **55**

dealer's brand See "private brands."

dear money Condition during which high-interest rates prevail. Also a period when goods and services are readily available at lower prices.

death benefit A benefit payable to the survivors or a beneficiary of a member upon his death while a member of a retirement plan.   **32**

death duties Inheritance taxes. Estate taxes.

death rate The number of deaths per thousand population per year for a stated area.

death taxes Taxes imposed on property or on the transfer of property at the owner's death; a general term covering estate taxes, inheritance taxes and other succession or transfer taxes.   **30**

debasement Reducing the quality, purity, or content, or otherwise altering the accepted intrinsic value of the coinage of a realm.   **1**

debenture An obligation not secured by a specific lien on property; usually an unsecured note or bond of a corporation.   **40**

debenture stock Stock issued under a contract to pay a specified return at specified intervals. In this sense, it may be considered a special type of preferred stock. It is to be distinguished from debentures which represent a bond in form as compared with a share of stock.   **19**

debit In an accounting sense, an entry which will increase an asset or expense account and will decrease a liability or income account. In insurance, accounts receivable. Compare "credit."

debt A contract evidencing an amount owed by one party to another for money, goods, or services.   **44**

debtee A creditor.

debt financing The long-term borrowing of money by a business, usually in exchange for debt securities or a note, for the purpose of obtaining working capital or other funds necessary to operational needs or for the purpose of retiring current or other indebtedness.   **60**

debt limit The maximum amount of gross or net debt legally permitted.   **29**

debt monetization The situation whereby the debt of a nation becomes the base for an increase in the money in circulation.

debtor A person or company who owes money.   **38**

debtor nation A country which on a net basis owes more to foreigners than it is owed by them. Such a nation would tend to have an "unfavorable" balance of trade.

debt service The amount of principal and interest that falls due within a stated period such as a year which must be paid by a debtor.

deceased account An account carried on deposit in a bank in the name and title of a deceased person. As soon as the death of a depositor is ascertained, the bank segregates the account, and withholds payment until authorized by a court of law to make such payment to the legal heirs. Tax waivers and authorized claims to the deposited account are known to the bank before payment may be made.   **1**

decedent A deceased person.   **1**

decentralization 1) The distribution of power and administration from a central authority to regional and local governing bodies.

2) Dispersion from a center, as the outward growth or movement of a retail center.

3) The redistribution of population and industry from the urban areas to outlying, suburban districts.

declaration date The date on which the directors of a corporation authorize the payment of a dividend; to be distinguished from the date of payment of the dividend.   **22**

declaration of dividend That action on the part of the board of directors of a corporation in which the decision is reached to pay the stockholders of the corporation a portion of the earnings or surplus of the firm.

declaration of trust An acknowledgment, usually but not necessarily in writing, by one holding or taking title to property that he holds the property in trust for the benefit of someone else.　　30

declaratory judgment The judgment or decision of a court interpreting an instrument or declaring what the law on the given matter is under a statutory proceeding that authorizes the court to enter such a judgment in a case that is not being litigated.　　22

decreasing costs The situation in which the per unit cost of production declines. This is generally associated with increased production when a business is operating below normal capacity.

decree The decision of a court of equity, admiralty, probate, or divorce; to be distinguished from the judgment of a court of law.　　33

dedicate To put aside one's private property for some public purpose, such as to make a private road public.　　5

deductible coverage clause Provision that in return for a reduced rate the insured will assume losses below a specified amount.　　52

deductive method A technique of scientific investigation in which a premise which has been accepted to be true becomes the basis of additional logical reasoning.

deed A written transfer of title to property, usually real estate.　　31

deed, administrator's A deed by a person lawfully appointed to manage and settle the estate of a deceased person who has left no executor.　　15

deed, committee A deed by a committee or commission appointed by a court of competent jurisdiction to sell a property.　　15

deed, executor's A deed by a person named by the decedent in his will to manage and settle his estate.　　15

deed, mortgaged A deed by way of mortgage which has the effect of a mortgage on the property conveyed and imposes a lien on the granted estate.　　15

deed of assignment The document which is used to appoint an assignee such as an individual or a fiduciary institution to take over an insolvent firm. The assignment states the powers and functions of the appointed firm or individual.

deed of trust An instrument that conveys or transfers to a trustee the title to property as security for the payment of a debt, giving the trustee the power to sell the property in order to satisfy the debt in the event of default on the part of the debtor. The instrument becomes void on the payment of the debt when due. **33**

defalcation The misappropriation or embezzlement of money or property by one to whom it has been entrusted, usually, by reason of his employment. **29**

default Failure to meet a legal obligation. **35**

defeasible Capable of being annulled or rendered void; as a defeasible title to property. **22**

defendant A person required to make answer in an action or suit in law or equity or in a criminal action. **35**

defensive portfolio An aggregate of investments which are unlikely to fluctuate much in value either up or down; for example, high-grade bonds and preferred stocks. **44**

deferred availability This term is used in Federal Reserve Bank statements. At all times there are checks traveling throughout the United States in the process of collection for member banks of the Federal Reserve System. These are contingent assets and are designated "deferred availability items." **1**

deferred charges Expenditures which are not chargeable to the fiscal period in which made but are carried on the asset side of the balance sheet pending amortization or other disposition; for example, discount on bonds issued. **29**

deferred credits Credit balances or items which will be spread over following accounting periods either as additions to revenue or as reductions of expenses. Examples are taxes collected in advance and premiums on bonds issued. **29**

deferred demand Demand for goods or services which cannot be met because the goods or services are not available. It is expected that if they do become available, the deferred demand will be met.

deferred income The income account which is used to record income which has been paid in advance but not as yet earned. The prepayment of rent or insurance are illustrations of items that become deferred income for the recipient.

deferred stock Rare in the United States. Found in England. A

111

security below regular common stock in priority of dividends. The dividend is not payable until a period of time or some event, such as earnings of a certain size, has come about.

deficiency judgment A court order authorizing collection from a debtor of any part of a debt that remains unsatisfied after foreclosure and sale of collateral.　　　　　　　　　　**33**

deficit 1) The excess of liabilities over assets (negative net worth); a term used indicating obligations or expenditures for items which are in excess of the amount allotted for those items in a financial budget.

2) The excess of obligations and expenditures as a whole affecting a given budget period which is in excess of the budget established for the period.　　　　　　　　　　　　　　**1**

deficit financing The process or methods used to meet a deficit. The term has most frequently been used during recent years in connection with the government's procedure in meeting its operating deficits through the sale of large quantities of bonds.　　　　　　　　　　　　　　　　　　　　**34**

definitive A permanent certificate, generally engraved, which replaces a temporary stock or bond certificate which is generally printed in a way that will not meet the standards of the security exchange upon which the security may be traded.

deflation An economic condition generally characterized by declining prices and depressed business. For contrast see "inflation."

deflationary gap The difference between government and private spending at a given time and the amount of government and private spending needed to produce full employment. Under Keynesian economists' proposals, the government spending would be increased sufficiently to stimulate the private sector so that the two combined would eliminate the deflationary gap.

deflator A divisor or statistical device which attempts to remove the influence of some increase such as the changing value of money. To get "real" or "constant" value, changing prices must be tied to a base period, and that part of change in price which is caused by inflation or similar distortion should be removed by the use of a deflator.

degressive tax A progressive tax in which each progressive step is at a lower rate than the previous step.

delayed opening A situation caused by an accumulation of buy or sell orders before the opening of a stock exchange. Efforts are made to find counterbalancing offers, usually with institutions, firms, or individuals who have a large interest in the security, to prevent the opening price from varying sharply from the previous day's close. The specialist in the stock will often sell some of his inventory in the security, or "short" it, to help arrange a reasonable opening price.   **44**

delcredere agent Agent who indemnifies his principal in the event of loss to the principal because of the extension of credit to a third party by the agent.   **5**

delinquency Failure to pay an obligation when due; sometimes this term is extended to cover the amount of the delinquency.   **31**

delinquent tax A tax still unpaid after its due date. The taxpayer or his property may be assessed a penalty or lien or be foreclosed for nonpayment of taxes.

delist The infrequent suspension or cancellation of privileges accorded a listed security. This may occur if an issue fails to maintain its listing requirements, such as the appropriate number of stockholders or number of shares outstanding. **44**

delivery 1) The transfer of the possession of a thing from one person to another.   **5**
2) The certificate representing shares bought "regular way" on the New York Stock Exchange normally is delivered to the purchaser's broker on the fourth business day after the transaction. If a seller wants to delay delivery of the certificates, he may have his broker offer the stock "seller's option," instead of "regular way," and he may specify the number of days, from five up to sixty, for delivery. A stock offered "seller's option" may command a lesser price than if offered "regular way." See "bid," "cash sale," "offer," and "transfer." **2**

delivery notice 1) A formal notice certifying that delivery of something will occur on a certain date, or has already occurred.
2) The notification of delivery of the actual commodity on the contract, issued by the seller of the futures to the buyer. **9**

delivery points In commodities dealing, those locations designated by futures exchanges at which the commodity covered by a futures contract may be delivered in fulfillment of the contract. **9**

demand The amount of a good or service that will be purchased

113

at various prices at a given time in a market. In another sense, it may be the amount of a good or services that will be purchased at the current price in a market. The first concept is one of a schedule of demand while the latter is one of a point of demand.

demand bill A sight bill of exchange.

demand deposit Deposits that are payable on demand at any time the depositor elects. The Federal Reserve Board and the various state laws define these deposits as being payable within 30 days after deposit. They are drawn against by check, and no notice of withdrawal is necessary. **23**

demand draft A draft that is payable on demand. Also called sight draft. **25**

demand loan A loan with no fixed maturity date, payable upon demand of the bank. Borrower is billed at specified intervals for the interest due the bank. **23**

demand note A promissory note payable on demand of the holder of the note as payee or transferee. **22**

demand rates A method of charge for electric service based upon the customer's installation, or maximum demand, or a function of the use or size of that installation.

de minimis doctrine The doctrine that "the law cares nothing for trifling matters." It has been involved in suits contesting "portal pay" under the Wage-Hour Law and the application of a federal statute to predominantly local activities. **12**

demonetization To divert from the character of standard money.

demonstrative legacy A gift of a specific amount or thing which is payable out of a designated asset which, in the event that asset is inadequate, the general assets of the estate may be used to pay the legacy.

demurrer A pleading which admits the facts but denies that they have legal effect. **35**

department store A retail store which handles a wide variety of lines of goods, such as, women's ready-to-wear and accessories, men's and boys' wear, piece goods, smallwares, and house furnishings, and which is organized into separate departments for purposes of promotion, service, and control. **13**

dependency allowance A payment or tax reduction for individuals who have dependents as defined by the government or other determining body.

dependent A person who is dependent for support upon another;

to be distinguished from one who merely derives a benefit from the earnings of another. **22**

depletion Reduction, through removal or use of an asset; an exhaustion of natural resources such as mineral deposits, timber, and water. **15**

depletion allowance The provision of the Internal Revenue Code that wasting assets such as oil wells, mines, quarries, shell banks, etc., may deduct from taxable income a percentage of the income from the asset.

deposit Money placed with a banking or other institution, or with a person either as a general deposit subject to check, or as a special deposit made for some specified purpose; securities lodged with a banking or other institution or with a person for some particular purpose; sums deposited by customers for electric meters, water meters, etc., and by contractors and others to accompany and guarantee their bids. Money put down to insure and guarantee the fulfillment of an agreement, such as a deposit offered to hold an apartment for a specific length of time.

deposit administration plan 1) A type of pension plan, usually under a master group annuity contract, providing for the accumulation of contributions in an undivided fund out of which annuities are purchased as the individual members of the group retire.
2) An insured pension arrangement. Periodic contributions of the employer are not allocated to the purchase of annuities for a particular employee until he is ready to retire. A feature of the plan is that the employer may hire his own independent actuarial consultants. **53**

depositary One who receives a deposit of money, securities, instruments, or other property. **30**

deposit currency The effect of a typical loan from a bank. The bank credits the borrower's account with the amount of the loan. This, in turn, may be withdrawn by check or cash.

deposit function The business of receiving money on deposit for safekeeping and convenience. This function includes the receiving of demand deposits subject to check and the receiving of savings (time) deposits at interest. **25**

deposit funds Those funds which are established to account for collections that are either (a) held in suspense temporarily and later refunded or paid into some other fund of the government, or (b) held by the government as banker or agent for others. Such funds are not available for paying salaries, expenses, grants, or other expenditures of the government and, therefore, are excluded from total budget receipts or expenditures. **7**

deposit insurance See "Federal Deposit Insurance Corporation." **1**

deposition The written testimony of a witness, under oath, before a qualified officer, to be used in place of the oral testimony of the witness at a trial. **30**

deposit line That approximate-average amount which a depositor tends to keep in his bank account. With a knowledge of the deposit line, a lending officer can judge not only the probable profitability of an account but also can relate it to a loan application.

deposit loan Most loans are made by the banker crediting the borrower's account with a "loan deposit" in the amount of the loan as distinguished from presenting the borrower with currency when granting a loan.

depositor One who makes a deposit of funds in a financial institution. **59**

depository A bank in which funds or securities are deposited by others, usually under the terms of a specific depository agreement. Also, a bank in which government funds are deposited or in which other banks are permitted by law to maintain required reserves. The term "depository" and "depositary" have come to be used interchangeably in banking. **25**

deposit slip An itemized memorandum of the cash and other funds which a customer (depositor) presents to the receiving teller of a financial institution for credit to his account. **25**

depreciable cost The value of a fixed asset that is subject to depreciation. Sometimes this is the original cost, and sometimes it is the original cost less an estimated salvage value. **28**

depreciated money 1) Money or currency which will not buy the same amount of goods and services that it did at some past period of time.

2) Money or currency which is at a discount from the standard money.

depreciation 1) Expiration in service life of fixed assets, other than wasting assets, attributable to wear and tear through use

116

and lapse of time, obsolescence, inadequacy, or other physical or functional cause.

2) The portion of the cost of a fixed asset other than a wasting asset charged as an expense during a particular period.   **29**

depreciation, accelerated Higher than normal rate of depreciation either for tax purposes or because of greater than normal use.

depression A sustained period of falling prices, characterized by excess of supply over demand, accumulating inventories, falling employment and rising welfare costs, deflation, abnormal commercial and industrial plant contraction, uneven drop in personal incomes, and fear and caution on the part of the public.   **15**

derelict Personal property which has been abandoned by the owner.   **35**

derivative deposit The typical result of a commercial loan is the action of the bank in crediting the account of the borrower with the amount of the loan. This deposit is derived from the loan.

derived demand That need for a good or service which has come about as a result of the demand for another good or service.

descent The passing of property by inheritance. See "devolution."   **30**

descriptive labeling To state the attributes of a good without the use of objective standards such as grades.

desk jobbers Same as drop shippers.

de son tort "Of his own wrongdoing." An expression found in such phrases as executor de son tort and guardian de son tort.   **30**

destructive competition See "cutthroat competition."

deterioration Physical wear-out; decay, impairment, wasting away, and wear and tear through action of the elements, age, and use.   **15**

devaluation The reduction in the value of the precious or semi-precious metal content of a monetary unit or the reduction in the exchange value of a nation's currency as a result of action by some agency such as a central bank, an exchange stabilization fund or the International Monetary Fund.

development 1) The gradual unfolding by which something such as a plan or a method comes to be.

2) Applying scientific and technologic knowledge to create

117

new or modify existing products and processes so they will best achieve stated performance and economic requirements.

3) A photographic image.

4) A real-estate investment enterprise, usually on a large-scale basis.

devise 1) To contrive, invent, or bequeath something.

2) A gift of real property by will; to be distinguished from bequest.

3) A will, or a clause in a will.

devolution The passing of property by inheritance; a general term that includes both descent of real property and distribution of personal property. **22**

diagonal expansion The increase in a firm's activity by such devices as the utilization of by-products or addition of a closely related line.

difference account In bookkeeping, an account carried in the general ledger where all differences from the true balances, such as averages and shortages, of the firm are recorded.

differential 1) Relation to a distinction or difference.

2) A difference in a wage rate for similar work done of comparable quality, which reflects a variable such as the race or sex of the worker, location, etc.

3) In investment trading, refers to the odd-lot differential, or compensation, received by an odd-lot broker for his services. A differential is added to the price of buy orders and subtracted from the price of sell orders.

differential duty See "preferential duty" and "discriminating duty."

diffusion theory of taxation The concept that a tax is transferred on to other than the original taxpayer by such techniques as price changes, increases in rents and even lower wages to employees of the taxpayer. While it is true that some taxes may be transferred by the taxpayer, not all fall in this class.

digested securities Stocks and bonds that have been sold to investors who are not expected to sell the securities in the near future.

dilution 1) The watering down or weakening of something.

2) The reduction in the value of an asset such as a stock. See "watered stock."

diminishing-returns theory Concept that when the proportions of land, capital or labor used in production are changed, a point will be reached when an additional unit of land, labor or capital will not increase production as much as the previous unit.

diminishing-utility theory Concept that a point is reached when an additional unit of goods or services will not have the same utility to the recipient as the previous unit.

direct advertising Advertising that is sent or given right to the customer, rather than being generally given or exposed to the public. A letter is direct, a newspaper ad is not. **38**

direct cost An expense that is free from any intervening conditions. An immediate cost as compared with an indirect cost.

direct earnings In cases where a firm has subsidiary companies, the direct earnings of the parent company are the amounts earned by it without the upstream dividends of the subsidiaries.

direct financing The obtaining of equity or debt capital without the use of a middleman or underwriter. See "direct placement."

direct heir A person in the direct line of the decedent; as father, mother, son, daughter. See "collateral heir" and "heir." **30**

direct labor The amount of the wages paid to employees whose time may be charged to specific finished products. **16**

direct mail Marketing goods directly to the consumer through the mail.

direct marketing Technique of distribution in which goods go from producer to consumer without going through a middleman.

direct obligation An obligation of the drawer or maker of the instrument as distinguished from the indirect obligation of an endorser of the instrument.

director 1) One who is charged with administering, leading, or supervising something.
2) Person elected by shareholders at the annual meeting to direct company policies. The directors appoint the president, vice presidents and all other operating officers. Directors decide, among other matters, if and when dividends shall be paid. **2**

directorate Refers to a corporation's board of directors. **44**

direct placement The selling directly of a security issue to a financial institution such as an insurance company, and bypassing the middleman-investment-banker by the issuer of the securities. Insurance companies have purchased many direct placements.   **5**

direct production The creation of utility without the use of capital, using only land and labor or, in rare cases, only labor.

direct reduction mortgage (d.r.m.) A direct reduction mortgage is liquidated over the life of the mortgage in equal monthly payments. Each monthly payment consists of an amount to cover interest, reduction in principal, taxes and insurance. The interest is computed on an outstanding principal balance monthly. As the principal balance is reduced the amount of interest becomes less, thereby providing a larger portion of the monthly payment to be applied to the reduction of principal. As taxes and insurance are paid by the mortgagee (lending association), these disbursements are added to the principal balance. This procedure follows throughout the life of the mortgage.   **1**

direct selling The process whereby the producer sells to the user, ultimate consumer, or retailer without intervening middlemen.   **13**

direct strike The refraining from work by the employees of a firm because of a grievance against their employer.

direct tax A levy which the taxed individual or firm may not transfer to someone else in the form of higher prices, rent or interest charge.

direct verification A method of bank audit whereby the auditor of a bank sends a request for the verification of the balances of deposits or loans as of a stated date to the depositors or borrowers. Verifications are returned directly to the auditor confirming the correctness of balances or listing discrepancies.   **1**

disability benefit A feature added to a life insurance policy providing for waiver of premium and sometimes payment of monthly income upon the furnishing of proof that the insured has become totally and permanently disabled.   **53**

disabling injury An injury which causes loss of working time beyond the day or shift on which the injury occurs.   **51, 52**

disbursement Money paid out in discharge of a debt or an expense; to be distinguished from distribution.   **30**

disbursement schedule A list or tabular statement of the amounts to be disbursed on specific dates in accordance with agreements entered into in a mortgage-loan type of transaction.   **33**

discharge 1) To unload, free, dismiss.

2) Ending of the employment relationship by act of the employer. See "constructive discharge." **12**

3) An explosion.

discharge of bankruptcy An order which terminates bankruptcy proceedings, usually relieving the debtor of all legal responsibility for certain specified obligations. **35**

disclaimer A document, or a clause within a document, which renounces or repudiates the liability of an otherwise responsible party, in the event of a noncompliance on the part of another party to other certain conditions within the instrument, or in the event of other named external conditions, or losses incurred due to the delivery of goods being in disagreement with the weight or count made by the shipper of the goods. **1**

discontinuous market A market which exists for unlisted securities as distinguished from the supposedly continuous market for listed securities, such as those on the New York Stock Exchange. **44**

discount 1) A deduction from the stated or list price of something.

2) A deduction given for prompt payment.

3) Interest deducted from the face value of a note at the time a loan is made. On other loans interest is collected at the time a note is paid. **23**

4) The amount by which a security is priced below par; that is, the opposite of premium. A $1,000 bond with a market price of $950 has a discount of $50. **49**

discounted value Present value of future payments due or receivable, computed on the basis of a given rate of interest. **42**

discount house 1) A retail establishment which sells brand-name merchandise at a lower price than the general retailer. To accomplish this, some of the customary services such as credit and delivery may not be available.

2) One of the functions of a commercial credit company.

discounting the news The adjustment in stock prices which takes place in anticipation of prospects and developments. Thus when a new development occurs as expected, the prices are not affected as they might have been. **44**

discount market That part of the money market in which commercial paper is traded. Institutions in the discount market include commercial banks, note dealers, commercial paper houses and discount houses. In addition, the Federal Reserve Banks by their rediscounting function are important factors in the market.

discount on securities The amount or percentage by which a security (a bond or a share of stock) is bought or sold for less than its face, or par, value; opposed to premium on securities. 30

discount rate That interest rate which a lender charges when it discounts an obligation such as a note or bill of exchange. The discount rate will vary by type of borrower, security, maturity, the supply and demand for funds in the market and the policy of the lender.

discretionary trust 1) A trust which entitles the beneficiary only to so much of the income or principal as the trustee in its uncontrolled discretion shall see fit to give him or to apply to his use. 30

2) An investment company which is not limited in its policy to any one class, or type, of stock or security but may invest in any or all of a broad range of securities.

discriminating duty See "preferential duty."

discrimination An unfair distinction such as unequal treatment of workers, whether by the disparate application of hiring or employment rules or of the conditions of employment, because of race, creed, sex, or union membership or activity. In many cases, discrimination is an "unfair labor practice" under federal or state laws. 12

discriminatory taxes Contributions exacted by the government for the purpose of helping special interests. The tax is imposed on those the special interests oppose.

dishoarding The consumption from a stockpile which had been increased previously above its normal level.

dishonor 1) The refusal of the drawee to accept or to pay a check, draft, or bill of exchange when it is presented to him for acceptance or for payment, as the case may be.

2) The refusal of the maker to pay a note when it is presented to him for payment. 25

disinflation The attempt to reduce the price level to a normal and not deflated level.

disinvestment Negative investment—the disposal of a piece of capital or the failure to maintain a capital good that is being worn out or used up.

dismissal wage Generally a lump-sum payment made to a worker whose employment is permanently ended for causes beyond the worker's control by an employer and which is in addition to any back wages or salary due the worker.   **12**

disposable personal income Personal income less personal taxes and nontax payments to government.   **7**

dissaving The reduction in net worth by spending more than current income.

distant delivery Delivery scheduled to be made during one of the more distant months ahead, and at least two months away.

distressed sale A forced liquidation of a thing. The assumption is that the seller does not receive as high a price for his good as he would under normal selling conditions.

distribution 1) The dividing up of something among several or many parties, such as profits to stockholders or owners, or money to creditors.

2) In law, the apportionment by a court of the personal property (or its proceeds) of one who died intestate among those entitled to receive the property according to the applicable statute of distribution; to be distinguished from disbursement.   **30**

3) The division of the aggregate income of any society among its members, or among the factors of production. Dispersal of goods throughout the community.   **38**

4) Selling, over a period of time, of a large block of stock without unduly depressing the market price.   **45**

distribution clause See "pro rata distribution."

distributors Middlemen; wholesalers.

disutility Distress or negative utility.

diversification 1) To be going in many different ways or directions, rather than being limited to just a few or one area.

2) Spreading investments among different companies in different fields. Diversification is also offered by the securities of many individual companies because of the wide range of their activities.   **45**

divest To annul; to take away a vested right.   **22**

divided coverage Division of insurance that would normally be covered by one insurance policy between two or more companies.   **52**

dividends The proportion of the net earnings of a corporation paid to the stockholders as their share of the profits. Dividends become payable only when declared by the board of directors. They are commonly distributed at regular intervals (quarterly, semiannually, or annually).   **25**

division of labor The employment of workers in such a way that each does a relatively simple and limited number of operations. The product frequently is on an assembly line or conveyor belt. Each worker, after completing his phase of the total job, passes it to the next until its final completion.

divisor A mathematical device to correct a time series which has become distorted because of a change in the base weights. A time series of security prices, such as the Dow Jones averages, must be corrected by the use of a divisor every time there is a stock split or dividend in any company which is included in their average.

documentary draft A draft accompanied by a shipping document, bill of lading, insurance certificate, etc., these documents having intrinsic value. Instructions for disposition of the document usually accompany the draft.   **23**

dole Welfare payments.

dollar Monetary unit of Canada, Ethiopia, Liberia and the United States.

dollar acceptance A bill of exchange or acceptance which may be drawn in a foreign or domestic country but is payable in dollars. While Canada, Ethiopia, Liberia and the United States all have the dollar as their monetary unit, it is generally assumed that the dollar is a United States dollar.

dollar bill of exchange See "dollar acceptance."

dollar-cost averaging The systematic investment in investment company shares of the same amount of money at regular intervals over a period of years regardless of the prices of such shares at the time of purchase.   **14**

dollar gap (dollar deficit) The difference in dollars for a nation which has not earned as many dollars as it has spent in a given period of time.

dollar stabilization 1) Those acts by monetary authorities such as the International Monetary Fund, the Exchange Stabilization Fund, the Federal Reserve Board, and the United States Treasury which have as their purpose the reduction in the fluctuation of the international exchange value of the dollar. 2) It also has been used to designate an idea of economist

Irving Fisher which would result in a compensated dollar which would be tied to commodities rather than gold.

domestic acceptance In a strict sense, any acceptance which has the drawer, the drawee and the place of payment within the same state. However, the term is generally loosely used to refer to any acceptance which has the drawer, drawee and the place of payment in the United States.

domestic bill Any of numerous documents such as sight or time drafts which are drawn and payable within the same state. In a looser sense, any of numerous documents which are drawn and payable in the United States.

domestic exchange As distinguished from foreign exchange, any acceptance, check, draft or similar document which is drawn and payable in the United States. In a foreign nation, any acceptance, check, draft or similar document which is drawn and payable in that nation would be considered as domestic exchange.

domicile The place where one has his true, fixed, and permanent home, and to which, whenever he is absent, he has the intention of returning. 5

donated stock Capital stock which is fully paid and has been returned as a gift to the issuing corporation.

donated surplus In accounting, a capital surplus account that contains a record of the par value of donated stock that is in the treasury of the corporation and of the proceeds from donated stock that has been sold. 16

double budget A system of segregating capital expenditures from recurring expense items so that an annual income statement will not be distorted during those years of heavy capital investment.

double-entry bookkeeping That system of bookkeeping under which both the debit and the credit elements of each transaction are recorded. 16

double indemnity Feature of some insurance policies that provides for twice the face amount of the policy to be paid if death results from stated but generally accidental causes. 5

double indemnity, health and accident Payment of an additional amount on accident insurance policies if death results from an injury sustained under certain conditions; as wrecking of a common carrier. 42

double indemnity, life Accidental death benefit, available at

125

nominal cost in connection with life insurance policies, providing for payment of double the face amount if death occurs as a result of an accident. **42**

double taxation 1) A taxing body imposing two taxes on what is essentially the same thing.

2) Double taxation of dividends—the federal government taxes corporate profits once as corporate income; any part of the remaining profits distributed as dividends to stockholders is taxed again as income to the recipient stockholder. **2**

dower The right which a widow has in some states to share in the real property of her deceased husband. See "curtesy." **33**

Dow-Jones averages Those averages of industrials, rails and utilities which are published by *The Wall Street Journal* and publications using their service. The figures refer to stock market quotations of the securities which make up the averages.

down payment The cash payment that the purchaser of merchandise sold on an installment-payment plan is required to make at the time of the sale.

down period The period of time during which a plant is closed for maintenance or repairs.

Dow theory A theory of market analysis based upon the performance of the Dow-Jones industrial and rail stock price averages. **2**

draft Bill of exchange—a signed written order addressed by one person (the drawer) to another person (the drawee) directing the latter to pay a specified sum of money to the order of a third person (the payee). **25**

drawback The return to an importer of the duties collected on imported goods which were intended for and are reshipped to another nation.

drawee The party who is directed to pay the sum specified in a check, draft, or bill of exchange. **25**

drawer Any party or company who draws a draft or check upon another party for the payment of funds. **23**

drawing account Money available to owners or salesmen to be used for expenses which will be deducted from future earnings. **38**

drayage The cost of moving articles in a for-hire vehicle.

drive An attempt to manipulate prices of securities or commodities by the concerted efforts of sellers to force prices down. Such action is illegal if proven.

drop shipper A wholesaler who does not store goods though he does take title. Also called desk jobber.

dry goods Textile fabrics; things made from cotton, wool, rayon, nylon, silk, etc.   **38**

dry trust See "passive trust."

dual-pay system Wage plan with two systems of computing pay in which the employee is allowed to choose the one which will give him the most compensation.

dual unionism Situation existing when the jurisdictional claims of one union infringe upon the jurisdiction of another union.

due bill A statement of an amount that is owed.

due date The date upon which a note, draft, bond, coupon, etc., becomes payable; the maturity date.   **23**

dump 1) To discard, get rid of, scrap.
2) The sale of a large amount of goods or securities in a disorganizing way, frequently with little regard to price or impact on the market.

Dun and Bradstreet Largest and oldest existing agency supplying information and credit ratings on and for all types of business concerns.   **23**

duopoly A market situation in which there are only two producers or sellers of a similar product.

duosony A market situation in which only two buyers are seeking a similar product.

durable goods Products into which are built long series of continuing services; products that last and continue to serve; usually applied to "hard goods"—metal, wood, etc.   **59**

duress Compulsion or constraint by force or fear of personal violence, prosecution, or imprisonment which induces a person to do what he does not want to do or to refrain from doing something he has a legal right to do. Sometimes the word is used with reference to the making of a will, as that it was made under duress.   **22**

dutch auction A sale by an auctioneer in which he offers the merchandise at a high price and lowers the price until a bidder responds and purchases.

duty A customs duty or tax on imports.

dynamic economy Situation in which an economy is characterized by growth and change.

dynamiter The expression for a nomadic "securities" salesman who attempts to sell fraudulent securities over the telephone. **44**

E

each way A transaction in which a securities broker executes the buying and selling, receiving a commission for each of the two functions. **44**

earmarked gold Gold in the fiduciary possession of one nation's central bank for another nation's central bank, treasury or stabilization fund.

earned income The amount received for goods or services delivered and for which no future liability is anticipated.

earned premium Premium for that portion of an insurance policy period which has expired and for which protection was provided. **42**

earned surplus The undistributed corporation profits resulting from the regular operations of the business. **16**

earnest money Money which is paid as an evidence of good faith or intent to complete a transaction and may be forfeited by the willful failure to complete the transaction. **5**

earning asset Any item of value which is producing income for the owner.

earning-capacity standard The capitalized value standard. The annual earnings of a business divided by an appropriate interest rate. The rate is estimated by the risk involved in the business. A very risky business would be capitalized at a higher percentage than a more stable business.

earnings Synonym for "net income," particularly over a period of years. In the singular, the term is often combined with another word, as in the expression "earning power," referring to the demonstrated ability of an enterprise to earn net income. **17**

earnings report A statement, also called an income statement, issued by a company showing its earnings or losses over a given period. The earnings report lists the income earned, expenses, and the net result. See "balance sheet." **2**

easement The acquired, or reserved, privilege or right of use of

128

property the ownership of which is held by another, such as the right of passage. **29**

easy money That condition in which interest rates are low and loans are relatively readily obtained.

ecclesiastical corporation A nonprofit corporation established by churchmen for a religious, educational or charitable purpose.

econometrics A school of economics devoted to use of mathematics and other measurements of economic data for the purpose of increasing the understanding of that field.

economic 1) Pertaining to the production, distribution and consumption of wealth to the material means of satisfying human needs and desires. **59**
2) Concerning the administration of the income and expenditure of a household, business, community, government, or other organization.

economic demand The desire to buy backed by the necessary money to make active purchasing possible—an actual "offer to buy at price" market situation. **59**

economic determinism The concept that economic factors cause social change.

economic friction Any human characteristic which distorts and reduces the operation of economic principles. Religion, taboos and customs may serve as examples of economic friction.

economic good Any service or thing that has utility and is not free.

economic harmony Concept that the profit system as determined for the individual actually works out for the best interest of society as a whole.

economic imperialism The use of large-scale power on the part of an organization to buy or sell to dominate a subject and to force the subject, individual, firm, or nation to take additional steps of cooperation or submission.

economic law Not a law in the legal sense but rather a generalization about economic relationships and probabilities.

economic man A hypothetical individual who is considered reasonably intelligent and informed and who will make his decisions to maximize the utilities of a situation. He is considered to be rational and not to make impulsive and noneconomic decisions.

economic mobilization The concentration of the people and business firms of an area upon some activity such as a war or depression so that production is directed to meet the goal such as winning the war or improving business conditions.

economic nationalism The policy of a country to produce all the goods and services it consumes.

economic planning A relative term to indicate a scheme or method of obtaining some economic goal. Such planning may be done by an individual, firm or nation. The degree of planning may vary from the modest establishment of some goal such as a rate of growth for gross national product to the almost complete regimentation of all the productive forces in a nation.

economic rent A philosophic concept of the true value of a property as compared with the contract rent which would be expressed in monetary units and might not be necessarily indicative of the true value, being possibly either over or under the economic rent.   5

economics The study of the factors which affect the production, distribution and consumption of wealth and of the use of the earth's resources to satisfy the needs and desires of man.   **59**

economic sanctions The provision for securing conformity to a position, decree or law by economic steps such as boycott, embargo, credit controls or trade restrictions.

economic strikes Strikes called to force changes in wages, hours, or other working conditions, rather than in protest against unfair labor practices.   **12**

economic system The orderly collection of economic principles, laws and attitudes into a plan for the operation of a society. The system may be established by governmental legislation or developed by evolutionary steps. The three major economic systems today are capitalism, socialism, and communism with many nations modifying a system to their own particular level of economic need or development.

economic union The treaty between signing nations to adopt and follow similar economic steps such as customs, taxation and other such economic policies.

economic warfare The use of such economic devices as control of credit, raw material, transportation, copyrights, patents, foreign exchange, blacklists, and economic pressure on neutral nations to stop trading with an enemy for the purpose of weakening and thus conquering the enemy.

economic wealth Those scarce material things that man finds of use. While businessmen consider money, securities and mortgages as being wealth, the economist contends that these are instruments that represent wealth and not wealth itself.

economies of scale Efficiencies which result from the producer having the proper proportions of land, labor and machinery to meet a given market.

economy of abundance That state of economic activity characterized by full employment and the satisfaction of material wants at a level of plenty.

economy of scarcity That state of economic activity at less than full employment and where consumers are unable to satisfy reasonable material wants.

effective date The date on which something goes into effect such as a contract or agreement, insurance policy, etc.

effective demand The ability to pay for goods or services that are desired.

effective interest rate or yield The rate or earnings on a bond investment based on the actual price paid for the bond, the coupon rate, the maturity date, and the length of time between interest dates; in contrast with the nominal interest rate.   **29**

Eight-Hour Law Federal statute limiting the straight-time hours of work of laborers and mechanics on public works contracts.   **12**

ejectment An action brought to regain possession of real property from a party wrongfully in possession of it.

elastic demand Demand which fluctuates at a greater proportionate rate than the rate of change of price for a product.

elastic money A currency or money supply which increases or decreases with the needs of the economy.

elastic supply Supply which fluctuates at a greater proportionate rate than the rate of change of price for a product.

election The choice of an alternative right or course. Thus, the right of a widow to take the share of her deceased husband's estate to which she is entitled under the law, despite a contrary provision in the will, is known as the widow's election.   **30**

eleemosynary Pertaining or devoted to nonprofit purposes or charity; as, an eleemosynary institution.   **30**

eleemosynary corporation A corporation devoted to giving relief to the poor, or to some other charitable purpose.

eligible paper Those documents, securities, notes and bills which are acceptable by a financial institution such as the Federal Reserve Bank for rediscounting purposes.

Elkins Act "An act to further regulate commerce with foreign nations and among the states." One of the important provisions of this act makes it a misdemeanor, punishable by heavy penalties, to accept or receive rebates, concessions, or discriminations as there defined. **19**

embargo Any prohibition imposed by law upon commerce either in general or in one or more of its branches. **38**

embezzlement The fraudulent appropriation to one's own use of the money or property entrusted to his care. **29**

Emerson Efficiency System An incentive plan whereby a direct laborer is paid a minimum guarantee until his production reaches two-thirds of standard. Beyond that point, he is paid a rapidly increasing bonus. In addition, when his production exceeds 100% of standard, he is paid an additional bonus (usually 20%) on the total time. Generally, this bonus is calculated monthly, rather than on individual jobs. This is done to discourage alternate spurts and lags in the workers' output. **28**

eminent domain The inherent right of certain legally constituted governing bodies to take title to a possession of real property, with just compensation to its owner, for the public good. **29**

emolument The remuneration connected with a service or office such as fee, or salary.

emphyteutic lease A perpetual lease in which the grantee has the right of alienation or descent provided that payment of the rent is maintained in a prompt manner.

employee benefits Advantages besides salary or wage that an employee may have through his employment. Sometimes called fringe benefits. **5**

employee services Maintaining the general welfare of employees on the job and assisting them with problems related to their security and personal well-being. **20**

employees' trust A trust established by an employer (usually a corporation) for the benefit of employees. **30**

emporium The chief market of an area or products.

encroachment 1) The act of trespassing upon the domain of another. Partial or gradual invasion or intrusion.

2) Encroachment of low-value district upon high-class residential section. **54**

encumbrance 1) Something which holds back or weighs down. 2) A lien or claim against title to property which, unless removed, prevents the passing of full and complete title. See "unencumbered property." **33**

end money That money or fund that may be used should an activity or project exceed the original budget. A contingency fund.

endorsement 1) A show of support, a verification. Backing up. 2) A signature on the back of a negotiable instrument, made primarily for the purpose of transferring the rights of the holder to some other person. For variations see "indorsee," "indorser." **31**

endowment Gift to an institution for a specific purpose such as money or property given to hospitals for research purposes. **38**

endowment fund A fund whose principal must be maintained inviolate but whose income may be expended. **29**

enforced liquidation In investment trading, condition caused by the failure of a security owner to maintain sufficient equity in his margin account. **44**

Engel's Law The economic concept that the proportion of a family's budget that goes for food goes up as the income goes down.

entail The system of land ownership and succession which may restrict the inheritance of land to a particular class of heirs such as the eldest son.

entity That which exists as separate and complete in itself. A corporation is an entity, separate and distinct from its stockholders. **30**

entrepreneur One who assumes the financial risk of the initiation, operation and management of a given business or undertaking. **1**

environment 1) The total surrounding conditions of influence and atmosphere. 2) The sum total of economic, physical, and social influencing factors which affect the desirability of a property, and hence its value. **15**

equalization fund See "exchange stabilization fund."

equalization of assessments The periodic review of real property values in a political division such as a county. As a result of the review by trained land appraisers, new values are given the various plots of land and the tax burden is equitably apportioned.

equation price The price reached by the adjusting action of competition in any market at any time, or in a unit of time, such that the demand and supply become equal at that price.   **19**

equilibrium Economic or physical condition which tends to maintain itself in the same situation.

equimarginal principle The amount of money, or the quantity of a good or service that an individual feels he should receive for some other good or service.

equipment Physical property of a more or less permanent nature ordinarily useful in carrying on operations, other than land, buildings, or improvements to either of them. Examples are machinery, tools, trucks, cars, ships, furniture, and furnishings.   **29**

equipment trust A corporate trust established for the purpose of financing the purchase of equipment; commonly resorted to by railroads for the purpose of rolling stock.   **30**

equipment trust certificate A type of security, generally issued by a railroad, to pay for new equipment. Title to the equipment, such as a locomotive, is held by a trustee until the notes are paid off. An equipment trust certificate is usually secured by a first lien on the equipment.   **2**

equitable charge A charge on property imposed by and enforceable in a court of equity, as distinguished from a charge enforceable in a court of law.   **30**

equitable ownership The estate or interest of a person who has a beneficial right in property the legal ownership of which is in another person. A beneficiary of trust has an equitable estate or interest in the trust property.   **30**

equitable title A right to the benefits of property which is recognized by and enforceable only in a court of equity; to be distinguished from legal title.   **22**

equities A term used synonymously with common stocks or capital stocks to designate securities that are owned capital rather than owed capital. The stockholders' equity in a company may be stated inclusive or exclusive of preferred stock.   **40**

equity 1) An interest of an ownership nature, as distinguished from an interest of a creditor nature. The value of collateral over and above the amount of the obligation it secures.

2) A system of legal principles and rules developed to supplement and correct a system of law that had become too narrow and rigid in scope and application. Its characteristic is flexibility and its aim is the administration of justice.   **33**

equity capital Money furnished by owners of the business.   **38**

equity financing The acquisition of money for capital or operating purposes in exchange for a share or shares in the business being financed.   **60**

equity of redemption The right of an owner of a mortgaged or encumbered property to recover the right transferred by the mortgage or other lien upon satisfaction of the debt either before or after foreclosure.   **33**

equity rate Rate applied to very large insurance risks that have had outstandingly good or bad records of claims so that the ordinary rates would not truly represent the risk.   **5**

equity trading See "leverage."

escalator clause Union-contract provision for the raising and lowering of wages according to changes in the cost-of-living index or similar standard.   **12**

escape clause A provision in maintenance-of-membership union contracts giving union members an "escape period" during which they can resign membership. Members who do not resign must remain members for the duration of the contract.   **12**

escheat The reversion of land to the state by the failure of persons legally entitled to hold the same. Also, the reversion to the state of certain funds after a stated period of inactivity pertaining to them, or of other property the ownership of which is unknown or in doubt.   **29**

escrow A written agreement among three or more persons, under which documents or property is deposited with one of the persons as custodian to be delivered to the grantee only upon the fulfillment of certain specified conditions.   **31**

escrow funds As applied to mortgage loans, represents reserves established for the payment of taxes and insurance when due. Reserves are collected monthly by the mortgagee as part of the regular payment.   **23**

essential industry An industry declared to be necessary by the government for a stated purpose such as national defense.

establishment 1) A place of business; often used to denote a business enterprise but in law now interpreted as one building or plot of ground; thus, a "firm" or "business" may have "establishments."   **59**

    2) A permanent civil or military government or organization; the status quo.

estate 1) The right, title, or interest which a person has in any property; to be distinguished from the property itself which is the subject matter of the interest.

    2) A large palatial private residence usually consisting of extensive grounds and several buildings.

    3) The property of a decedent.   **22**

estate tax A tax imposed on a decedent's estate as such and not on the distributive shares of the estate or on the right to receive the shares; to be distinguished from an inheritance tax.   **30**

estimate 1) In appraising, an opinion developed from analysis of an adequate data program by one qualified to develop such an opinion; hence, the opinion of an informed person.

    2) A preliminary opinion of the approximate cost of doing certain work. See "guess."   **15**

estoppel The legal principle which precludes a person from alleging in an action what is contrary to his previous action or admission or which bars him from denying a misrepresentation of a fact when another person has acted upon that misrepresentation to his detriment. The person so precluded or barred is said to be estopped.   **30**

estovers Materials or supplies that a tenant is permitted to take from the custody of the landlord in order to make necessary repairs and prevent constructive eviction. It would include such things as tools, necessary fuel, and certain repair materials.   **5**

eviction The depriving by due process of law of a person or persons from the possession of land in keeping with the judgment of the court.   **5**

excess-profits tax A levy designed to take away from a business "abnormal" profits which have resulted from some emergency situation such as war.

excess reserves A term used to designate the amount of funds held in reserve by banks in excess of the legal minimum requirements, whether the funds are on deposit in the Federal Reserve Bank, in a bank approved as a depository, or in the cash reserve carried within its own vaults.   **1**

exchange 1) An organization or place for transacting business or settling accounts between parties at some distance from each other.

2) An organization for trading in securities or commodities.

3) The volume of funds available for use in another city or country.

4) An amount charged for the collection of a check or other financial instrument.

exchange acquisition A method of filling an order to buy a large block of stock on the floor of the exchange. Under certain circumstances, a member-broker can facilitate the purchase of a block by soliciting orders to sell. All orders to sell the security are lumped together and offset with the buy order in the regular auction market. The price to the buyer may be on a net basis or on a commission basis.   **2**

exchange charge A fee or service charge made by the drawee bank on the presenting bank for its services in paying negotiable instruments. The Federal Reserve Act forbids drawee banks to make such charges against Federal Reserve Banks on checks in process of collection. The reason is to assure that check money will be payable throughout the country at its face value.   **8**

exchange controls Various governmental restrictions limiting the right to exchange one nation's currency into another nation's currency.

exchange rate The price of one nation's currency expressed in terms of another nation's currency.

exchange stabilization (or) **equalization fund** The sum of money, or the organization handling the money, used to purchase or sell gold, foreign exchange, and domestic currency for the purposes of keeping the exchange rate within a very limited range. See "exchange rate."

exchequer That account of the Chancellor of the Exchequer of the United Kingdom which is used to handle the revenues and payments of the kingdom. The account is maintained in the Bank of England. It roughly corresponds with the United States Treasury Department's accounts in the twelve Federal Reserve Banks.

excise tax A tax levied by the federal and state governments upon the manufacture, sale, or consumption of certain commodities, or a tax levied on the right, privilege, or permission to engage in a certain business, trade, occupation, or sport. **1**

exclusion 1) A restriction or limitation.

2) Provision of part of the insurance contract limiting the scope of the coverage. Certain causes and conditions, listed in the policy, which are not covered. **52**

exclusive listing An agreement providing that a specific broker shall be the sole agent of the owner of a property, giving the broker the sole right to sell or rent the property within a specified time.

ex coupon A security without the interest coupon, *i.e.,* the current interest coupon has been detached. **44**

ex dividend When a dividend is declared by a corporation, it is payable on a designated date to stockholders of record as of a stated date. When stock is sold prior to the stated date, the dividend belongs to the buyer and not to the seller. When the stock is sold subsequent to the stated date and prior to the date of payment, the dividend belongs to the seller and not to the buyer. It is then said to sell ex dividend. (The New York Stock Exchange, however, has a special rule to the effect that the stock becomes ex dividend three business days prior to the stated date. Most other exchanges follow the New York rule.) **22**

execution A formal judicial order which directs a public officer, usually a sheriff, to execute or carry into effect a final judgment or decree of a court. **22**

executive The individual engaged in the administrative function, be it private or public, who plans and controls the execution of the activity.

executor A person or an institution named by an individual in his will to settle his estate in accordance with the terms of his will. **25**

exemplified copy A copy of a record of document witnessed or sealed or certified to as required by law for the purposes of a particular transaction. **30**

ex gratia payment Settlement of a claim which an insurance company does not think it is legally obligated to pay to prevent an even larger expense of defending itself in the courts. Strike suits or threats of suit may result in an ex gratia payment. **5**

exhaust price That price at which a broker is forced to sell a security which was margined and subsequently has dropped in price. Prior to reaching the exhaust price, the broker will request his customer to provide additional margin or cover. In the event that the customer does not provide the needed margin, the security will be sold by the broker when the stock drops to the exhaust price so that the broker himself will not suffer any loss.

ex officio By virtue of his office.   **5**

exoneration 1) The act of clearing, freeing from blame, acquitting.

2) The act of relieving one of what otherwise would be or might be a liability or a duty.   **22**

expansion 1) That phase of a business cycle or fluctuation in which there is an increase in industrial activity. Periods of expansion are associated with recovery and prosperity.

2) A broadening or extending of the operation or territory of a business or organization.

ex parte Ordinarily implies a hearing or examination in the presence of, or on papers filed by one party and in the absence of, and often without notice to, the other.   **35**

expediting charges Funds expended to replace or repair damage to prevent even larger claims.   **5**

expendable 1) That which is capable of being consumed or used up in production or service.

2) That which can be sacrificed or given up.

expenditure An actual payment or the creation of an obligation to make a future payment for some benefit, item, or service received.   **1**

expense In its broadest sense it includes all expired costs which are deductible from revenues. Narrower use of the term refers to such items as operating, selling or administrative expenses, interest, and taxes.   **17**

expense loading The practice in insurance rate making denoting the amount which is added to the pure premium to provide for the expense of the insurance company.   **52**

expense ratio The ratio of expenses to income.   **42**

expiry In insurance, termination of a term policy at the end of the term period.   **58**

explicit interest The amount of money or goods paid on a loan.

export Goods shipped outside a country. To ship goods outside a country.   **5**

139

export bounty That premium or subsidy paid to an exporter of covered goods. The subsidy is generally paid by the government for the purpose of stimulating an industry.

Export-Import Bank That governmental agency formed in 1934, and expanded in 1945, to engage in the general banking business but not to compete with private banking activities in helping exports and imports of the United States. Most of such help is tied to price-supported agricultural products.

export license The document issued by a government which will permit a stated amount of the described commodity to be exported. Items such as gold, arms, munitions and drugs may require such a license.

express trust A trust stated orally or in writing with the terms of the trust definitely prescribed; to be distinguished from a resulting trust or a constructive trust. **30**

expropriation The act or process whereby private property is taken for public purpose or use, or the rights therein modified by a sovereignty or any entity vested with the necessary legal authority, *e.g.,* where property is acquired under eminent domain. **54**

ex rights Without the rights. Corporations raising additional money may do so by offering their stockholders the right to subscribe to new or additional stock, usually at a discount from the prevailing market price. The buyer of a stock selling ex rights is not entitled to the rights. See "ex dividend" and "rights." **2**

extended coverage A clause in an insurance policy or of an endorsement of a policy which provides extra or additional coverage for other hazards or risks than those provided for under the basic provisions of the policy. **52**

extensive cultivation In contradistinction to intensive cultivation, it is the use of limited labor and machinery on agricultural land.

external economies Reduction in costs of a firm which have resulted from outside factors over which the firm has no control.

extractive industry A business activity such as mining and quarrying which takes natural resources from their site and thus depletes the natural resource.

extra dividend A supplementary dividend in cash or stock. A dividend in addition to the one which a firm has regularly been paying. **44**

140

extrapolation A method of estimating a value which is outside the known values.

ex warrants Without warrants. A security trading ex warrants indicates that the warrants have been retained or exercised by the seller. **44**

F

fabricated materials Those industrial goods which become a part of the finished product and which have undergone processing beyond that required for raw materials but not so much as finished parts. **13**

face of the note The amount stated on the note. It is also known as the principal. **16**

face value The principal value of a note, bond, or other instrument. The value upon which interest is computed, if an interest-bearing instrument. **23**

facilitating agency An organization which assists but does not take title to goods. A stock exchange or common carrier is a facilitating agency.

fact-finding board A group of persons appointed by an organization such as a business or a government to investigate, collect and make known the facts regarding a specific situation or problem.

factor 1) A type of commission merchant who often advances funds to the consignor, identified chiefly with the raw cotton and naval stores trades.

2) A specialized commercial banker, performing the function of financing for producers of, and dealers in, many varieties of products and occasionally combining this function with that of selling. The term "factor" was formerly synonymous with "commission merchant." **13**

factorage The earnings or commission of a factor.

factor cost The market price of a product from which is deducted all costs that are not factors of production such as transfer payments and depreciation.

factoring A means of advancing credit whereby the factor purchases at a discount and without recourse the accounts receivable of a firm. The factor assumes complete responsibility for credit investigation and collection.

factors of production Land, capital, labor, and management when used to produce wealth.

faculty principle of taxation The ability-to-pay theory of taxation.

fad A craze or fashion of short duration.

failure of issue Failure, by nonexistence or death, of lineal descendants (children, grandchildren, and on down the line). **30**

fair-employment practices Policy of firing, promoting, etc., without regard for race, sex, or religious background. **12**

Fair Labor Standards Act The federal Wage-Hour Law which establishes minimum-wage and overtime-pay requirements and child-labor restrictions. **12**

fair-market value A legal term variously interpreted by the courts but in general connoting a price obtainable in the market which is fair and reasonable in view of the conditions currently existing. **5**

fair return An income on invested capital used in the activity that will permit the business to raise additional capital for normal growth.

fair trade laws Federal and state legislation on resale price agreements generally designed to restrict price cutting by establishing minimum retail prices for products whose manufacturers comply with the provisions of the fair trade laws.

fair value 1) Value that is reasonable and consistent with all the known facts. **54**
2) Under the Investment Company Act, value determined in good faith by the board of directors for those securities and assets for which there is no market quotation readily available. **3**

false pretense Refers to any untrue statements or representations made with the intention of obtaining something of value such as property or money. **52**

family A group of one or more persons occupying a single dwelling unit, as distinguished from a group occupying a boarding house, rooming house, club, hotel, sorority or fraternity house. **10**

Fannie Mae Nickname. See "Federal National Mortgage Association."

farm bloc The senators and representatives of states with extensive agricultural interests who tend to vote on agricultural legislation as a group or bloc.

farm cooperative An association of farmers for the purpose of marketing and/or purchasing goods for its members.

Farm Credit Administration Established in 1933, it comprises twelve Federal Land Banks, twelve Federal Intermediate Credit Banks, twelve Production Credit Corporations, twelve District Banks for Cooperatives, the Federal Farm Mortgage Corporation and related agencies.

Farmers Home Administration Created in 1946 to aid in the financing of farm homes and improvements; it also helps finance purchase of seed, equipment, fertilizer, and livestock.

farmers' market A privately owned retail center with central management that rents booth space usually on a short-term basis to a large number of merchants. Generally located in a suburban or rural area, it has simple facilities, ample parking, and large assortments of low-priced nonfood merchandise as well as food lines. It enjoys a low overhead and heavy traffic. A carnival atmosphere prevails, and an auction is frequently featured.   **24**

farm surpluses Those agricultural products which have been acquired under loan or support programs by the government.

fascism While usually regarded as a political system, fascism, in the business sense, worked through a mercantilistic guild system of "sindacati" or controlled unions organized along occupational lines and "corporazioni" which were similar to producers' guilds. The deaths of Hitler and Mussolini in 1945 and the defeat of the Axis powers brought about the end of this system.

fashion cycle The tendency for certain goods to have surges of popularity and sales followed by periods of disinterest and poor sales.

fas price An amount charged an importer which includes such expenses as insurance, warehousing, trucking, and lighterage up to the loading tackle of the ship. All risk of ownership rests with the seller up to the loading on the vessel.   **5**

favorable balance of trade A situation in which the value of the merchandise and service exports exceed the merchandise and service imports for a nation for a period of time. The difference is made up by shipment of gold, obtaining holdings of foreign exchange or making of foreign investments.

featherbedding Labor practices that are not productive or which result in the employee being paid for work which he did not do.

feature Refers to the more active stocks in the general list. **44**

Federal Advisory Council Twelve men, one from each Federal Reserve District, who have no power except to give advice to the Board of Governors of the Federal Reserve System regarding business conditions and related economic factors.

federal credit union A cooperative association organized under the Federal Credit Union Act for the purpose of accepting savings from its members, making loans to them at low interest rates, and rendering other financial services to its members. Cooperatives offering similar services also operate under state charters. **1**

Federal Crop Insurance Corporation Facility for insurance of growing crops by an instrumentality of the United States Government. No element of compulsion is involved. **5**

federal debt limit A limit imposed by law (Second Liberty Bond Act, as amended) on the aggregate face amount of outstanding obligations issued, or guaranteed as to principal and interest, by the United States except such guaranteed obligations as may be held by the Secretary of the Treasury. **7**

Federal Deposit Insurance Corporation A corporation established by federal authority to provide insurance of demand and time deposits in participating banks up to a maximum of $100,000 for each depositor. **25**

federal funds 1) Funds owned or set aside for use by a federal government such as the United States or Switzerland.

2) Bank deposits at the Federal Reserve Banks or at correspondent banks. Banks, which find themselves with temporary excess reserves not needed for transactions purposes, can lend these balances, overnight or for a few days, to banks which have temporary reserve deficiencies. **46**

Federal Home Loan Bank System A system established in 1932 to serve as a mortgage credit reserve system for home mortgage lending institutions. Members may obtain advances on home mortgage collateral and may borrow from Federal Home Loan Banks under certain conditions. **34**

Federal Housing Administration An instrumentality of the

United States Government that provides an insurance protection to mortgage holders of mortgages issued under its supervision.	**5**

Federal Intermediate Credit Banks Twelve regional banks established by Congress for the purpose of providing intermediate credit for ranchers and farmers by rediscounting the agricultural
paper of financial institutions.

federal labor union A union which was affiliated directly with the American Federation of Labor prior to its merger with the Congress of Industrial Organizations and which had no national officers except those of the American Federation of Labor's executive council.	**12**

Federal Land Banks Twelve regional banks established by Congress for such purposes as providing long-term mortgage loans to farmers through National Farm Loan Associations.

Federal Mediation and Conciliation Service Independent agency created by the Taft-Hartley Act in 1947 to attempt to settle labor disputes which substantially affect interstate commerce.	**12**

Federal National Mortgage Association A corporation organized in 1938 under the provisions of the National Housing Act of 1934, as amended. It provides a secondary mortgage market for the purchase and sale of Federal Housing Administration insured and Veterans Administration guaranteed loans.	**33**

Federal Open Market Committee The Board of Governors of the Federal Reserve System plus the president of the New York Federal Reserve Bank and four of the remaining Federal Reserve Bank presidents from the other eleven Federal Reserve Banks. The four are chosen on a rotating basis. The committee determines the broad policy of open market operations which are conducted through the Federal Reserve Bank of New York as agent for the system.

Federal Power Commission The governmental agency established in 1920 to regulate interstate operations of private utilities in such things as issuance of securities, rates and site location.

Federal Reserve Act As amended, this act establishes and provides for the operation of the Federal Reserve System. See "Federal Reserve Banks" and "Federal Reserve System."

Federal Reserve agent The Class "C" director and chairman of the board of directors of a Federal Reserve District Bank whose major function is safeguarding the collateral for Federal Reserve notes in his possession.

Federal Reserve Banks (Twelve in number plus branches.) Federal banking corporations that deal principally with their member banks and with the government. They deal with the general public only to a limited extent. They act as agents in maintaining reserves, issuing money in the form of bank notes, and lending money to other banks.

Federal Reserve Board The seven-member Board of Governors of the Federal Reserve System located in Washington, D.C. Members are appointed for fourteen-year terms by the President with Senate approval and devote their full time to board business. No two members come from the same district. One term expires every two years.   44

Federal Reserve cities The head office and number of each of the twelve Federal Reserve Banks follows: 1. Boston, 2. New York, 3. Philadelphia, 4. Cleveland, 5. Richmond, 6. Atlanta, 7. Chicago, 8. St. Louis, 9. Minneapolis, 10. Kansas City, 11. Dallas, 12. San Francisco. These are known as the twelve Federal Reserve cities.

Federal Reserve note A noninterest-bearing promissory note of a Federal Reserve Bank issued for general circulation as money and payable to the bearer on demand.   25

Federal Reserve System The central banking system of the United States, created by an act of Congress (Federal Reserve Act) in 1913. It consists of regional bankers' banks (twelve Federal Reserve Banks and their branches), which are controlled and supervised by the Board of Governors in Washington, and national and state member banks. It has wide powers in controlling credit and the flow of money, as well as regulating its member banks.

Federal Savings and Loan Association The title given to one of the associations established by the Home Owners Loan Act of 1933 and amended in the Home Owners Loan Act of 1934, approved on April 27, 1934. This act permitted existing and newly formed mutual savings banks and building and loan associations to come under a federal charter. Under the federal charter, these institutions are governed and regulated by the Federal Home Loan Bank Board.   1

146

Federal Savings and Loan Insurance Corporation An organization created in 1934 for the purpose of insuring the shares and accounts of all federal savings and loan associations and of such state-chartered savings and loan associations as apply for insurance and meet the requirements of the corporation. **34**

Federal Security Agency The United States agency formed in 1939 whose functions were absorbed in 1953 by the Department of Health, Education and Welfare.

Federal Tort Claims Act Permits the United States to be sued for damage to property or personal injuries under circumstances such that if the federal government were an individual it would be liable. Previous to this the concept of sovereignty that a government cannot be sued without its permission was in effect. **5**

Federal Trade Commission The United States agency formed in 1914 to prevent restraint of trade and unfair pricing and advertising in interstate commerce.

federal unemployment insurance tax Dual state and federal tax based on merit rating to provide insurance benefits for unemployment of covered individuals. **5**

fee Depending on the context, it may either be a remuneration for services or an inheritable estate in land. **54**

feeder line A transportation company which originates and funnels traffic to a major line.

fee simple An absolute fee, that is, an estate of inheritance without limitation to any particular class of heirs and with no restrictions upon alienation; sometimes known as fee simple absolute; the largest estate a person may own. **30**

fee tail An estate limited to a particular class of heirs of the person to whom the property or estate is granted. **54**

fiat money Inconvertible and irredeemable money issued by a government but given the status of being legal tender.

fictitious trade style A designation of a business conducted by one or more persons using a name not containing the surname of that person or those persons. **35**

fiduciary An individual, corporation, or association, such as a bank or trust company, to whom certain property is given to hold in trust, according to the trust agreement under which this property is held. The property may be utilized, or invested, for the benefit of the property owner to the best ability of the fiduciary. Administrators and executors of estates, and trustees of organizations are common examples of fiduciaries. Investments of trust funds, unless specified in the trust indenture, are usually restricted by law.　　　　　　　　　　**1**

fiduciary money or standard Currency not secured in full by precious metals. Credit money.

fiduciary service A service performed by an individual or a corporation acting in a trust capacity. A banking institution authorized to do a trust business may perform fiduciary services, for example, by acting as executor or administrator of estates, guardian of minors, and trustee under wills.　　　　　　**25**

fieldman An individual employee working away from the head or home office in the territory served by his company.　　**5**

field warehouse receipt A receipt issued by a field warehouseman for inventory or for other property stored on the owner's premises. The part of the owner's premises on which the property is stored must be leased to the warehouseman to comply with the Federal Warehouse Receipts Act. Banks accepting field warehouse receipts as collateral for loans are, therefore, protected by having legal possession of the property pledged.　　　　　　　　　　　　　　　　　**1**

fifo See "first in, first out."

finance As a noun, the system by which the income of a company is raised and administered. As a verb, to conduct financial operations or to furnish money. Deals with methods for supplying capital needed to acquire, develop, and operate real property.　　　　　　　　　　　　　　　　　　**5**

finance bill A draft drawn by a bank on a bank in another country against securities held by the foreign bank.

finance company A discount house or commercial credit company. At times it is also used to refer to a personal loan company.

financial guaranty A type of bond in which the insurer guarantees that it will pay a fixed or determinable sum of money.　**5**

financial insolvency That situation in which a firm, individual, government, or other organization is not able to pay its debts as they mature even though the assets may exceed the liabilities.

financial investment The purchase of sound stocks or bonds as compared to real investment in a capital asset such as real estate or plant and machinery.

148

financial services 1) All related services provided by banks and financial institutions to their customers.

2) Those financial organizations established to rate securities, publish investor services, etc., such as Moody's Investor's Service and Standard and Poor's Corporation. **44**

financial solvency That situation in which a business is able to meet its current debts with its current assets.

financial statement A summary of figure facts showing the financial condition of a business. It is an itemized listing of assets (what the business owns), liabilities (what the business owes), and net worth of capital account (the owners' equity in the business). A balance sheet of a bank is called a statement of condition. **25**

finder's fee The amount an intermediary between a lender and a borrower obtains for bringing the two together, provided that financing is consummated.

fine The penalty charged the violator by a government or authority such as a union for breaking a law or rule.

finished goods Goods that have gone through the manufacturing process and that have been made ready for sale. **16**

finks Workers hired during a strike primarily for the purpose of defeating the strike. **12**

firm-commitment offering A securities issue whereby the risk of selling the entire issue is assumed by the underwriting brokers. Some agreements specify only a "best efforts" approach without the assumption of risk by the underwriters. **44**

first in, first out Accounting method of valuing inventory on the basis of first in, first out. That is, an entire inventory may have been acquired at slightly different prices and time intervals. The accountant upon receiving the notice of a sale of part of that inventory will compute his cost and profit on the oldest or first price for his markup. This method is referred to as "fifo." For contrast see "lifo," or "last in, first out."

first lien The best and highest priority claim against an asset.

first mortgage The senior mortgage, thus having precedent and priority over all other mortgages taken out on a property. **54**

fiscal 1) Financial matters, in general.

2) Of or pertaining to the public treasury or revenue. **38**

fiscal agent 1) In general, a person or organization serving as another's financial agent.

2) An agent for a corporation or organization to handle cer-

tain matters relating specifically to taxes in connection with an issue of bonds.

3) An agent for a national, state or municipal government or governmental body to pay its bonds and coupons or to perform certain other duties related to financial matters.   **30**

fiscal monopoly A commercial monopoly operated by a government for revenue and profit.

fiscal period Any period at the end of which a unit determines its financial condition, the results of its operations, and closes its books.   **29**

fiscal policy In a general sense, a government's activities concerned with taxes, receipts, debt expenditures, currency and trust funds.

fiscal year The accounting year of a firm, government, or other organization.   **2**

five percenter Those individuals or firms who expedite the obtaining of federal contracts by business firms for a fee. The fee is 5% of the contract obtained.

fixed capital Capital invested in fixed assets, such as land, buildings, machinery, etc.   **1**

fixed charges Expenses the amount of which is more or less fixed.   **29**

fixed costs Those indirect or overhead expenses of a business activity which do not vary with the volume of activity.

fixed debt A permanent debt extending over a length of time, such as that represented by bonds.   **44**

fixed income Any constant income which does not fluctuate over time, such as that from bonds, annuities and preferred stocks.   **44**

fixed investment trust An investment company established as a nondiscretionary trust and which is limited to a stated and agreed upon list of securities.

fixed-price contract An agreement by which the buyer pays the seller or producer a stipulated amount.

fixed shift Established working period; same hours of work over an extensive period.   **12**

fixing the price 1) Setting a price for something in advance (as through an agreement between producers or by government edict) rather than through the free enterprise system.

2) The computation of the price at which a spot commodity

will be billed. The price is determined after a call sale permits a differential to be established with a specific futures contract.

fixtures Appurtenances which are affixed to the building or land and generally in such a way that they cannot be moved without causing damage to either the property or themselves. **54**

flat (After a market quotation for a bond.) No accrued interest to be paid by the purchaser to the seller; issues in default and, usually, issues on which interest payments are contingent on earnings quoted on that basis. **22**

fleece The taking advantage of a poorly informed individual by a person conversant with security market conditions.

fleet of companies Many different companies are affiliated with others under the same management. These groups of companies are called fleets.

flexible schedule Situation in which work period and working hours are not fixed but vary in accordance with production requirements. **12**

flexible tariff A schedule of duties which the Tariff Commission may adjust within certain maximum ranges as their discretion would indicate.

flight of capital The movement of capital, which has generally been converted into a liquid asset, from one place to another to avoid loss or to increase gain.

float Checks, in the process of being collected and converted into cash, which represent funds not available to the bank for investment purposes, although immediate credit is usually given to the depositor. Float is an important factor in analyzing customer accounts in order to compute service charges. **30**

floating capital Capital which is identified as being in the form of current assets rather than fixed assets.

floating debt Liabilities (except bonds) payable on demand or at any early date; for example, accounts payable, bank loans, notes or warrants. **29**

floating supply The amount of a security or commodity which is in the hands of speculators and traders as distinguished from investors or users of the commodity.

floor The huge trading area where stocks and bonds are bought and sold on a stock or commodities exchange. **2**

floor broker Any person who, in or surrounding any pit, ring, post, or other place provided by a contract market for the meeting of persons similarly engaged, engages in executing for others any order for the purchase or sale of commodity or security on or subject to the rules of any contract market, and who for such services receives or accepts a prescribed fee or brokerage. **9**

floor-plan financing A type of financing which supplies the capital to permit a dealer in a certain product or products to acquire samples of the product or products to display for sale, and which is liquidated when the sale is consummated. **1**

floor trader Any member of a stock or commodity exchange who trades on the floor for his own account. **2**

flow chart 1) A visual device which shows the movement of some product, item, authority or other economic factor from one point or place to another.

2) In electronic data processing, a symbolic representation of program logic or computer processing.

fluid savings Savings in a liquid form such as cash or demand deposits which may be used at the discretion of the holder.

fly-by-night An activity which is not considered to be sound and which is expected to move under cover of darkness to avoid payment to creditors.

for a turn A speculative transaction made to obtain a quick, and frequently small, profit on the sale of securities.

for cash Cash transactions generally require the purchaser to pay for the product or item prior to or no later than delivery.

forced loan A sum of money borrowed against the will or judgment of the lender.

forced sale The act of selling property under compulsion as to time and place. Usually a sale made by virtue of a court order, ordinarily at public auction. **54**

forecasting Predicting reasonable probabilities about the future of something, such as sales of a product, economic conditions, etc. **38**

foreclosure The process by which a mortgagor of real or personal property, or other owner of property subject to a lien, is deprived of his interest therein. The usual modern method is sale of the property by court proceedings or outside of court. **34**

foreign agency An agency of a domestically domiciled firm which is located outside the country. The major consideration is that the legal relationship is one of agency as compared to branch or subsidiary operation.

foreign bill A bill drawn in one state and payable in another state or country.

foreign bill of exchange The system by which the balances arising out of transactions between countries are settled. The currency used in making the settlement. **25**

foreign corporation A corporation organized under the laws of a state other than the state in which it is doing business. **30**

foreign correspondent 1) The firm or individual in a foreign nation which acts for a principal as an agent.

2) A reporter of news from a foreign source.

foreign deposits Those deposits which are payable at a financial institution outside the jurisdiction of the United States Government and payable in the currency of the country in which the depository is located. See "nostro account." **1**

foreign exchange The conversion of the money of one country into its equal of another country. **38**

foreign exchange rate The price relationship between the currencies of two countries. **25**

foreign trade zone A free port or area where foreign merchandise may be imported without being required to pay duties on the condition that it is not used domestically and is shipped to some other country.

forfeiture The automatic loss of cash, property, or rights, as a punishment for not complying with legal provisions and as compensation for the resulting damages or losses. The term should not be confused with "confiscation." The latter term designates the actual taking over of the forfeited property by the government. Even after property has been forfeited, it cannot be said to be confiscated until the governmental unit claims it. **29**

forgery The alteration of any document, instrument, or signature, with the intent to defraud or prejudice any individual constitutes forgery, which is a statutory crime, punishable by imprisonment. **1**

formula investing An investment technique. One formula calls for the shifting of funds from common shares to preferred shares or bonds as the market, on average, rises above a certain predetermined point—and the return of funds to common share investments as the market average declines. **2**

form utility The additional satisfaction of a human want that is created by changing the shape of some sort of product. A block of salt gains utility by being converted into small grains so that it may be used as a condiment. This gain is known as form utility.

forward exchange A means of hedging against the fluctuation of a foreign exchange rate by purchasing a bill of foreign exchange that is payable at some future or forward period of time.

forwarding 1) A procedure used to carry forward information from one page to another in an account or journal. Usually only the totals are "carried forward" and are so labeled. **16**
2) The sending of mail and messages arriving at a previous address to a current address or location.

forwarding agent That individual or company which handles the function of collecting and shipping merchandise for others.

foul bill of lading A bill of lading indicating that a damage or shortage existed at the time of shipment. **19**

foundation 1) The base or lowest part of a structure upon which everything else rests or is founded upon.
2) Basic principles or policies.
3) A permanent fund established by contributions from one source (as the Carnegie Foundation) or from many sources (as the Cleveland Foundation) for charitable, educational, religious or other benevolent uses or purposes. See "community trust." **30**

founders' stock Stock which is issued to the promoters or founders for their services in forming a new corporation.

fraction 1) A portion of a whole.
2) In investments, a term generally applied to holdings of less than one share, resulting from rights and stock dividends. Since they are not entitled to dividends, they are usually disposed of by sale or rounded out, by the purchase of additional fractions, to full shares. **22**

fractional currency Coins in the United States that have a value of less than one dollar. Also called fractional coins or fractional money.

fractional reserve The present system of commercial banking in the United States in which any bank is legally required to maintain only a part of any deposit in the form of reserves such as till cash or deposits with a central bank. The difference

154

between the required reserves and the actual reserves may then be lent to borrowers.

franchise 1) Liberty, freedom, right, privilege.

2) A special privilege granted by a government permitting the continuing use of public property, such as city streets, and usually involving the elements of monopoly and regulation. **29**

3) A right given by a corporation or business firm to another to sell or distribute a certain product or service in a given area or section, in return for some compensation or a share of the profits.

franchise clause In marine insurance, a policy feature providing that no claims below a stated amount are to be paid by the insurance company, but, if the claims are above that amount, the entire amount will be paid. This clause discourages the submission of small claims that cost more to process than the actual settlement amount. **5**

franchise tax The charge made by a governmental unit for the right to exercise a private monopoly such as a public utility or bus line.

franking The exemption from having to pay for the postage on United States mail which is granted to members of Congress and certain other departments and executives of the nation for certain uses of the mails.

fraud Deception or artifice used to deceive or cheat. **52**

free alongside (FAS) Seller's quoted price which includes delivery of material to the loading facility of the ship. See "fas price." **5**

free and open market A market in which supply and demand are expressed without restraint in terms of price. Contrast with a controlled market in which supply, demand and price may all be regulated. **2**

free banking Concept that any group of incorporators of a bank that can meet certain standards should be issued a charter. Since 1933 the concept of free banking has been altered to require showing necessity for the service.

free coinage The situation where the mint must coin all designated metals presented to the mint for that purpose. There may be a charge for minting the coin, and, in this sense, free coinage is not necessarily free of expense.

free good Anything which has use to man but is so available

155

that all can have it without expense or work. Daylight and air are two examples of free goods.

freehold estate A legal estate in land commonly referred to as an estate of inheritance. The two most important freehold estates are the fee simple estate and the life estate. See "chattel." **33**

free list in customs The enumeration of items that may be imported without payment of any duty.

free port See "foreign trade zone."

free ride The situation where an individual is in a position to take advantage of circumstances to obtain a profit without exposing himself to risk.

free silver See "free coinage."

free trade A situation in which customs duties and restrictions on exports or imports are absent and no governmental actions are permitted to interfere with foreign commerce.

frictional unemployment That situation where people are not working because of technical factors. A migratory farm laborer experiences frictional unemployment for the period in transit from one job to another even though he is assured of the job upon arrival.

fringe benefits See "employee benefits."

fringe issue Provisions in a labor agreement that involve compensation to the employee other than hourly wages or incentive earnings, such as vacations, overtime, sick leave, holidays, etc.

frozen account An account that has been suspended in payment until a court order or legal process again makes the account available for withdrawal. **1**

frozen credits Loans which would normally have been called and matured, but, due to economic conditions, it is recognized by the creditor that such a step would precipitate the bankruptcy of the debtor and thus preclude any substantial payment. As a result, such credits may be carried or extended, with the hope of liquidation when the debtor has recovered. Also described as frozen loans.

full coverage Any form of insurance which provides for payment, without deduction, of all losses up to the amount of the insurance occasioned by hazards covered. See "all risks insurance." **50, 51, 52**

full employment The situation when all able people who are in the labor market and wishing employment may find gainful work. During full employment people may, however, not be working for such technical reasons as frictional unemployment and vacations.

full faith and credit debt Usually state debt for which the credit of the government, implying the power of taxation, is unconditionally pledged.　　　　　　　　　　　　　　　　　　　7

full lot A "round" or "board" lot. Generally, 100 shares of stock traded on the New York Stock Exchange.

full stock An equity security with the par value of one hundred dollars.

fully paid stock Legally issued stock for which the corporation has received at least the amount of the par value in goods, services or money.

fully registered A term generally applied to bonds which are registered as to principal and income. In this form, a bond is not negotiable and interest is remitted by the disbursing agent to the registered owner.　　　　　　　　　　　　　　　22

function A more or less arbitrary subdivision of the total activity area, which, when the size or nature of the business justifies it, can best be performed by a specialist.　　　　　　　　20

functional financing See "compensatory fiscal policy."

functional obsolescence The reduction in the value of a real estate property because that property does not possess the technological features of more efficient or newer property.　　5

fund Stock; capital; cash or currency; to be distinguished from other kinds of property. As distinguished from a reserve, an asset or group of assets segregated for some specified purpose.　　　　　　　　　　　　　　　　　　　22

fundamental disequilibrium The material and continuing difference between the official exchange rate of a country's currency and the purchasing power of the currency.

funded debt Usually interest-bearing bonds of a company. Could include long-term bank loans. Does not include short-term loans, preferred or common stock.　　　　　　　　2

funded pension plan A systematic method used by the insurer of a pension insurance plan to accumulate the amount or fund which will be needed to meet the claims of the plan.　　5

funding The act of converting a shorter maturity debt into a longer maturity. Some authorities use the term to refer to the conversion of debt into equity but they appear to be in the minority.

157

future-exchange contract A contract for the purchase or sale of foreign exchange to be delivered at a future date and at a rate determined in the present. 25

futures Agreements to buy and receive or to sell and deliver a commodity at a future date, with these distinguishing features: All trades in the same contract, such as the grain contract, have the same unit of trading, 5,000 bushels; the terms of all trades are standardized; a trade, therefore, may be offset later by an opposite trade through the same clearing member; all trades must be made by open outcry in the pit within the hours prescribed; the contract has a basic grade but more than one grade is deliverable; delivery is made during a single calendar month; the trades are cleared through a clearinghouse daily. 9

G

gain Profits; winnings; advantage. To obtain, earn, or increase.

gain sharing A wage plan in which a bonus is paid for production in excess of a standard.

Gantt chart A device designed to display production data graphically.

garnishee The party upon whom a garnishment is served.

garnishment A notice summoning a third party, in whose hands the effects of the defendant are attached, not to pay the money or deliver the goods to the defendant but to appear in court and answer to the suit of the plaintiff to the extent of his liability to the defendant. 35

general audit An audit which embraces all financial transactions and records and which is made regularly at the close of an accounting period. 29

general depository A bank which is a member of the Federal Reserve System and which is permitted to handle deposits of the United States Treasury.

general fund The fund that is available for any legally authorized purpose and which is therefore used to account for all revenues and all activities not provided for in other funds. The general fund is used to finance the ordinary operations of a unit. 29

general ledger A company's general book of accounts in which all financial transactions are recorded or summarized.

general legacy A gift of personal property by will which is not a particular thing as distinguished from all others of the same kind; to be distinguished from specific legacy.   **22**

general loan and collateral agreement A continuing agreement under which an investment broker borrows on the security of stocks and bonds which are listed on an exchange. A broker's loan.

general management trust A trust not limited to a specific list of securities in which to invest.

general partnership A firm formed by two or more people, each having the power to bind the firm and all partners by his actions and in which all partners are fully liable for the debts of the partnership.

general property tax See "property tax."

general store A retail store which carries a variety of nonrelated items of merchandise, usually including groceries, hard goods, and soft goods, and which is not departmentalized.   **13**

general strike A situation in which many industries and business firms are struck by their workers with the attempt at paralysis of the business in the area.

general tariff A single-schedule tariff, that is, one single rate of duty on a product no matter what country exported it. It is also called a unilinear tariff.

gentlemen's agreement An unsigned, unsecured contract based upon the faith of both parties that each will perform.   **59**

geographic wage differentials Differences in wage rates based upon locations of plants or industries.   **12**

G.I. bill of rights The popular term for those privileges and benefits that veterans possess under the Servicemen's Readjustment Act of 1944 as amended.   **5**

gift The value of a donated asset acquired without cost to the recipient or regard to its donor. The use of the gift may or may not be restricted.   **29**

gift causa mortis A gift of personal property made by a person in expectation of death, completed by actual delivery of the property, and effective only if the donor dies; to be distinguished from gift inter vivos.   **30**

gift certificate Certificate issued by store or firm entitling recipient to purchase merchandise at its sales outlet.   **26**

gift inter vivos A gift of property between living persons. To make such a gift effective, there must be actual delivery of the property during the lifetime of the donor and without reference to his death.   30

gift tax An excise tax levied by the federal government and many states on the gift or transfer of property. Most taxes of gifts are progressive and have minimum exemptions.   5

gilt-edged High-grade bond issued by a company which has demonstrated its ability to earn a comfortable profit over a period of years and pay its bondholders their interest without interruption.   2

give an indication To express an interest in a new security issue by entering a firm buy order for a stated amount.   44

give an order 1) To issue a command or instruction expected to be followed.
2) An instruction to an investment broker to buy or sell a security in a certain amount which may, or may not, include specifications of a price or time limit.   44

glut To oversupply.   38

going concern A successful business with the prospects of continuing.

going-concern value An intangible value said to inhere in an operating plant or common carrier or utility with business established because it is an actual operation, as distinguished from one newly constituted and not yet in operation which has yet to establish its business and reputation.   19

gold bullion standard Sometimes called the rich man's standard because the paper currency of the nation which was on the gold bullion standard could be exchanged into gold freely but only in sizeable amounts such as a gold bar which might be worth over $5,000.

gold certificate account Gold certificates on hand and due from the Treasury. The certificates, on hand and due from the Treasury, are backed 100 percent by the United States Government. They count as legal reserve, the minimum the Reserve Banks are required to maintain being 25 percent of their combined Federal Reserve note and deposit liabilities.   4

gold exchange standard The monetary system in which a nation ties its currency to another nation's gold standard by providing that the first nation's currency may be exchanged for the currency of the nation that is on the gold standard. The exchange is pegged at a fixed rate which is maintained by the monetary authorities. This makes the one nation's gold do double-duty but will also permit the gold exchange nation to earn interest on funds which are not tied up in bold bullion or coin by purchasing bonds of the nation which is on the gold standard.

gold points The upper and lower limits in the rates of foreign exchange between two nations which are on the gold standard. When these limits or points are reached, it then becomes profitable to ship gold rather than purchase foreign exchange.

gold settlement fund The Interdistrict Settlement Fund. See "gold wire" for illustration of operation of the fund.

gold standard A monetary system with gold or specific weight as the unit of value.   **38**

gold stock Value of gold owned by a government.   **4**

gold wire A term used principally in Federal Reserve Banks to describe the telegraphic transfer of gold between Federal Reserve Banks through the medium of the Federal Reserve Board in Washington. These transfers arise from the settlement of interbank balances in the Federal Reserve System and occur daily. The gold involved is on deposit with the Treasurer of the United States.   **1**

good In an economic sense, anything which has utility. No value judgment is implied when used in the economic connotation.

good delivery Certain basic qualifications must be met before a security sold on the exchange may be delivered. The security must be in proper form to comply with the contract of sale and to transfer title by delivery to the purchaser. If these qualifications are met, then the security is ready for "good delivery."   **2**

goods and chattels The term commonly used to describe and identify all of the tangible (touchable) personal property in an estate, such as jewelry, furniture, tools, equipment.   **22**

goods in process Goods in a factory on which some operations have been performed but that have not been completed.   **16**

good until canceled (g.t.c.) An order or instruction given by the customer to his investment broker to be effective until the customer rescinds the order.

goodwill An intangible asset that represents the difference between the book value of a business and its purchase (or sale)

161

price when the latter is greater than the book value. It is based on reputation, established business, location, etc.   **16**

go public The public offering of securities for sale to raise money, get a market valuation for the stock, or distribute the holdings of the major stockholders. If the offering is large enough, it may come under Security and Exchange Commission regulation.   **44**

government depository Any bank which has been selected and approved to receive deposits of a government or agency of a government. Generally, the term is used to distinguish a bank which is designated as a depository for the United States Government.

governments 1) Those administrative bodies which rule, control and direct the actions of their members, citizens, etc.

2) As used in the United States, all types of securities issued by the Federal Government (United States Treasury obligations), including, in its broad concept, securities issued by agencies of the Federal Government.   **40**

grace period A formally specified extension of time beyond the due date for payment of insurance premiums, taxes or other obligations, or for performing a specific duty, such as renewing a driver's license.   **22**

graded tax A local tax structure designed to stimulate construction and land utilization by taxing unimproved land at a higher rate or base than improved land.

grade labeling The inclusion on a label or container of an objective designation which may be compared with a recognized standard. Meat labeled Prime or Choice and milk labeled Grade A or B are examples of this type.

grading Grading is the process of sorting individual units of a product according to predetermined standards or classes.   **13**

graduation 1) The formal recognition of a student's completing a course and/or meeting specific requirements.

2) A division of any space into small regular points.   **38**

graft Financial or other gain through the abuse of one's position or influence.   **38**

grain exchanges Those commodity exchanges upon which trading in spot and futures of grain takes place.

grain pit That portion of the trading area of a commodity or grain exchange in which the pit traders or commodity brokers transact their business. The physical appearance is of a series

162

of concentric rings with each ring representing a different contract period.

granger 1) A member of a farm organization called a grange. 2) A railroad which carries a substantial amount of grain.

grant To admit as true; to allow; to give.   **38**

grantee 1) One who receives a grant. 2) A person to whom property is transferred by deed or to whom property rights are granted by means of a trust instrument or some other document.   **30**

granter One who grants credit.   **35**

grantor A person who executes and delivers a deed or other instrument by which property rights are conveyed or otherwise transferred to another.   **31, 36**

grants-in-aid Sums of money given by the federal government to a state or local government for specified purposes. They represent federal support for a state or locally administered program.   **7**

graph A chart that is used to show mathematical figures in diagrammatic form.   **16**

gratuitous coinage The monetary system of unlimited coinage at no expense to the owner of the bullion which is presented for coinage at the mint. In contradistinction, seigniorage coinage results in a profit to the mint on the coins minted.

gratuity An unsolicited gift. A tip.

graveyard shift The shift employed from midnight until 8 a.m.

gray market A legal market in which goods in short supply can be purchased at premiums over normal trade prices.

greenbacks Technically, only the inconvertible notes issued during the Civil War period which were legal tender for all public and private debts except interest on national debt or import duties. Today, the term is used to refer to any of the paper money issues of the Federal Reserve Banks or the United States Treasury.

Green River ordinance A local law regulating door-to-door selling.

Gresham's Law The general theory is that if two kinds of money of equal nominal value are in circulation, the general public may prefer one over the other, because of metal content or because one is more easily mutilated or debased, and will tend to hoard the "good money" and spend the "bad money." This drives the "good money" out of circulation, while keeping the "bad money" or inferior money in circulation. The term also applies to available balances in depositors' accounts.   **1**

grievance An employee's or employer's dissatisfaction with some aspect of the employment relationship. May or may not be limited to dissatisfaction due to interpretation of the contract.

grievance procedure Grievance procedure of a union contract is an orderly way to resolve disputes by successive steps, usually beginning with negotiations between union stewards and foremen and ending with meetings between top union and company officials.   **18**

gross 1) Twelve dozen.
2) Coarse; common.   **38**

gross debt The total amount of debt without any reduction for such deductions as sinking funds.

gross income The whole, entire or total amount of income without having been subject to deduction.   **38**

gross interest The total price paid for the use of a thing which includes the cost of the capital and the cost of the administration of the transaction.

gross lease A lease of property under which the lessor agrees to meet all charges which would normally be incurred by the owner of that property.   **54**

gross margin (For purposes of marketing.) Sales revenue less the cost of goods sold (adjusted for inventory depreciation and merchandise shortages).   **13**

gross national debt The total outstanding debt of a national government including duplications and overlapping entries.

gross national product (GNP) The market value of the output of goods and services produced by the nation's economy in a year.   **24**

gross net premiums In insurance, computed by deducting return premiums from gross premiums, but not less reinsurance premiums.   **5**

gross profit The result of net sales revenue minus the cost of goods sold.   **1**

gross profit on sales The amount by which the net sales exceeds the cost of the merchandise sold.   **16**

gross sales The total sales of all merchandise sold to customers before deducting the returned sales.   **16**

gross yield The return obtained from an investment before deduction of costs and losses involved in procuring and managing the investment. See "net yield." **33**

ground rent A price paid each year or for a term of years for the right to occupy and improve a piece of land. **33**

group banking A form of banking enterprise whereby a group of people form a holding company for purpose of acquiring a majority of the capital stock of several banks in order to control their operations. **23**

group-bonus wage plan An incentive plan used where the efforts of more than one man are required to perform basically related direct labor operations. The incentive for the group as a whole is first computed and then distributed to the individuals on some equitable basis. **28**

group medicine A plan of medical insurance to provide such services as medical examinations and treatment of illness for a group such as employees of a company.

growth stock Stock that is characterized by the prospect of its increase in market value rather than by the amount of cash dividends it earns for the stockholder. **22**

guarantee To make oneself liable or responsible for the performance of something; a surety; a promise or pledge.

guaranteed annual wage A contractual obligation for an employer to provide an employee a minimum amount of income during a year. This amount may be less than a fully employed worker might earn but does provide at least an assured minimum.

guaranteed letter of credit A term used to describe those traveler's letters of credit or commercial letters of credit where the party requesting the credit issuance does not pay the bank in cash for the equivalent amount of the credit upon its issuance. Reimbursement to the bank is guaranteed by the applicant for this accommodation and is often backed by collateral security or the merchandise itself. **1**

guaranteed mortgage A mortgage on which there is a guarantee of payment of principal or interest or both. In years prior to 1930 this was frequently done by a mortgage guarantee corporation. Today most such mortgages are of the Federal Housing Administration or Veterans Administration variety. **5**

guaranteed mortgage certificate A document indicating a stated partial interest in a bond and mortgage which is held by a trustee. A mortgage loan company, in turn, guarantees such

165

certificates for a typical fee of about one half of one percent of the principal per year.

guaranteed stock A form of stock on which the dividends are guaranteed by some company other than the issuer. Such stocks are confined almost entirely to the railroad field. **22**

guaranteed wage plans Systems under which the employer states, in advance, that for a specific period he will pay a predetermined amount to, or retain in service at some employment or in any event with pay, a previously specified number of his workers, whether or not they have work to do. **12**

guaranty A written promise by one person (the guarantor) to be liable for the debt of another person (the principal debtor) in the event that the principal debtor fails to perform his obligation and provided the guarantor is notified of that fact by the creditor. A guaranty must be in writing to be enforceable at law. **25**

guaranty fund A fund which a mutual savings bank in certain states must create through subscriptions or out of earnings, in order to meet possible losses resulting from decline in value of investments or from other unforeseen contingencies. In other states such a fund is known as the surplus fund. **34**

guaranty stock Basic stock which is not withdrawable and which protects the interest of all other investors against losses. **31, 36**

guardian An individual appointed by a court to manage the affairs or person (or both) of a minor or a mentally incompetent individual. A corporation appointed by a court to manage the affairs of a minor or a mentally incompetent person. **25**

guardian ad litem A person appointed by a court to represent and defend a minor or an incompetent in connection with court proceedings; sometimes called a special guardian. **30**

guardian de son tort One who, although not a regularly appointed guardian, takes possession of an infant's or an incompetent's property and manages it as if he were guardian, thereby making himself accountable to the court. **30**

guess An opinion based on inaccurate, incomplete or uncertain data, and often without benefit of any supporting data. The opinion of an uninformed person. See "estimate." **15**

guild A group of people associated for a common objective; a fraternity.

H

habeas corpus A writ directing one who has custody of another to bring him before the court to determine the right to hold such person in custody. **35**

half stock A common stock or preferred stock having a par value of fifty dollars.

hallmark The indented mark made on gold and silver which shows the degree of purity and fineness of the metal.

handbills Small printed papers bearing announcements to be given out by hand; sometimes called dodgers. **38**

hand-to-mouth operation The technique of operating a business with the smallest amount of goods, labor, machinery, capital and other facilities adequate to take care of current and immediate requirements.

hard copy A visible record which may be read by the human eye. **23**

harden A firming of prices of stocks or commodities after a period in which prices have declined.

hard money Has three different meanings. The context will indicate which one to use: 1) A situation in which interest rates are high and loans are hard to arrange.
2) Metallic currency.
3) A nation's currency which is desired by foreigners in lieu of a "soft" currency which may be the domestic or other foreign currency.

hardware 1) The mechanical equipment necessary for conducting an activity, to be distinguished from the planning and theory that went into the activity.
2) The physical equipment or devices forming a computer and peripheral equipment. **41**

Hatch Act Federal statute which, as amended by the Taft-Hartley Act, forbids corporations or unions to make contributions or expenditures in connection with elections for certain federal offices. **12**

hazard A dangerous condition which may create or increase the probability of loss or injury.

head tax A poll tax or charge made upon any immigrant entering the United States.

167

health and welfare plan Plan providing insurance payments to employees in case of sickness or accident. **12**

health certificate Statement of health completed by an insured, usually as a request for reinstatement of a policy. **42**

health hazard Health reasons, personal and family, or occupational, indicative of an added insurance risk incurred above that considered standard. **42**

heavy industry One involved in manufacturing basic products such as metals or which manufactures equipment such as machines. **44**

heavy market A declining market caused by an inadequate supply of bids to buy securities to offset the supply of offerings. **44**

heavy returner A customer whose account shows an unduly large number of items returned for credit. **26**

hedge To offset against. Also, a security which has offsetting qualities. **3**

hedging A type of economic insurance used by dealers in commodities and securities, manufacturers and other producers to prevent loss due to price fluctuations. This is obtained by counterbalancing a present sale or purchase by a purchase or sale of a similar commodity, or of a different commodity, usually for delivery at some future date, the desired result being that the profit or loss on a current sale or purchase will be offset by the loss or profit on the future purchase or sale. **1**

heir A person who inherits real property; to be distinguished from next of kin and from distributee. An heir of the body is an heir in the direct line of the decedent. A son, for example, is the heir of the body of his father or mother. See "collateral heir," "direct heir" and "next of kin." **30**

heirs-at-law The persons who inherit the real property of a person who dies without a valid will disposing of his property. **22**

hereditament Any kind of property that is capable of being inherited. If the property is visible and tangible, it is a corporeal hereditament; if it is not, it is an incorporeal hereditament—for example, a right to rent or a promise to pay money. **30**

hidden assets Those assets publicly reported at different value than their true worth. May involve the risk of tax penalty as well as being merely misleading. **44**

hidden inflation That phase of inflation which is not revealed by economic indicators. Generally, hidden inflation takes the form of a reduction in quality.

hidden tax A governmental levy of which the ultimate user is unaware. Generally, an indirect tax.

hierarchy A specified rank or order of persons or things; thus, a series of persons or things classified by rank or order. **41**

higgling A situation in which the purchaser offers a low price and the seller asks a high price and, through bargaining, a third price somewhere between the two is arrived at to the agreement of the buyer and the seller.

high credit Highest amount of credit extended to a particular customer at one time. **26**

highest and best use The utilization of a property which will produce the highest or maximum net return over the life of the property. The term does not necessarily refer to an intensive development of the site but considers the site in terms of the maximum net return. **54**

high finance 1) Very complicated financial transactions such as associated with recapitalization of a complicated corporate structure as distinguished from low or simple financial transactions such as a small bank loan.

2) Borrowing to the maximum of one's credit.

3) The use of others' funds in a speculative way which may result in a loss to the owner of the funds.

high pressure Trying to force a customer to buy something he doesn't really want or need. **38**

hi-lo index A moving average of individual stocks that reach new highs and new lows each day. Often indicates a change in the market that some of the other market indicators will not show. Variations in the average of the new highs and lows may indicate a deteriorating or rebounding market in general while an average such as the Dow-Jones Industrials might show a neutral or even opposite action in the blue chip issues. **44**

hiring hall Headquarters from which a union fills requests for workers. **12**

hold-back pay That amount of a wage that an employer does not pay out even though it has been earned by the time payment is made.

holder in due course A person who has taken a negotiable instrument (check, note or bill of exchange) under the following conditions: That it is complete; that it is not overdue or to his knowledge previously dishonored; that he took it in good faith for value; and that at the time it was negotiated to him he had no notice of any infirmity in the instrument or defect in the title of the person negotiating it.   **23**

holder of record The owners of a corporation's securities as they appear in the records of the firm's transfer agent on a certain date. These individuals or organizations are then entitled to any benefits or dividends declared.   **44**

hold-harmless agreement Liability of one party is assumed by a second party; frequently the second party is an insurance company.   **5**

holding company A corporation which exercises control over other companies through title to their securities, primarily voting issues.   **19**

holding the market A stabilization or support of a particular security or commodity. The Securities Exchange Commission considers attempts to manipulate prices by "holding" or "stabilization" to be illegal, with the exception of reported stabilization of a new issue which has been cleared by the Securities Exchange Commission.

holdover tenant A tenant who remains in possession of leased property after the expiration of the lease term.   **5**

hold the line As used in price stabilization, it means the use of many devices to stop price increases.

holographic will A will entirely in the handwriting of the testator.   **30**

home economics Refers to that field of knowledge which deals with household management skills, *i.e.,* cooking, sewing, consumer purchasing, etc.

home loan A real estate loan for which the security is residential property.   **31, 36**

homestead The land and buildings thereon occupied by the owner as a home for himself and family, if any, and in most states protected to some extent by statute against the claims of creditors.   **22**

homestead association A term given in some states to an institution that operates as a savings and loan association. See "savings and loan association."   **34**

homework A piecework production system in which the entrepreneuer provides material to be processed in a person's home.

honor The payment of a demand negotiable instrument, or the acceptance for future payment of a time negotiable instrument, upon presentation. See "acceptance." **1**

horizontal expansion The establishment of facilities to permit a firm to expand its business in the same product it is producing or selling.

horizontal union Union which covers workers or groups of similar status though of different crafts or classes. **12**

hot money Funds which move from investment situation or institution to investment situation or institution in a short period of time generally to obtain a higher rate of return or greater safety and at times to avoid taxes or regulation. It may also be a designation for currency which was illegally acquired and subject to being traced.

hourly-rate wage plan A plan whereby the worker is paid a fixed amount per hour regardless of what he produces. **28**

house organ Newspaper or magazine published by and for associates of an organization. **42**

Housing Authority An agency set up by either the federal, state, or local government to construct or manage public housing generally for lower income group tenants. **5**

hypothecation Originally, a pledge to secure an obligation without delivery of title or possession; now, generally any pledge to secure an obligation, such as the hypothecation of securities for a loan. **30**

hypothesis The tentative explanation of a situation based upon the logical development of subject data.

I

idle money Uninvested, available funds. **1**

illegal-purpose doctrine Test applied by some courts in determining whether union activities, lawful in themselves, were invalid because of their objectives. **12**

illegal strike A strike that is called in violation of law, such as a strike that ignores "cooling-off" period restrictions or some absolute statutory ban, or a strike that disregards the "no strike" order or agreement of the parent or local union. **12**

illiquid An asset which cannot easily be converted into cash.

immediate beneficiary (Also called present beneficiary and primary beneficiary.) A beneficiary of a trust who is entitled to receive immediate benefits from the trust property, whether or not limited to income, opposed to ultimate beneficiary.   **30**

immediate order Also called a "fill or kill" order, or one that must be executed at a stipulated price as soon as it reaches the exchange floor, or be canceled.   **44**

immediate record A record of a transaction that is made at the time the transaction occurs.   **16**

immigrant remittances Any funds which immigrants may send out of the country. Generally, such remittances are minor factors in a nation's balance of payments.

impaired capital A condition in which the capital of a business is worth less than its stated capital.

impair investment A money, or near-money, expenditure which does not result in capital formation, being either for consumption or a transfer and acquisition of existing capital.

impartial chairman Term often applied to a permanent arbitrator, named for the life of the union contract, and usually selected by mutual agreement. The term indicates his function of presiding over the union contract and its observance by both parties.   **12**

imperfect competition The market situation where at least one trader can materially affect the market price of a product.

impersonal account An account in a set of books of record which is other than that of an individual or firm.

implied trust A trust created by operation of law or by judicial construction to be distinguished from an express trust.   **22**

implied warranty Representation, not in writing, that insurable conditions exist.   **5**

import To bring goods from another country into one's own country.   **5**

import credit A commercial letter of credit issued for the purpose of financing the importation of goods.   **25**

import license Permission obtained from a government to import stated quantities of enumerated goods.

import quota The amount of a product which a nation will permit to be imported during a stated period.

import rate A railroad transport rate established specifically for application on import traffic and generally less, when so published, than domestic rate.   **19**

impost To classify so as to establish a customs duty.

imprest fund (petty cash fund) A system commonly employed in business which provides a fund of a designated amount (by debiting petty cash and crediting cash) out of which payments for expenses of small amounts are made. **1**

improper improvement Improvements which do not conform to the best utilization of the site. **54**

improvements Buildings, other structures and other attachments or annexations to land which are intended to remain so attached or annexed, such as sidewalks, trees, drives, tunnels, drains and sewers. **29**

impulse item Things bought on sudden decision, not standard items of purchase. Novelties, luxuries, etc. **38**

imputed An estimate of value in the event that a cash payment is not made for a good or service.

imputed interest An estimate of value, charge of interest due for the use of capital even though a cash payment is not made. Implicit interest.

inactive corporation One which neither operates property nor administers its financial affairs. If it maintains an organization, it does so only for the purpose of complying with legal requirements and maintaining title to property or franchises. **19**

inactive stock An issue traded on an exchange or in the over-the-counter market in which there is a relatively low volume of transactions. Volume may be no more than a few hundred shares a week or even less. On the New York Stock Exchange most inactive stocks are traded in 10-share units rather than the customary 100. See "round lot." **2**

inactive trust A trust in which the trustee has no duty except to hold title to the property. **22**

incentive wages Method of wage payment by which workers receive extra pay for extra production. **12**

inchoate Not yet completed. Contracts are inchoate until executed by all the parties who should join in their execution, and a widow's right to dower is inchoate so long as her husband lives. **5**

incidence of taxation The individual or firm that actually has the burden of a tax even though not formally paying it.

in-clearing items Items received by a bank as a result of a clearinghouse exchange are commonly called incoming clearings, or shorted to "in-clearings." **23**

income A stream of benefits generally measured in terms of money as of a certain time; a flow of services. It is the source of value. Loosely, the money a person or company has coming in from any source. Exactly, income is made up of the amount received from both earnings and investments. **54**

income fund Investment company whose primary objective is generous current income. May be balanced fund, common stock fund, bond fund or preferred stock fund. **3**

income return The amount of annual income paid on an investment. The percent obtained by dividing the amount of annual income paid on an investment by the cost or purchase price.

income statement A record of income and expense relating to the operations of a business; a summary of transactions from the sale of goods or services. Operating statement and profit and loss statement are other terms that are sometimes applied to this accounting record. **25**

income tax That tax, federal, state or local, which is levied on the income of individuals or firms.

incompetent One who is legally incapable of managing his affairs because of mental (not physical) deficiency. **30**

incontestable clause Standard policy provision. A policy cannot be contested by the insurer after a given length of time. See "contestable clause." **42**

inconvertible money Irredeemable money. Money which may not be converted into the standard. United States money is inconvertible since it is not redeemable in gold.

incorporate To form into a corporation; become a corporation. **38**

incorporation by reference Reference in one document to the contents of another document in such a manner as to give legal effect to the material to which reference is made. **30**

increasing costs A production situation in which the cost per production unit goes up as production volume goes up.

increasing returns A situation in which production is increased even though there has been no increase in the various factors of production such as land, labor, capital or management. This may be due to a more efficient utilization of one or more of the factors. The term is also used to describe a situation in which an additional unit of any of the factors of production results in an increase in production more than was caused by a prior unit of the same factor.

174

increment That which is gained or added. **22**

incremental cost The cost of one more unit; marginal cost.

incumbrance A lien or liability attached to real property. See "encumbrance." **35**

indefeasible Incapable of being annulled or rendered void; as, an indefeasible title to property. **30**

indemnity That which is given as compensation or security for loss. **35**

indent A foreign order for merchandise with or without restrictions such as price, quality or mode of shipment.

indenture A written agreement under which bonds or debentures are issued, setting forth maturity date, interest rate, security and other terms. **2**

independent contractor One who agrees to perform certain actions for another and is responsible only for the results but not subject to direction of the party hiring him. **52**

independent union A labor organization, not company-dominated, which is not affiliated with the AFL-CIO and remains independent of any federation. **12**

indeterminate appropriation An appropriation which is not limited either to any definite period of time or to any definite amount, or to both time and amount. **29**

indifference curve A schedule of the changing rate of substitution of a good or service for another good or service. The schedule is plotted on a chart.

indifference map The plotted series of indifference curves or schedules.

indirect cost Also called overhead, fixed cost or supplementary cost. A cost which does not vary with the volume of activity. A real estate tax is an example of an indirect cost.

indirect exchange The technique used in arbitrage of foreign exchange in buying foreign exchange in one market and promptly selling it in another market at a rate that will yield a profit over the purchase price plus the expenses of the transaction.

indirect export An export which is handled by a middleman rather than the producer.

indirect labor The amount of the wages paid to employees who work in the factory but whose time may not be charged to specific finished products. **16**

indirect production The modern system of production which involves the use of capital and tools. Thus, to make most products one first makes a machine to make the product. Only in a very primitive society does one find direct production.

indirect standard The monetary system which does not directly convert its currency into a standard metal such as gold or silver but permits, as a right of ownership, the exchange of the domestic currency into the currency of a nation that is on a metal standard. The ratio of exchange is established and maintained with only infrequent changes.

indirect tax A levy by a governmental unit which can easily be passed on to some other individual or firm. To the individual or firm that bears the final burden of the tax it is an indirect tax.

individual income tax Income taxes may be on the income of people or companies such as corporations. That portion of the total collection of taxes paid by people. It is either a state or federal tax and also has progressive features after a minimum deduction.

individualism The economic social structure which is characterized by free enterprise and the right of private property as well as a profit system.

individual proprietorship A business owned by one person. The individual owner has all the rights to profits from the business as well as all the liabilities and losses.

indorsee The holder of a negotiable instrument to whom it has been transferred by indorsement. **25**

indorsement See "endorsement."

indorser A person who signs his name on the back of a negotiable instrument, such as a check, draft, or promissory note, for the purpose of transferring his title to the instrument or of guaranteeing payment. **25**

induced consumption The increased purchases which are derived from consumers as a result of capital investment. To build a plant, direct and indirect employees must be hired; these, upon being paid, buy consumer goods. These goods, in turn, provide income and thus consumption for the related activities.

induced investment The capital investment in such forms as plant and machinery produced as a result of increases in spending by consumers.

176

inductive method Logical reasoning from observed data which permits a hypothesis.

industrial bank A financial institution that derives its funds through a form of savings known as "investment shares" and invests these funds by specializing in the financing of businesses through the assignment of pledged accounts receivable. **1**

industrial goods Goods which are destined for use in producing other goods or rendering services as contrasted with goods destined to be sold to the ultimate consumer. **13**

industrial loans Loans outstanding to industrial borrowers under an amendment to the Federal Reserve Act which authorized the Federal Reserve Banks to make loans to certain business firms unable to get credit from other financial institutions on reasonable terms. This authority was terminated in August 1959. **4**

industrial plant reserve Any productive facility for manufacturing defense material subject to administration by a government agency for that purpose.

industrial relations Insuring that the working relationships between management and employees and the job satisfaction of and work opportunities for the company's personnel are developed and maintained in the best interests of the company and its employees. **20**

industrial research The systematic investigation of opportunities for improvement of products or production in a commercial or business sense. Applied research as compared with pure research which does not require a materialistic goal.

industrial revolution That period starting in the late 18th century in which rapid advancements were made in production largely due to the use of steam and machinery.

industrial union A union whose membership includes any worker in a particular industry, regardless of the particular skills the members are exercising. Membership is secured largely from semiskilled and unskilled workers. **12**

industry A particular branch of trade or manufacture.

industry-wide bargaining The labor relations activity designed to set a pattern of policy for an entire industry and the employees in that industry.

inelastic demand Demand which does not change at a proportionate rate with the rate of change in price.

inelastic supply Supply which does not change at a proportionate rate with the rate of change in price.

infant A person not of legal age, which at common law was twenty-one years, but which in some states has been changed by statute; the same as a minor.   **30**

infant industry A relatively new business activity for which at times the plea is made for governmental help either in the form of subsidy such as feeder airlines receive or for tariff protection such as granted the chemical industry for a period after World War I.

inferior goods Products and services which, as income increases, tend to be consumed in smaller amounts.

infirmity Any known act, or visible omission in detail, in the creation or transfer of title that would invalidate an instrument is known as an infirmity.   **1**

inflation A rapid and sharp increase in the general price level generally associated with an increase in the supply or velocity of money.

inflationary gap The amount by which government and private spending exceeds the amount needed to maintain a stable price level and full employment.

inflationary spiral That condition in the rapidly increasing price level which leads workers to demand higher wages, which increases costs, which in turn leads sellers and producers to ask even higher prices.

infringement The act of violating; breach nonfulfillment.   **38**

inherent vice A condition in property which causes deterioration or damage; for example, the painting of damp wood.   **52**

inheritance That estate in property, technically real property but in general usage any property, which has come about through a bequest by will or devise or through intestate descent.

inheritance tax A tax on the right to receive property by inheritance; to be distinguished from an estate tax.   **30**

injunction An order of a court of equity directing a person to do or refrain from doing some act.   **35**

in kind Generally refers to payment of a loss through replacing the damage to a destroyed property with the same type of property, the option generally being with the insuring company.   **52**

in loco parentis In the place of a parent. A phrase meaning a

178

person who takes the place of a child's parent, usually one who is not a legally appointed guardian. **22**

input 1) That which is put in or inserted into.

2) Information or data transferred or to be transferred from an external storage medium into the internal storage of the computer.

3) Describing the routines which direct input as defined in (2) or the devices from which such information is available to the computer.

4) The device or collective set of devices necessary for input as defined in (2). **41**

input area Same as block or input (2). **41**

insanity A mental condition, or impairment, which results in a person's being declared legally incompetent. **42**

inscribed Those particular government bonds such as Series E savings bonds whose records are maintained by the Federal Reserve Banks rather than the United States Treasury.

insider reports The monthly reports required by the Securities and Exchange Commission that must be filed by the officers, directors and stockholders who own more than 10% of any corporation whose securities are listed on a national securities exchange. Included are records of all purchases and sales made during the previous month and the total number of shares held at the end of the month. These reports, along with the information on what action investment funds are taking, make it possible to know which securities have gained or lost favor with people who are close to the market. **44**

insolvency The inability to pay one's debts in the ordinary course of business. **35**

installation equipment Those industrial goods that do not become part of the physical product and which are exhausted only after repeated use, such as boilers, linotype machines, power lathes, and bank vaults. **13**

installment A part payment. **38**

installment sales Sales that are made on terms by which the customer pays part of the selling price at the time of sale and signs a written contract covering the settlement of the balance in periodic payments. **16**

institutionalism The increase of governmental activities affecting the social existence of a people.

institution economics That school of economics which stresses

179

the importance of the social environment or institutions on the economic behavior of individuals.

instrument A written document that gives formal expression to a legal act or agreement. **33**

instrumental capital Goods which may be used to produce capital such as machine tools.

instrumentalities A term often applied to agencies of the federal government and whose obligations are not the direct obligation of the federal government. However, there is an implied support; for example, Federal Land Bank bonds. **22**

insurable interest Such an interest in the subject matter of life or property insurance as will entitle the person possessing the interest to obtain insurance on it. **30**

insurance The contractual relationship which exists when one party, for a consideration, agrees to reimburse another for loss caused by designated contingencies. **50**

insurance, accident Insurance against the loss of earning power sustained through disabling accident, only. **42**

insurance, accounts receivable Insurance against loss due to inability to collect outstanding accounts receivable because of damage to or destruction of records by a peril insured against. **5**

insurance, all-risk A name given to a policy which covers against the loss caused by all perils except those which are specifically excluded by the terms of the policy. Ordinary policies, contrarywise, name the peril or perils which are specifically covered in that policy. **50, 52**

insurance, assessment Plan of insurance for which either the amount of insurance, or the number and amount of assessments or premiums, are variable. **42**

insurance, automobile liability Indemnity policy for legal liability for bodily injury or damage to others arising from accidents of ownership or operation of an automobile. **5**

insurance, business Accident and sickness coverage issued primarily to indemnify a business against loss of time because of the disability of a key employee. **5**

insurance, business interruption Protection for the owner of a business from losses which would be sustained during a period when the business is not operating due to such occurrences as fire or other hazards. **52**

insurance carrier The insurance company, since it assumes the financial responsibility for the risks of the policyholders.   **52**

insurance, casualty Insurance protection for accident or injury to persons or property.   **42**

insurance, combination policy An insurance policy, or more often, two policies printed on one joined sheet, which provides coverage against several hazards under the one document.   **50**

insurance, commercial Accident and sickness insurance intended primarily to be sold to workers in commerce and business as contrasted to industrial workers.   **5**

insurance, concurrent Insurance under two or more identical contracts, varying only in amount or policy dates.   **42**

insurance, cooperative Refers to mutual associations such as fraternal, employee, industrial or trade union groups. The profit motive is not the factor in this type of insurance but rather the accomplishment of some social end or goal.   **5**

insurance coverage The total amount of insurance carried.   **54**

insurance, credit Two different types of insurance. 1) Issued by insurance companies on accounts receivables. Claim payment is made if the account receivable proves uncollectable.
2) A type of insurance more properly called credit life insurance.   **5**

insurance, credit life Life insurance issued by a life insurance company on the lives of borrowers to cover payment of loans (usually small loans repayable in installments) in case of death.   **5**

insurance, employer's liability Protects an employer against the claims for damages which arise out of the injuries to employees in the course of their work. A workmen's compensation policy insures the employer against liability under state compensation laws. Employer's liability insurance provides protection in cases not covered by the compensation laws.   **52**

insurance, endowment Provides for payment of the face amount to the insured on maturity, or to the beneficiary on prior death of the insured. Combination of pure endowment and term insurance.   **42**

insurance, excess A policy or bond covering the insured against certain hazards, which applies only to loss or damage in excess of a stated amount.   **50**

insurance, extended term A form of insurance available as a

181

nonforfeiture option. It provides the original amount of insurance for a limited period of time. **51, 53**

insurance, family income Insurance that provides an income (usually $10 monthly per $1000 of insurance) to the beneficiary to the end of a specified period from the inception of the insurance if the insured dies within that period. The face amount of the insurance is paid at the end of the income period or when the insured dies after the end of the period. **51**

insurance, fire Contract prescribed by each state subject to modification by endorsements insuring against direct loss by fire, lightning and other defined causes. **5**

insurance, fleet policy An insurance contract covering a number of automobiles, usually owned by companies who provide them for certain employees.

insurance, floater policy A policy under the terms of which protection follows movable property, covering it wherever it may be; *e.g.,* a policy on tourists' baggage. **50**

insurance, fraternal A system of cooperative protection furnished by a fraternal order to its members on a nonprofit basis. **52**

insurance, government Protection issued by the United States Government in amounts up to $10,000, to those who have served or are serving in the armed forces, intended to cover the added hazards of war. The insurance is usually issued on a term basis with the option of converting to a permanent plan. **42**

insurance, graded premium life A type of modified life insurance in which the premiums increase each year for the first several years and then level off. **5**

insurance, group Any insurance plan by which a number of employees (and their dependents) or other homogeneous groups, are insured under a single policy, issued to their employer or leader with individual certificates given to each insured individual or family unit. **50**

insurance, group creditor Contract issued to the creditor on the lives of his debtors to pay the amount of the indebtedness in the event of death. **5**

insurance, group disability Provides benefits for a group of individuals, usually employees of the covered company, to compensate for losses such as time lost because of accident, or sickness, hospitalization cost, medical or surgical expense. **52**

nsurance, guaranteed premium reduction (gpr) Policies for which an annual reduction in premiums is available as specified in the contract. **42**

nsurance, health Insurance for loss due to disability sustained because of disease. **42**

nsurance, homeowner's policy A form of package policy including fire and allied lines, theft insurance and comprehensive personal liability. **5**

nsurance, industrial Insurance designed primarily for hourly wage workers exposed to some degree of occupational hazard and having difficulty in accumulating an amount of money to pay an annual or semiannual premium. **5**

nsurance, joint life Insurance on two or more persons, the benefits of which are payable on the first death. **51**

nsurance, keyman Protection of a business firm against the financial loss caused by the death of or disablement of a vital member of the firm. **5**

nsurance, level premium Insurance for which the cost is distributed evenly over the period during which premiums are paid. **53**

nsurance, liability Insurance provided by casualty and surety companies as a protection against the loss of property or of the earning power of an individual or company. **1**

nsurance, life Insurance providing for payment of a specified amount on the insured's death either to his estate or to a designated beneficiary. **51**

nsurance, limited payment life Whole of life insurance for which number of premiums payable is limited, and after which the policy becomes fully paid. **42**

nsurance, limited policy A policy providing insurance against specified types of accidents or restricted in indemnity payments as contrasted with full coverage policies. **50**

nsurance, major medical expense Contractual protection for large surgical, hospital, or medical expenses. **5**

nsurance, marine That form of coverage which is primarily concerned with the protection of goods in transit and the means of transportation. This term is applied in common usage to risks involving ocean transit. **50**

nsurance, mortgage Title II of the 1934 National Housing Act provided a system of insurance on mortgage loans popularly known as FHA or Federal Housing Administration insurance. Insurance companies have declining term policies on the life of the mortgagor which are popularly called mortgage insurance.

insurance, nonassessable Insurance under which the premium rate is guaranteed and no additional assessments may be required. **42**

insurance, noncancellable A policy which the insurer is obligated to continue in force during the period for which the policy was written, and so long as payment of premiums is made when due. **42**

insurance, old age and survivors See "Social Security Act."

insurance, ordinary Life insurance on an annual premium basis as distinguished from industrial or group insurance. Term loosely used for whole life insurance. **42**

insurance, over- Insurance of an amount in excess of possible loss. **42**

insurance, overlapping Insurance coverage from two or more policies or companies which in part duplicate the insurance of certain risks. **5**

insurance, paid-up Policy for which all required premiums have been paid, and under which the company is liable for benefits as provided by the terms of the policy. **42**

insurance, participating Insurance issued by a mutual or mixed company providing for participation in dividend distribution. **42**

insurance, partnership Insurance coverage on the lives of business partners, the purpose being to enable the remaining partner, on death of the other, to purchase the business and to cushion the loss of executive ability. **42**

insurance policy Written or printed document stating terms and conditions of insurance. **38**

insurance premium Charge by the insurance company to individual or company for the insurance contract. **5**

insurance, products liability Protection provided against claims arising from the utilization of the covered product manufactured, sold, handled or distributed by the insured or others trading under his name if the accident occurs after possession has been relinquished to others and away from premises owned, rented or controlled by the insured. **50, 52**

184

insurance, protection and indemnity Insurance against loss due to claims for damages against vessel owners or operators not covered by the basic marine insurance contract, often written by mutual associations called clubs.   **51**

insurance, renewable term Term insurance providing the right to renew at the end of the term for another term or terms, without evidence of insurability.   **53**

insurance, replacement Insurance under which the loss payable is the replacement cost of the property new. The excess over the depreciated replacement cost is payable only if the property is actually replaced.   **51**

insurance, retirement income Insurance payable on death before a specified age, with provision of a life annuity certain if the insured attains that age.   **51**

insurance, schedule of The list of individual items covered under one policy as the various buildings, animals and other property in farm insurance or the list of the rings, bracelets, etc., insured under a jewelry floater.   **50**

insurance, self- The systematic provision of a fund to provide for the loss which the individual or firm may have. The endeavor of one who is subject to a risk to lay aside sums periodically which in time will provide a fund to cover any loss which occurs.   **52**

insurance, single premium A life insurance contract that provides that for the consideration of a premium paid only once, the insurance company will assume the liability on the contract.   **5**

insurance, social Old age benefit insurance, federal unemployment insurance, state unemployment insurance, and disability insurance are examples of social insurance. The insurance is generally established by state or federal government with progressive benefits for the less favorably situated social groups.   **5**

insurance, specific A policy coverage that goes into detail as to the description of the property covered as compared to a blanket coverage, applying separately to specifically named objects or locations.   **50**

insurance, straight life A plan of insurance for the whole of life with premium payable until death. See "insurance, ordinary."   **51, 53**

insurance, substandard Coverage issued to those who do not qualify for insurance at regular rates, usually due to being high risks.

insurance, term A plan of insurance payable at death providing death occurs within a specified period. In fire and accident insurance it is a policy contract for a period of more than one year. **50, 53**

insurance, title Insurance against financial loss resulting from claims arising out of defects in the title to real property, which are existent but undisclosed at the time the policy is issued by the title company. **22**

insurance trust A trust composed partly or wholly of life insurance policy contracts. **30**

insurance, under- A condition in which not enough insurance is carried to cover the insurable value, and especially to satisfy a coinsurance clause. Insurance less in amount than the possible loss to which it applies. **50, 51**

insurance, unemployment A form of social security that pays a weekly income to workers while they are unemployed. **38**

insurance, whole life A plan of insurance for the whole of life, payable at death. **53, 58**

insurance, workmen's compensation Social insurance that provides that employees may collect from their employer for injuries sustained in the course of their employment. **5**

insured An individual or business organization protected in case of some loss or damage, under the terms of the insurance policy. **58**

insured pension plans Retirement and other employee benefit plans, the source of the benefits of which is life insurance paid for wholly or partially by the employer. **22**

insurer The party to the insurance contract who promises to pay losses or render service. **51**

intangible property Property which cannot be touched or realized with the senses, such as a legally enforceable right. The right possessed by the holder of a promissory note or bond is intangible property, the paper and writing being only the evidence of that right. **30**

intensive cultivation Use of large proportions of fertilizer, machinery, labor and other capital on relatively limited agricultural acreage.

interchangeable parts Those segments of a whole product, which being duplicated could be reassembled at random and fit together and operate efficiently.

interdistrict settlement fund That part of the Federal Reserve System, located in Washington, D.C., which serves as a clearinghouse for the twelve Federal Reserve Banks in settling the difference between the debits and credits each of the banks has with the other eleven, thus minimizing the need to transfer funds. The fund is settled daily.

interest The sum paid for the use of borrowed money or credit.   **33**

interest rate A percentage that expresses the relationship between the interest for one year and the principal.   **16**

interim certificate A temporary document which serves the purchaser of a new issue of securities as proof of ownership until such time as the engraved certificate is available.

interlocking directors Directors of two or more similar corporations who simultaneously hold office in the corporations. The inference generally is that this device will tie the policies of the two companies together and reduce the competition between them.

intermediate goods Capital goods which do not directly satisfy a consumer need.

internal audit A routine and continuous check on the accuracy of all accounting records.   **28**

internal control 1) To have control come from within the organization or firm.
2) A plan of organization under which employees' duties are so arranged and records and procedures so designed as to make it possible to exercise effective accounting control over assets, liabilities, revenues and expenditures.   **29**

internal improvement Any governmental capital expenditure such as a dam, bridge, or road within the boundaries of the government.

internal national debt The sum total of all the private and public indebtedness of a domestic nature of a nation as distinguished from the external debt or foreign debt.

internal revenue For the United States Government: All receipts from federal taxes excluding the amounts collected as customs. For a business: All receipts from the operation of the business. This would not include such amounts as earnings on outside investments.

187

Internal Revenue Service That agency of the government which collects and administers the collection of the internal revenue taxes.

international balance of payments The sum total of all the receipts of a nation from the other nations of the world and all the payments made by that nation to all the other nations of the world. If the nation has received more than it has paid it is described as having a favorable balance of payments.

International Bank for Reconstruction and Development See "World Bank."

international double taxation The situation in which two sovereign powers tax a property or income. To prevent this inequity most modern nations have tax treaties which result in the reduction of the tax burden of the individual or company who would otherwise be subject to full double taxation.

international economics The section of the broad field of economics which concerns itself with balances of payments, foreign exchange, international capital movements and related subject areas.

international gold bullion standard A gold bullion standard with the limitation that gold may be freely obtained in the form of bullion only for purposes of export. This prevents it from being hoarded for domestic purposes and gives a central bank greater control over the limited amount of gold.

International Monetary Fund A companion institution to the nations with foreign exchange to meet temporary needs in their balance of international payments and thus avoid nationalistic trade barriers and currency depreciation.

International Trade Organization Affiliate of the United Nations whose purpose is to help trade between the various nations by encouragement of tariff reduction and other such steps which will help international trade.

international union Union whose membership includes employees in at least one other country in addition to the United States, usually Canada.

international unit A statistical device used to put data from various nations on a uniform base so that the different economies may be compared.

interpleader A court procedure under which a bank or other stakeholder, in order to be protected from possible double liability, acknowledges its obligation to make payment, or to turn over property, and compels the rival claimants to litigate their respective rights. **34**

interpolation The computation of an intermediate value of a number or quantity between a series of stated values or numbers.

interrogatory In law, a question placed in writing by one party with the intention of allowing another party to reply.

in terrorem clause A provision of a will or trust agreement intended or, at any rate, calculated to frighten a possible beneficiary into doing or refraining from doing something at the peril of forfeiting his possible benefits—such as a provision that would disinherit any named or potential beneficiary who contested the will. **22**

interstate carrier A common carrier doing business across state boundaries. **50**

interstate commerce A very broad term used to refer not only to shipments of goods between states but also to the methods of transportation and manufacture of goods which move over state borders.

interstate Commerce Act Comprises the original act to regulate commerce, approved February 4, 1887, and many amendments. **19**

interstate Commerce Commission The agency created by the Congress in 1887 to obtain reports, establish rate structures and prevent discrimination and other abuses from railroads. Amendments since then have increased the powers of the commission to include pipe lines, motor lines, and interstate barge and boat lines under their control provided they fall within the broad definition of interstate commerce.

inter vivos trust A trust created during the settlor's lifetime; the same as a living trust; to be distinguished from trust under will or testamentary trust. **22**

intestate A person who dies without making a will; not disposed of by will. **35**

intestate succession The descent and distribution of property of a person who dies without a valid will. **22**

intrastate commerce Business in one state only; never crossing state lines. **38**

intrastate traffic Traffic moving wholly within one state, that is, originating and terminating in the same state and not passing en route outside the state. **19**

intrinsic value The value possessed by a particular thing considered in itself. **1**

invention Something discovered or originated. **38**

inventory A detailed list showing quantities, descriptions and values of property and goods, and frequently also units of measure and unit prices. **29**

inventory control 1) An internal system for keeping adequate inventory at hand.

2) A governmental device used in emergencies to regulate inventories for the purpose of better utilization of the goods and to prevent hoarding.

inventory valuation adjustment 1) A method of removing the influence of price inflation from inventories stated in monetary units. This may be done by the use of various price indexes.

2) Corporate profits and income of an unincorporated enterprise include inventory profit or loss in customary business accounting. Current output in the national income accounts, however, includes only the value of the change in volume in inventories. The adjustment is that which is necessary to take account of this departure from business accounting. No valuation adjustment is necessary for farm inventories because farm income is measured exclusive of inventory profits. **7**

investment The use of money for the purpose of making more money, to gain income or increase capital, or both. Safety of principal is an important consideration. **2**

investment banking The business of underwriting and distributing corporate and government securities. **25**

investment bill A discounted bill of exchange held to maturity as an investment.

investment certificate Certificate issued by associations which shows the amount of money an individual has invested with them. They do not carry any stockholders' liability and have no voting rights. Not to be confused with investment accounts. **31, 36**

investment company A financial institution through which investors pool their money to obtain supervision and diversification of their investments. **3**

Investment Company Act Federal statute enacted in 1940 for the registration and regulation of investment companies. **3**

investment counselor One who is professionally engaged in rendering investment advisory and supervisory services. **2**

investment credit The long term extension of funds for purchase of such fixed assets as machinery, buildings or land as compared with the furnishing of working capital credit for inventory or accounts receivable and wages.

investment portfolio The list of the various securities owned by a bank, an individual, a business enterprise, or other organization.

investment ratings A number of investment services such as Moody's, Fitch's, Standard & Poor's, Value Line, etc., rate securities by various devices such as letters, numbers, or similar devices. In addition, bank examiners and "legal list" states assign investment classifications to securities. These ratings attempt to assign securities to certain general classes of quality or investment attributes.

investment trust A company which uses its capital to invest in other companies.   **2**

invisible export See "invisible items of trade."

invisible hand Concept advanced by classical school and Adam Smith that by acting for one's own self-interest and guided by a profit motive, the greatest production and good would result.

invisible items of trade Those nontangible items that are part of a balance of payments. Such expenditures as purchase of foreign insurance, foreign shipping, tourist expenditures and remittances by immigrants to their former countries are the major invisible items of trade.

invoice An itemized statement of merchandise or services bought or sold with the date, terms, methods of shipment if any, cost, and any other pertinent details.

involuntary bankruptcy An individual or firm judicially declared insolvent as a result of a petition filed with a competent court by the required number of unpaid and past-due creditors.

irish dividend A trade term which refers to the imposition of an assessment on a security rather than a dividend.

iron law of wages See "brazen law of wages."

irredeemable money Inconvertible money which cannot be exchanged for standard money.

irrevocable letter of credit A contract by the issuer to accept drafts as conditioned by the contract and to charge them against their account. The letter is good (irrevocable) for a stated period of time.

191

irrevocable trust A trust that cannot be altered by the person who created the trust. **5**

irrigation The use of any artificial means of bringing water to agricultural land.

issue 1) Any of a company's securities, or the act of distributing such securities. **2**

2) All persons who have descended from a common ancestor; a broader term than children. **30**

issued stock That portion of the authorized stock which is treasury stock or outstanding in the possession of the stockholders as distinguished from unissued stock.

itemized appropriation A restriction of an appropriation to be made only for and in the amounts itemized.

J

jerry-built Built cheaply, flimsily, and sometimes temporarily.

job account An account pertaining either to an operation which occurs regularly (a "standing order") or to a specific piece of work (a "job order"), showing all charges for material and labor used and other expenses incurred, together with any allowances or other credit. **29**

jobber 1) A middleman who buys from wholesale dealers and sells to retailers. **38**

2) A merchant dealing in special, odd, or job lots.

job classification Job ratings based on analysis of the requirements of the work. **12**

job description Written summary of the important features and requirements of a job. Usually based on a job analysis.

job evaluation System for fixing the relative value of jobs as they exist in a plant or office. **12**

job lot 1) An odd assortment of various merchandise.

2) A form of contract having a smaller unit of trading than the regular contract. **9**

joinder A joining of parties as plaintiffs or defendants in a suit at law. **29**

joint account An account owned by two or more people, subject to check or withdrawal by all signatures of all joint owners. **1**

joint agreement The contract between union and management where more than one union or employer is involved.

joint and several Obligations which are enforceable against each and all of several persons.   **35**

joint costs The manufacturing costs of two or more products which, by the nature of production, are processed together.

joint demand The type of demand in which two or more products or services must be brought together if utility is to be produced.

joint rate A joint charge made by two or more companies for providing the use of their facilities.

joint return The federal and/or state income tax report for a husband and wife to file their income jointly rather than individually.

joint stock company A form of business organization in which the capital contribution of the partners is represented by transferable shares. It differs from the corporate form of organization in that each of the partners has unlimited liability, and is similar from the standpoint that death or transfer of membership does not terminate operations.   **44**

joint tenancy An estate held by two or more persons in which the interest of anyone dying passes to the surviving tenant.   **35**

joint venture Something undertaken by two or more parties.

journal A book in which any of the records of a business are first written.   **16**

journeyman Worker in a traditional craft who has gone through an apprenticeship and mastered the type of work involved in the craft; qualified craftsman.   **12**

judgment 1) An opinion or discretion.
2) The decision or sentence of a court of law; to be distinguished from a decree. The obligation created by such a decision or sentence.   **33**

judgment creditor The creditor who has been granted a judgment against a debtor by an appropriate court of jurisdiction.

judgment debtor The debtor against whom a judgment has been obtained, which has been recorded.

judgment lien A charge rendered in a state or federal court on a piece of land or personal property against one who owes a debt. When applied to personal property it is generally termed an attachment.   **31, 36**

judgment note A note given by a debtor to a creditor acknowledging the debt and one which, if remaining unpaid at maturity, authorizes the creditor to appear in a court at law and confess judgment without process to the maker. **1**

judicial settlement The settlement of an account in accordance with the order, judgment or decree of a proper court, the effect of which in many states is determined by statute. **30**

junior interest 1) A legal right that is subordinate to another interest.

2) A mortgage participation junior to another participation. **5**

junior lien A lien placed upon a property that has a senior lien already made and recorded. The rights are enforceable only after the previous liens have been satisfied. **54**

jurat Either a person under oath, or a memorandum added to an affidavit stating when, before whom, and, in some jurisdictions, where, the oath was taken. **22**

jurisdiction Legal right, power, or authority to hear and determine a case; as, the jurisdiction of a court. **30**

jurisdictional dispute 1) A conflict over who or what body has the legal authority to preside or govern in a specific area.

2) A conflict that may involve either a dispute between two unions, as to which shall represent a group of employees in collective bargaining, or as to which union's members shall perform a certain type of work. **12**

jurisdictional strike Work stoppage as a result of a jurisdictional dispute.

K

kameralism A broad concept of mercantilism concerned with not only the production of wealth by a state but also with how the wealth may be best used. Also spelled "cameralism."

key industry A dominant industry in its field or in the general economy. **44**

Keynesian An economic concept similar in logic or reasoning to the theories of John Maynard Keynes, British economist of major importance during the 1930's and 1940's. One of his ideas calls for large governmental spending and deficits during business recessions as a counter-cyclical device. Another states that wages not only are a cost of business but also are a major factor in demand; thus increased wages lead to increased production to meet the demand.

kickback 1) An illegal or dishonest rebate secretly given a buyer by a seller for granting the order or contract, such as a payoff given to a crooked politician for a defense contract.
2) An illegal payment made by a worker to someone in a position of firing him so that he will not be laid off or given unpleasant duties.

kin Persons of the same blood or members of the same family.   **22**

kind In the phrase "distribution in kind," distribution of the property itself and not the cash value of the property.   **30**

kindred Persons related by blood.   **30**

kinked curve A supply or demand schedule or similar plotted curve which is characterized by a sharp bend.

kiting Technique of drawing checks against deposits that have to clear through the banking system. Kiting takes advantage of the time needed for checks to clear and permits the kiter to use funds that are not his.   **5**

Knights of Labor One of the first large American unions or federations of unions. Nineteenth century precursor of the American Federation of Labor.   **12**

L

labor Manual workers; manual exertion; a factor of production.

labor agreement A trade agreement. The contractual relationship between the employer and the union representing his employees which covers the conditions of employment which will prevail for the period of the contract.

labor force All persons 14 years of age or over in the United States who are employed or able, willing, and seeking work. Civilian labor force excludes all who are members of the armed forces and in institutions.   **7**

labor grade A technique of job evaluation in which levels of skill required for the various jobs are established.

Labor Management Relations Act (Taft-Hartley Act) Federal statute which amends the National Labor Relations Act to regulate some union activities, authorizes damage suits for collective bargaining violations and certain strikes and boycotts, and sets up procedures for trying to settle "national emergency strikes."   **12**

labor piracy Practice of attracting laborers away from another employer by offering more attractive wages and benefits.

labor relations Term ordinarily used to denote all matters arising out of the employer-employee relationship which involve collective action on the part of the employees; most intimately associated with collective bargaining and concerted activities.   **12**

labor-saving machinery Mechanical devices that reduce the need for workers and create problems of technological unemployment.   **12**

labor theory of value The theory that the value of anything is closely related to the amount of labor required to make it.

labor turnover The ratio or percentage which is computed by dividing the average number of employees for the covered period by the number of newly hired employees. This indicates the ratio of new employees to the average number of workers usually employed. This figure may also be adjusted for an annual rate.

labor union Any organization of employees which has as its purpose the improvement of the condition of its members. The union may act as the representative of its members in negotiating with employers.

laches A defendant in a lawsuit may plead laches as his defense if he can prove that he has suffered from the fact that the plaintiff delayed in bringing suit.   **5**

laissez-faire Economic system in which very little government control is exercised over business.

lamb A novice at speculation, inexperienced, and quite likely to be shorn or lose on his investments.

lame duck 1) A speculator whose venture has not succeeded.
2) An elected official who is still in office but whose position has been filled by another who will take over at a later date. The term refers to the official's inability to speak from a position of meaningful authority or influence as he might have during his actual term of office.

land In a legal sense, the solid part of the surface of the earth as distinguished from water; any ground, soil, or earth whatsoever, regarded as the subject of ownership, and everything annexed to it, whether by nature; *e.g.,* trees, and everything in or on the earth, such as minerals and running water, or annexed to it by man, as buildings, fences, etc. In an economic sense, land consists of all those elements in the wealth of a nation which are supposed to be furnished by nature, as distinguished from those improvements which owe their value to the labor and organizing power of man.　　　　**54**

Land Bank 1) An agricultural program which has as its purpose the retirement of land from active agricultural purposes by a government subsidy to encourage the transfer of use into such activities as tree cultivation. Also called "Soil Bank."
2) A Federal Land Bank.
3) A state cooperative to assist savings and loan associations.
4) A bank which instead of having capital uses land as the basis for issuing currency and extending credit such as the Land Bank founded in New England in 1740.

land contract A legal instrument to deliver a deed to the property given to the purchaser of the real estate, who customarily pays a small portion of the purchase price when the contract is signed and agrees to pay additional sums at specified intervals and in specified amounts until the total purchase price is paid. Since the possession of the land, that is, the ownership, does not become final until the whole payments have been made, this serves as a means of financing some properties in certain states.　　　　**54**

land grant The land given to an individual or organization by the federal government for the purpose of stimulating or accomplishing certain goals.

land improvements Physical changes in, or construction of, a more or less permanent nature attached to or appurtenant to land, of such character as to increase its utility and/or value.　　　　**54**

land patent The document used by the United States Government to transfer title of a land grant to the new owner.

land tax A property tax on real estate.

land trust An unincorporated association for holding real property by putting the title in one or more trustees for the benefit of the members whose interests are evidenced by land trust certificates.　　　　**22**

land trust certificate An instrument which grants participation in benefits of the ownership of real estate, while the title remains in a trustee. 5

land-value tax The levy by a governmental unit on the value of the land alone. The land value is an appraised value rather than one sales value.

lapping Theft from one customer being covered by theft from another, generally by means of false entries in books of accounts. 5

lapse (noun) The falling of a gift into the residuary estate by reason of the death of the legatee or devisee during the testator's lifetime. Such a gift is known as a lapsed legacy or lapsed devise. 30

larceny Theft; taking and carrying away the goods of another. 38

last in, first out An accounting technique which assigns the value of an inventory from the cost of the most recent purchases. The balance sheet valuation of inventory is computed on the purchase price of earlier purchases and thus minimizes income taxes in periods of inflation. For contrast see "first in, first out" (fifo).

last will The will last executed by a person. Since all former wills ordinarily are revoked by the last one, the term is used to emphasize the fact that it is the latest and, therefore, the effective will of the maker. 30

late charge A special fee demanded in connection with any payment on a mortgage loan or other obligation that is not made when due. 33

lawful money All forms of money which, by federal law, is endowed with legal tender for the payment of all debts, both public and private. See "legal tender." 1

layaway Goods purchased to be called for at a later date. A deposit is put down and the balance paid when the goods are picked up. 38

lay days The stated period of time a chartered vessel without any penalty may stay in a port for purposes of loading and unloading. 5

layoff Temporary, prolonged or final separation as a result of lack of work or business. 12

layoff loan Generally considered to be one within the legal limit

of the country bank but taken by the city bank to assist a
country bank that is highly loaned up.

leakage That reduction from a theoretical financial potential
caused by friction or a similar economic factor.

learner A worker undergoing a usually short period of training
in a trade that ordinarily requires less skill than those for
which a regular apprenticeship is demanded.   **12**

lease A contract by which the possession and use of real estate
or other property is conveyed for a certain specified term and
at a specified rent.   **31, 36**

leaseback A technique of financing and handling real estate.
The original owner sells the property and simultaneously
leases it back. There are a number of advantages and disadvantages to such a practice. Advantages include frequent tax
savings; disadvantages include loss of a hedge in a period of
inflation.

leased department Part or subdivision of a store which is rented
to an independent operator as a concession.

leaseholds Rights to the use of real estate by virtue of the lease,
usually for a specified term of years, for which a consideration
is paid, as distinguished from the ownership of the real
estate.   **29**

ledger A record of final entry in bookkeeping.   **1**

legacy A gift of personal property by will; the same as a bequest.
A person receiving such a gift is called a legatee.   **30**

legal entity A thing, other than a person, that exists, can sue, be
sued, and otherwise dealt with as if it were a natural person; in
this sense, a corporation, a state, or a city is a legal entity. **22**

legal interest That maximum interest rate established by state
law which is used in contracts which have omitted mention of
a rate.

legal investment An investment that conforms to the requirements of the statutes. A term used principally with reference
to investments by trustees and other fiduciaries and by savings
banks; often abbreviated to legals. To be distinguished from an
authorized investment.   **30**

legal list A list of investments selected by various states in
which certain institutions and fiduciaries, such as insurance
companies and banks, may invest. Legal lists are restricted to
high-quality securities meeting certain specifications. See
"prudent man law."   **2**

legal person Description of a corporation's condition of being subject to laws just as if it were a person.

legal rate of interest The maximum rate of interest that is permitted by the laws of the state having jurisdiction over the legality of a transaction. Interest in excess of this legal rate is termed usury. See "usury." **1**

legal reserve 1) The minimum reserve which an insurance company must keep to meet future claims and obligations as they are calculated under the state insurance code. **58**
2) A bank's legal reserve is the portion of its deposits (demand and time) which it is required by law to maintain in the form of cash or readily available balances to meet the demands of depositors. **25**

legal security That stock or bond which a fiduciary such as a trust company or trustee may purchase and hold for beneficiaries. In some states these are published in a legal list.

legal tender Coin or currency required by law to be accepted in payment of obligations. **31, 36**

lender One who makes a trade of putting money to interest; a money lender. **38**

lessee One who possesses the right to use or occupy a property under a lease; the tenant. **54**

lessor The person, corporation, or other legal entity that leases property to a lessee. **22**

letter of attorney A written document which evidences a power of attorney. **30**

letter of credit An instrument issued by a bank to an individual or corporation by which the bank substitutes its own credit for that of the individual or corporation. **25**

letter of trust A letter of lien. A letter which states that the signer-agent is holding merchandise or property for a seller until such times as the seller is paid for the goods.

letter patent A sealed and signed document from a government which grants a special right, privilege, property, or title such as the exclusive right to make or sell an invention.

letters testamentary A certificate of authority to settle a particular estate issued to an executor by the appointing court. **34**

level charge plan An investment accumulation plan under which the selling charges are spread over the entire life of the investment program. **3**

level of living The plane or standard of living. The material goods and services enjoyed by a person or group.

leverage 1) In securities investment, the effect on the per share earnings of the common stock of a company when large sums must be paid for bond interest or preferred stock dividends, or both, before the common stock is entitled to share in earnings. Leverage may be advantageous for the common stock when earnings are good but may work against the common stock when earnings decline. **2**

2) Financial leverage refers to the controlling of a certain amount of investment worth with a smaller amount of money, such as controlling a land investment with a down payment, receiving the benefits of appreciation while making payments.

levy (verb) To impose taxes or special assessments. (noun) The total of taxes or special assessments imposed by a governmental unit. **29**

liability A debt or responsibility that is owed or assumed.

liability, capital A comprehensive term which includes all long-term indebtedness of a corporation which is represented by the outstanding capital stock (liability to owners) and mortgages and bonded indebtedness (liability to outside creditors). **1**

liability, central The grouping together on one record of all liabilities of a borrower, such as loans both direct and indirect, consumer credit, letters of credit, guarantees, and other accommodations. The purpose of this record is to prevent over-extensions of credit to the borrower. **1**

liability, common law A party's responsibility for injuries or damage imposed upon a second party because of the first party's actions, by that part of the law based upon custom and usage as established by the courts, as distinguished from liability under statutes passed by a legislative body. **5**

liability, contingent A liability which is dependent upon certain events occurring before it becomes an active liability. **22**

liability, contractual Liability over and above that which would be imposed by law which a person assumes under the terms of a contract. **52**

liability, corporate profits tax Federal and state taxes levied on corporate earnings of a given year. This measures taxes for the year in which they are incurred, not necessarily for the year in which they are paid. **7**

liability, cumulative When one bond is canceled and another issued to take its place and the first bond has a discovery period, the surety company is exposed to the possibility of a loss equal to the aggregate sum of the two bonds. **50**

liability, current Those pecuniary obligations ordinarily intended to be paid in the usual course of business within a relatively short time, normally within a year, out of earnings. **15**

liability, deposit The total of time, demand and certificate of deposits as well as other special deposits such as Christmas Club, Vacation Club and escrow accounts which a bank owes its customers.

liability, direct A known primary obligation requiring the payment of a certain sum of money either now or at some determinable future date. See "prime maker." **1**

liability, fixed A long-term debt; recurring expenses. **38**

liability, indirect A secondary, or contingent, liability assumed by the indorsement or guaranty of an obligation for which another party is primarily liable. **25**

liability, indirect business tax and nontax All tax liabilities incurred by business, except for corporate income and social insurance taxes, plus general government nontax revenues for business. Nontax liabilities consist mainly of certain charges for government products and services, of fines and penalties, of donations, and of special assessments by state and local governments. Note that tax and nontax liability consists of payments incurred, not payments made. **7**

liability, joint Liability for which more than one person or company share responsibility. **5**

liability, legal An obligation enforceable by law most often considered in a monetary sense. **52**

liability, limited Responsibility in event of bankruptcy limited to the amount invested in the business. **38**

liability limits The sum or sums beyond which a liability insurance company does not protect the insured on a particular policy. **50**

liability, primary A direct liability as differentiated from an indirect or contingent liability.

liability, secondary A contingent liability.

liaison The contact maintained between units, in order to ensure concerted action. **38**

libel To spread false statements about another which tend to injure his reputation. **38**

license The document embodying the formal permission from a legally constituted governing authority to carry on a certain activity, the conduct of which would otherwise be illegal. Usually used for revenue and/or regulatory purposes.

lien A charge or claim against the property of another until some claim against that person is paid or satisfied. **31, 36**

life estate A freehold interest in land, the duration of which is confined to the life of one or more persons or contingent upon certain happenings. **54**

life expectancy The length of time a person of a given age may be expected to live according to the statistical tables that have been worked out. **22**

life table A tabulated statement presenting mortality and survivor characteristics of a given population. **5**

life tenant One who owns an estate in real property for his own lifetime or for another person's lifetime or for an indefinite period bounded by a lifetime. **30**

lifo See "last in, first out."

limited (ltd.) A corporation. While mostly associated with British or Canadian business firms using the corporate form and thus having limited liability, the term is sometimes used in the United States and has the same meaning.

limited audit An audit in which the effectiveness of the system of internal control and the mathematical accuracy, legality, propriety, and completeness of all transactions are determined by examining only selected items. **29**

limited depositary A Federal Reserve System member bank which under stated restrictions may receive governmental deposits.

limited-function wholesaler A merchant middleman who sells to retailers and other merchants and/or to industrial, institutional, and commercial users but who does not sell in significant amounts to ultimate consumers. **13**

limited order In investment trading, an order in which the client has set restrictions as contrasted to a market order. See "market order." **9**

limited partner A member of a partnership who as a result of giving up an active voice in management and publicly an-

nouncing in the legally required way that he is a limited partner acquires limited liability.

limited partnership A partnership consisting of both general and special partners, with at least one member, the manager, being fully responsible for all debts. **44**

limping standard A monetary standard in which designated silver coins are considered as unlimited legal tender and thus do not have to be redeemed in gold though the paper currency is so redeemable.

lineal descendant A person in the direct line of descent, as child or grandchild; opposed to collateral heir. **30**

line of credit A term applied to a maximum amount of credit which a bank will extend to a particular borrower (usually a business concern) over a stated period, subject to certain conditions which must be met by the borrower, such as maintaining a specified balance in his checking account. **25**

liquidation The process of paying the liabilities of a business, selling the assets, and distributing the remaining cash to the owner or owners of the business. **16**

liquidity 1) A term used to describe the solvency of a business, and which has special reference to the degree of readiness in which assets can be converted into cash without loss. **1**
2) The ability of the market in a particular security to absorb a reasonable amount of buying or selling at reasonable price changes. **2**

liquidity preference The tendency for people to keep their assets in a form that is cash or easily converted into cash rather than in a frozen form.

lis pendens Notice of a pending suit. **15**

listed securities Securities that have been accepted for trading on a recognized securities exchange. **40**

listing The record of property for sale or lease and services being booked or sold by a broker or agent who has been authorized in writing by the owners and/or managers to act as their agent or representative. **54**

list price The posted, published price which may at times be reduced by such devices as volume discounts, commissions, discounts for prompt payment, or other rebate.

litigation The act of carrying on a lawsuit. **5**

little steel All steel manufacturers in the United States except USX.

living trust A trust that becomes operative during the lifetime of the settlor; opposed to a trust under will. The same as a trust inter vivos. **30**

Lloyd's Association A group of individual insurance underwriters who make contributions to a common fund. The individual contributors are liable for the amount of the risk placed after their respective names in the policy in proportion to their contribution. Any individual underwriter is not liable for the others' assumed risk or loss. **52**

Lloyd's of London An insurance carrier in the nature of a board of trade or insurance mart, where individual underwriters gather for the purpose of quoting rates and accepting insurance on all manner of risks. Lloyd's is bound by few restrictive regulations and is free to develop special coverages to meet nearly all manner of insurance situations. **42**

loan Money advanced to a borrower usually to be repaid with interest, and evidenced by notes, bonds, etc. **31, 36**

loanable funds interest theory Theory that the supply and demand of money determine interest rates.

loan crowd Those members of a stock exchange who will lend securities for those who have sold short.

loaned flat When stocks are sold short the seller must borrow them to make delivery. If he is able to borrow them without making a payment of interest for them he is dealing in a stock that is "loaned flat."

loaned stock Stock which has been loaned to a short seller or his broker in order to fulfill the terms of a short-selling contract by delivering shares. **44**

loan interest Explicit interest. The amount paid for the use of capital or money.

loan rate The charge at which loan funds can be had at a given time and at a given lending source. **59**

loan shark A lender of funds at a rate higher than the maximum legal rate.

loan value The largest amount that can be borrowed on an item, such as the wholesale price of a car or the security of the cash value of a life insurance policy. The idea is for the lender not to be overcommitted in the event of default on the part of the borrower. **5**

local rate The amount charged within a limited geographic district for goods or services.

local union The basic unit in union organization. The local has its own constitution and bylaws, and elects its own officers, but it is chartered by the international with which it is affiliated.   **12**

locked-in An investor is said to be locked-in when he has a profit on a security he owns but does not sell because his profit would immediately become subject to the capital gains tax. See "capital gain."   **2**

lockout Shutdown of a plant by the employer to discourage union membership or activity.   **12**

lockup Refers to securities that have been withdrawn from circulation and placed in a safe-deposit box for purposes of long-term investment.   **44**

Lombard Street The London financial area similar to Wall Street in New York or LaSalle Street in Chicago.

long 1) Signifies ownership of securities. "I am long 100 United States Steel" means the speaker owns 100 shares. See "short."   **2**

2) One is said to be net "long" of the futures market if he has bought more contracts than he has sold—the opposite of "short."   **9**

long and short haul clause The Fourth Section of the Interstate Commerce Act, Part I, which prohibits a transportation line from charging more for a shorter than for a longer haul over the same route, except by special permission of the Interstate Commerce Commission, hence the term "Long and Short Haul Clauses."   **19**

long position A market attitude of one who actually owns securities, that is, one who is expecting a rise in prices or holding for income as opposed to one who has a short position.   **44**

long term A period of six months or more as opposed to the short or near-term period of less than six months. Long-term securities profits are accorded a more favorable tax treatment than short-term gains.   **44**

long-term trend 1) A pattern to be studied or analyzed for a period of six months or more.

2) The basic direction in which market prices seem likely to move over a period of time in the future.   **44**

loss leaders (price leaders) Items which a dealer sells at very low prices, sometimes below cost, in order to increase store traffic. The dealer hopes the people who come to buy the low-priced items will buy enough other goods at profitable prices to more than make up for the loss he suffers on the leaders. **24**

loss-payable clause A clause in an insurance contract providing for payment of a loss, for which the insurer is liable to the insured, to someone other than the insured, such as a bank holding a lien on an auto which it has financed. **51**

loss reserve That portion of the assets of an insurance company kept in a readily available form to meet probable claims. A fund provided for the payment of losses which have been incurred but are not yet due. **52**

lump-sum Full payment made in one sum, and at one time. **42**

lump-sum appropriation An appropriation made for a stated purpose, or for a named department, without specifying further the amounts that may be spent for specific activities or for particular objects of expenditure. **29**

luxuries Comforts and beauties of life beyond what is really necessary for normal living. **38**

luxury tax A levy upon products which are not deemed to be necessities, such as liquor, jewelry, tobacco, etc.

M

macroeconomics That school or phase of economics which concentrates on aggregates such as gross national product as compared with microeconomics which concentrates on the individual.

maintenance of membership A union security system under which an employee is not required to join the union, but if he does, or, if already a member, he fails to resign during the "escape period," he binds himself to remain a member for the duration of the union contract. **12**

major trend The basic direction in which stock prices are moving over a period of time regardless of temporary movements contrary to trend. Also called the primary movement. **44**

make a market In investment trading, to stand ready to buy or sell, adjusting bid and offer prices to balance purchases and sales. **40**

maker Any individual, proprietorship, corporation, or other legal entity who signs a check, draft, note, or other type of negotiable instrument as a primary responsible party is known as the maker. **1**

make-work practices Labor policies that compel, through hiring of extra help, the spreading of available work. **12**

malingering A period of deliberate protraction of feigning disability. **5**

Malthusian population theory Concept that population increases by a geometric progression while the ability to add to the supply of food is at a slower arithmetic rate. The conclusion followed that a point would be reached when the amount of food available on a per capita basis would result in a population restriction.

managed currency A manipulated money. The currency is not permitted to respond to "natural laws" of such factors as gold points or supply and demand.

management The administration and policy makers of a business or other organization. In a corporation it is the board of directors, elected by the stockholders, and the officers of the corporation, appointed by the board of directors. **2**

management fee The amount paid to the investment adviser for its services. **14**

management stock 1) The stock owned by the management of a corporation.

2) Stock which having extra voting privileges can control a corporation.

manifest A document listing the contents, value, origin, destination, carrier and time a cargo is shipped.

manipulation 1) Operating or managing skillfully with the hands.

2) An illegal or false operation. Buying or selling a security for the purpose of creating false or misleading appearance of active trading or for the purpose of raising or depressing the price to induce purchase or sale by others. **2**

man-land ratio The number of people per unit of land as a method of measuring the density of population.

manorial system The feudal system.

manufacturer's agent An agent who generally operates on an extended contractual basis; sells with an exclusive territory; handles noncompeting but related lines of goods; and possesses limited authority with regard to prices and terms of sale. **13**

manufacturer's brand A manufacturer's or producer's brand usually enjoying wide territorial distribution. **13**

margin 1) A reserve amount or quantity. An excess of time or money over what is actually needed or required.

2) The amount deposited by a client with his broker to protect the broker against loss on contracts being carried or to be carried by the broker. **9**

marginal borrower The individual or firm which will cease to borrow if the loan rate of interest is increased.

marginal buyer A buyer who will quit the market if the price is raised.

marginal cost That amount of money one extra unit of production will add to the total cost of production.

marginal desirability See "marginal utility."

marginal efficiency of capital The relationship between the return and the cost of an additional unit of capital.

marginal land That which barely pays the cost of working or using. Land whereon the costs of operating approximately equal the gross income. **54**

marginal lender The individual or firm which will cease to lend if the loan rate of interest is decreased.

marginal producer The manufacturer who is just meeting his production costs at the price he is receiving for his product.

marginal productivity theory of wages Theory stating that labor's wages should be determined by the additional value added to the product, or by the added quantity produced by the last worker hired.

marginal propensity to consume The percentage of an additional unit of disposable income which is spent for consumption during a given time period.

marginal rate of substitution See "equimarginal principle."

marginal revenue The gross income, or sale price of an additional unit of production.

marginal seller The individual or firm which will drop out, or refuse to sell, in the event that the price of the product or service is reduced.

marginal trading The purchasing of a security or commodity in which the buyer does not pay for the transaction entirely with his own funds but rather borrows part of the purchase price.

marginal utility The amount of satisfaction gained by consuming an additional unit of good.

margin call A demand upon a customer to put up money or securities with the broker. The call is made when a purchase is made; also if a customer's equity in a margin account declines below a minimum standard set by the Exchange or by the firm. See "margin." 2

margin of cultivation That state of utilization of agricultural land in which the income produced by the last unit of labor, capital, or management will just meet the cost of the unit.

margin of safety The balance of income remaining after payment of fixed charges (or after payment of preferred dividends), expressed as a percentage of gross revenues (net sales); hence the approximate percentage by which gross revenues can decline or operating expenses can increase before the continued payment of bond interest (or of bond interest plus preferred dividends) is endangered. 40

marital deduction The portion of a decedent's estate that may be given to the surviving wife or husband without its becoming subject to the federal estate tax levied against the decedent's estate; a term that came into general use under the Internal Revenue Act of 1954. 22

Maritime Law Rules of conduct or action set forth by specific court (Admiralty) having jurisdiction on maritime questions and offenses. 5

markdown The reduction of an originally established selling price. 24

market 1) An aggregate composed of a prospective buyer (or buyers), and a seller (or sellers), that brings to focus the conditions and forces which determine prices.
2) The aggregate demand of the potential buyers of a commodity or service.
3) The place or area in which buyers and sellers function.
4) To perform business activities which direct the flow of goods and services from producer to consumer or user. 13

marketability The relative ease and quickness with which a good, property, commodity, or service can be sold; salability. 34

market analysis A subdivision of marketing research which involves the measurement of the extent of a market and the determination of its characteristics. 13

market demand The total quantity of a good which is demanded at any one time at a given price.

210

marketing Directing and encouraging the flow of goods from producer to consumer or user. **20**

marketing agreement 1) A price-fixing or similar arrangement between producers of like products. Usually illegal.

2) That system of agricultural products distribution and price-fixing permitted by law involving the approval of two-thirds of the producers and products covered by the agreement. Upon submission and acceptance by the United States Department of Agriculture the restrictions become binding not only on the agreeing majority but also on the disagreeing minority.

marketing cooperative One of over 7,000 organizations having over 2,000,000 members devoted to aiding their members market their products which are primarily agricultural in nature. Present tax provisions give them a distinct advantage over commercial corporations in the same field.

marketing research Gathering, recording and analyzing facts relating to the transfer and sale of products. **20**

market order An order to a stock broker from a client to buy or sell stocks or bonds at the price prevailing when the order reaches the market. **1**

market penetration Extent to which a given establishment, firm or plant shares or dominates the sales in a given market area. **24**

market price 1) That price which prevails in a market at a given period of time.

2) The point of intersection of a supply and a demand schedule of a market.

3) In the case of a security, market price is usually considered the last reported price at which the stock or bond sold. **2**

market value The price of a good, property, service, security, or commodity, as determined by current market transactions.

markup The amount added to the cost of merchandise or services when they are first priced to cover expenses and provide a profit; also called initial markup. **24**

Marxian Any economic or political concept believed to have been proposed by, or which follows the philosophy of Karl Marx—communism.

Massachusetts trust An unincorporated organization created for profit under a written instrument or declaration of trust, by the terms of which the property held in trust is managed by compensated trustees for the benefit of a person whose legal interests are represented by transferable certificates of participation or shares; also called business trust.   **30**

mass picketing Patrolling by large numbers of closely ranked persons, often strikers, preventing access to company premises and often conveying threats of violence.   **12**

mass production Production by machinery; assembly line; in great quantity.   **59**

master's deed A deed issued by a master in chancery in satisfaction of a judgment and under a court order.   **5**

matched and lost When two bids to buy the same stock are made on the trading floor simultaneously, and each bid is equal to or larger than the amount of stock offered, both bids are considered to be on an equal basis. So the two bidders flip a coin to decide who buys the stock. Also applies to offers to sell.   **2**

material cost That cost of a product which is due only to the cost of raw material and would not include such indirect expenses as wages, rent, interest and management costs.

mathematical economics The use of mathematical formulas and symbols to try to express principles of economics. Econometrics.

matrix An array of quantities in a prescribed form; in mathematics, usually capable of being subject to a mathematical operation by means of an operator or other matrix according to prescribed rules.   **41**

mature economy That stage of development of a nation's economy where a decline in the rate of growth has occurred on a relatively permanent basis. During the 1930's a number of economists described the United States as a mature economy. However, the 1950's and 1960's seem to indicate that they mistook a cyclical reversal for a long-term trend.

maturity The time when a note, draft, acceptance, bond, insurance policy or other instrument becomes due for payments.

maturity date The date upon which a financial obligation or other contract becomes due for payments or expires.   **31, 36**

maturity value The amount that must be paid on the date a financial obligation becomes due.   **16**

maximum The greatest quantity, value, or degree possible.   **38**

maximum-hour legislation Part of the Fair Labor Standards Act of 1938 as amended, which covers employees in interstate commerce and restricts regular hourly minimum rates to a forty-hour week. Hours in excess of 40 are reimbursed at a rate of 150% of the regular rate.

maximum-minimum tariff system A tariff which uses two schedules of duties. The high or maximum tariff may be invoked as a penalty while the low or minimum tariff may be used for favored nations' imports.

mean See "arithmetic mean."

measured day rate A technique for piecework compensation based upon the employees' production for the preceding day.

mechanic's lien A claim against title to property placed by or for the benefit of one who has performed labor or has furnished material in improving the property.   **34**

median See "average, median."

mediator Serves as a referee to help people decide for themselves, but does not impose a binding decision. Advises with worker and employer in labor disputes.   **38**

medium of exchange Any commodity (commonly money) which is widely accepted in payment for goods and services and in settlement of debts, and is accepted without reference to the standing of the person who offers it in payment.   **34**

melon Slang financial term meaning extraordinary profits waiting to be divided.   **44**

member bank The term applied to any bank, either national or state, that is a member of the Federal Reserve System. A state bank that is not a member of the system is termed a nonmember bank.   **25**

member corporation A securities brokerage firm, organized as a corporation, with at least one member of the New York Stock Exchange who is a director and a holder of voting stock in the corporation.   **2**

member firm A securities brokerage firm organized as a partnership and having at least one general partner who is a member of the New York Stock Exchange.   **2**

memorandum account The record of an account maintained by a bank which is not included in its assets or liabilities. An example is the record of a bad debt written off, on which subsequent recoveries are anticipated.   **1**

memorandum buying A marketing and selling technique in which the producer is not paid for his goods until the retailer has sold the merchandise to the consumer.

mercantile Engaged in trade or commerce. 38

mercantile agency That organization such as Dun and Bradstreet or local credit bureau which supplies credit information on applicants for credit to its members. In addition, the agency may also perform other functions, such as collection of past-due accounts and trade-collection statistics.

mercantilism The system of business from about 1550 to 1850 in England in which great emphasis was put on retention of a favorable balance of trade.

merchandise Goods bought for the purpose of resale. 38

merchandise turnover The number of times that a business buys and sells a stock of goods during a year. 16

merchandising The process of distributing a product or a service by systematic and carefully planned promotion and directed sales effort. 33

merchantable Salable in the ordinary way; fit for ordinary uses to which it is put. 5

merchantman A vessel which carries freight, or passengers, or both, and is not a part of a navy.

merchant marine A nation's facilities and equipment for carrying on trade and international commerce on the ocean.

merchant middleman A middleman who takes title to the goods he stocks and sells. 13

merger When two or more businesses join together and form a single company. 38

merit rating 1) In insurance, a system used in measuring the differences of a specific risk from some moral, or other standard, in order to correct the manual rate for that risk. 52
2) In personnel administration, the regular review of an employee's performance. Merit rating may be for purposes of promotion, layoff, firing or training.

meter rate Applies to any method of charge for utility service based solely upon quantity. The quantity is expressed in units, as, kilowatt hours of electricity used. 21

meter rate, straight-line The term "straight-line" indicates that the price charged per unit is constant, *i.e.,* does not vary on account of an increase or decrease in the number of units. 21

metes and bounds A method of describing land through the use of boundaries and measurements of a parcel of real estate. 5

microeconomics The approach to the study of economics which concentrates attention on individuals or single products or goods. For contrast see "macroeconomics."

middleman A business concern that specializes in performing functions or rendering services immediately involved in the purchase and/or sale of goods in the process of their flow from producer to consumer.   **13**

milking The excessive exploitation of something such as the assets of a firm either through very high dividends or payments of bonus or salary to management.

mineral rights The right or title to all or to certain, specified minerals in a given tract of land.   **22**

minimum The least amount, quantity, or degree.   **38**

minimum rate 1) In insurance rating, a general class for risks of low hazard, with many units in the class. Opposed to "schedule rate" and "specific rate." See "class rate."   **50, 51**
2) In public utility rates, it is the rate established by the regulatory body below which a utility may not charge for a service.

minimum wage Lowest amount of money that may be paid to workers, as prescribed by law.   **38**

minor A person under legal age, that is, under the age at which he or she is accorded full civil rights; the same as an infant.   **30**

minor coins The five-cent and one-cent pieces.

mint The establishment or place where coins are made from metal under the supervision of an authorized governmental official.

mintage The fee collected by the mint for making coins from metal.

mint par of exchange The figure derived by dividing the pure gold or silver weight of the monetary unit of one nation by the pure similar metal of the monetary unit of the other nation.

mint price of gold Thirty-five dollars per fine troy ounce of gold.

mint ratio The ratio of the weight of gold which is in a monetary unit to the weight of silver in the same monetary unit provided that the nation is on a bimetallic standard.

minute book A book in which is kept an official record of the proceedings of various meetings such as stockholders' meetings and board of directors' meetings.   **16**

misdemeanor A minor crime punishable by fine, or jail sentence, or both, as contrasted with a felony.

missionary salesman A salesman employed by a manufacturer to make contact with and work with the customers of his distributors, usually for the purpose of developing goodwill and stimulating demand, helping or inducing them to promote the sale of his employer's goods, helping them train their salesmen to do so, and often taking orders for delivery by such distributors. **13**

mixed accounts In accounting and bookkeeping, accounts whose balances are part asset and part expense or part liability and part income. **16**

mixed economy Most western economies today are mixed economies in that they have characteristics of both capitalism and socialism in varying degrees.

mixed property Property which has some of the attributes of both real property and personal property, such as fixtures and keys to a house. **30**

mode See "average, mode."

model A representation of a thing in miniature or, in the case of economics, in mathematical terms.

modified union shop Provision in a contract that requires all new employees to join the union within a stated period after employment, but does not require present employees to join the union. However, all employees who are or who become union members must retain membership in good standing as a condition of employment.

monetary reserves The amount of gold and silver held by the Treasury or monetary authorities to secure the issue of credit money in circulation. The U.S. is no longer on the gold standard.

monetary standard The standard upon which a country's money is issued.

monetary system Description of the legal standard money of a nation and the related legislation on reserves, coinage, and methods of redemption and conversion.

monetary unit A country's unit of money.

money Those things which are generally acceptable in any society, and which pass freely from hand to hand as mediums of exchange. **38**

money broker An individual or firm, sometimes called a "finder" who brings those needing money to those who lend money and for this expects a fee. See "finder's fee."

money in circulation Total amount of currency and coin outside the Treasury and the Federal Reserve Banks. **4**

money market Market for short-term, high-grade, open-market assets.

money order Money orders are instruments commonly purchased for a fee by people who do not maintain checking accounts, but who wish to send money to distant points. **1**

money rates Those rates of interest which lenders are charging various classes of borrowers.

money wage That amount paid to an employee in money.

monometallism A single-standard monetary system in which one metal, generally gold, is given free and unlimited coinage.

monopolistic competition That situation in which one or two buyers or sellers can influence the price of a product in a market.

monopoly Exclusive control of a commodity or service in a particular market. **38**

monopsony A buyers' monopoly.

monthly investment plan A methodical investment technique introduced by members of the New York Stock Exchange in 1954 to allow a public investor to acquire stock on a regular, convenient basis, with payments ranging from $40 every three months to $1000 every month. **44**

moonlighting The act of holding more than one job.

moral hazard Refers to the risk resulting from the personal habits of the insured which may increase the possibility of loss due to carelessness or dishonesty. **50, 52**

moratorium That period of time, generally some emergency such as war, depression, or bank holiday, during which the normal activities and transactions of everyday life, either personal or business, are temporarily postponed.

more-favorable-terms clause That part of a union contract in which the union agrees not to negotiate any more favorable terms with the employer's competitors than the employer has agreed to. In this case, the term refers to favoring an employer and not the union.

morning loan Loans made by banks to stockbrokers on an unsecured basis for the purpose of the broker handling his stock deliveries until reimbursed by his customer.

Morris plan bank A bank which concentrates on relatively small loans and consumer credit involving insurance on the life of the debtor.

mortality table A table showing the probable death rate per year, and expectation of life at any given age. **42**

mortgage An instrument by which the borrower (mortgagor) gives the lender (mortgagee) a lien on real estate as security for a loan. The borrower continues to use the property, and when the loan is repaid, the lien is removed. **25**

mortgage banker A banker who specializes in mortgage financing; an operator of a mortgage financing company. They also disburse funds for taxes, insurance, etc., as escrow agents. **1**

mortgage certificate An interest in a mortgage evidenced by the instrument, generally a fractional portion of the mortgage, which certifies as to the agreement between the mortgagees who hold the certificates and the mortgagor as to such terms as principal, amount, date of payment, and place of payment. **54**

mortgage clause Clause in an insurance policy which makes the proceeds payable to the holder of a mortgage on the insured property to the extent of his interest in that property. **52**

mortgage company Mortgage financing companies are mortgagees themselves, as well as being mortgage agents for other large mortgagees. Serving as mortgage agents, these mortgage bankers collect payments, maintain complete mortgage records, and make remittances to the mortgagees for a set fee or service charge. **1**

mortgagee The institution, group or person which lends the money in a mortgage transaction. **31, 36**

mortgage loan A loan secured by a mortgage on real estate. Also called a real estate loan. **25**

mortgage, open-end A mortgage which permits the mortgagee to make additional advances, to be added to the principal balance and to be secured by the mortgage, without prejudice to the position of the mortgagee as a senior lienor or encumbrancer. **15**

mortgagor An owner of property who executes a mortgage pledging that property as security for a debt. **33**

most-favored-nation clause That part of an international commercial treaty in which the signatory nations agree to grant to no other nation trade concessions or duties more favorable than granted to the signatory nations.

Motor Carrier Act Federal statute under which the Interstate Commerce Commission may regulate hours of service of interstate passenger and freight motor vehicle operators.　　**12**

multicraft union A union which members of several different crafts, trades, or occupations may join.

multilateral agreement The accord of more than two individuals, firms, governments, or parties.

multilinear tariff A tariff which has a separate schedule of duties for each nation or group of nations. Also called multiple tariff.

multiple currency system A method of control for foreign exchange. The domestic currency may only be exchanged into foreign currency through a government agency or controlled bank. The rate of exchange will vary according to the product or use being made of the exchange. Generally, essentials such as farm machinery and tools are given a more favorable rate than luxuries.

multiple expansion of deposits (or credit) The nature of operation of a fractional reserve commercial banking system such as is found in the United States. A bank with excess reserves makes a loan and thus creates a deposit; when the deposit is withdrawn and spent it tends to be deposited in a bank creating excess reserves which, in turn, may be lent and cause a multiple expansion of credit or deposits. The rate of expansion is determined by the reserve requirement. A 10% reserve requirement in theory could have an expansion of ten times, while a 20% would have a five times expansion potential.

multiple tariff See "multilinear tariff."

multiplier principle The ratio between the increase in income and the increase in the formation of new capital used by followers of Keynes to recommend large-scale government spending during depressions as a means of increasing national income.

municipal Pertaining to the local government of a town or city.　　**38**

municipal corporation An incorporated political subdivision such as a town, county or city.

municipal improvement certificates Certificates issued in lieu of bonds for the financing of special improvements.　　**29**

municipals A word which in its broad sense designates the securities of any state, or of any political subdivision of a state, including cities, counties, towns, villages, districts and authorities. **40**

municipal socialism The situation in which a municipality owns and operates one or more utilities such as transit lines, waterworks, power generators, or gas producers.

muniments Those elements which improve, strengthen, or fortify the rights in property. **5**

mutual benefit associations Fraternal societies, social groups, other organizations, or corporations for the relief of members of the group operating on a corporate or assessment insurance plan. The features of this plan provide that the payment of losses is not met by fixed premiums payable in advance, but by assessments intended to liquidate specific losses. **5**

mutual company A company with a corporate form but no stock; profits being dispersed on the basis of the amount of business a member did with the company.

mutual fund The shorter and more popular term for an open-end investment company. **14**

mutual insurance companies Companies with no capital stock, owned by policyholders. Trustees of the company are chosen by the policyholders. The earnings of the company, over and above the payments of the losses and operating expenses and reserves, are the property of the policyholders. **52**

mutual mortgage insurance fund A fund (established under the provisions of the National Housing Act) into which mortgage insurance premiums and other specified revenue of the Federal Housing Administration are paid and from which losses are met. **33**

mutual savings bank A bank that is owned by the depositors and managed for them by a self-perpetuating board of trustees. It has no capital stock and therefore no stockholders. **25**

N

narrow market A thin market. A condition in the securities' market characterized by low volume of trading and slight variation in quotations.

National Advisory Council on International Monetary and Financial Problems Comprised of the Secretary of State, the

Secretary of the Treasury, the Secretary of Commerce, Chairman of the Board of Governors of the Federal Reserve System and the Export-Import Bank. Its function is to coordinate the policies of the United States in the World Bank and the International Monetary Fund.

National Association of Securities Dealers A voluntary association of brokers and dealers handling over-the-counter securities, formed after the Maloney Act of 1938. This special legislation was passed to regulate the over-the-counter market. The association has importance to members because they receive reduced commission from each other. **44**

national bank A corporation organized under a federal banking law (National Bank Act), and authorized to do a general or commercial banking business—that is, receive deposits subject to check, and make loans. It usually performs a variety of other functions as well. A national bank must have the word "national" in its corporate title. **25**

National Bank Act The legislation under which national banks were formed and operate. See "national bank."

national bank note A type of currency issued in the United States. National bank notes are backed by two types of United States Government bonds—2% consols of 1930, and the 2% Panama Canal bonds of 1916–36 and 1918–38. These bonds were called for redemption by the Bank Act of 1935, and so no further issuance of national bank notes was authorized. They are being retired from circulation. National bank notes are in denominations of 5, 10, 20, 50, and 100 dollars, and each has a brown seal and the issuing bank's charter number on its face. **1**

National Bankruptcy Act This act, as frequently amended, has established uniform laws on bankruptcy in all the states. In its present state it contains numerous chapters covering the procedures for handling the various bankrupt organizations ranging from individual through corporate, municipal, and railroad reorganization.

national brand A manufacturer's or producer's brand usually enjoying wide territorial distribution. **13**

National Bureau of Standards Part of the United States Department of Commerce. Works in areas of testing, standardization, measurement, and values.

national capitalism Economic and political system in which the national government exercises great control over the use of capital and may engage in competition with private enterprise in such sectors as power and utilities.

national debt The total amount owed by a national government.

national economy The entire economic life of a country.

national income A measure of the aggregate earnings of a nation's labor and property which result in the production of new goods and services in a given period of time.   7

National Industrial Recovery Act Legislation enacted in 1933 which established the Public Works Administration and the National Recovery Administration. Parts of the act were declared unconstitutional by the Supreme Court of the United States in 1935.

nationalization The conversion from private ownership and operation of a business activity to control and operation and, at times, ownership by a national government.

National Labor Relations Act Federal statute, originally known as the Wagner Act and now a part of the Taft-Hartley Act, which guarantees to employees in industries affecting interstate commerce the right to self-organization, to bargain collectively and to engage in concerted activities.   12

National Labor Relations Board (NLRB) Agency established to determine collective-bargaining representatives and prevent unfair labor practices.

national minimum A federal social welfare policy which establishes a standard of living below which people should not experience because of public charitable assistance and welfare, or social security.

national product See "gross national product."

national security exchange A stock and securities exchange classified as such by the Securities and Exchange Commission. Included are most of the larger exchanges in the United States. Only a few small exchanges are not designated as national security exchanges. Not to be confused with National Stock Exchange.

National Stock Exchange A stock exchange which was founded in 1960 in New York City. The third stock exchange in that city, the other two being the New York Stock Exchange and the American Stock Exchange. Not to be confused with national security exchange.

national union A union with local unions and members

throughout the United States but without foreign local unions or members.

national wealth The monetary sum of all the material assets owned by citizens and institutions of a country as of a stated time and which are within the borders of the nation, plus the material assets owned outside the nation. A number of nations assume a balance between assets owned abroad and assets within a nation owned by foreigners, and thus count all material assets, irrespective of ownership within their borders. Material assets are used to prevent duplication of counting assets such as currency or securities.

natural capital Land when used as a factor of production.

natural monopoly A situation characterized by the obviousness of having only one producer of a service rather than many competitors. Telephone communication, electrical production, and other utilities are typical natural monopolies. A natural monopoly may also come about because of unique mineral deposits, water flow, or soil characteristics. The owner of land upon which may be found minerals that are not to be found on other lands may be considered to have a natural monopoly.

natural order The philosophy of laissez-faire, as developed by the Physiocrats, under which each individual would do what would provide the greatest return with the least effort. This was considered to be natural and part of natural order or law.

natural rights The rights to life, liberty, and the pursuit of happiness provided the pursuit does not infringe upon the rights of others. Governments do not have the legal sanction to deny natural rights under the Declaration of Independence of the United States.

near-money Time deposits in commercial banks, savings and loan shares, Treasury bills, and other very liquid assets are considered near-money since they may be converted into money very easily.

negative investment See "disinvestment."

negative-pledge clause A covenant in an indenture to the effect that the corporation will not pledge any of its assets unless the notes or debentures outstanding under the particular indenture are at least equally secured by such pledge; also called the covenant of equal coverage. **22**

negligence Failure to do what a reasonably prudent individual would ordinarily do under the circumstances of a particular case, or doing what a prudent person would not have done. **50, 53**

negotiable Something which can be sold or transferred to another for money or in payment of a debt. **38**

neoclassical school of economics Also known as the Cambridge School. Has modified the classical school of Alfred Marshall and his predecessors to Adam Smith, by greater development of marginal utility and mathematics while rejecting the classical position on laissez-faire.

nepotism Practice by those in positions of power and influence such as corporate management or public office, of giving promotions, higher earnings, better jobs, and other benefits to employees who are their relatives or friends.

net cost 1) The actual cost of something, after all income or other financial gain is subtracted from the gross cost.
2) In insurance, the total premiums paid on a policy, minus any dividends, and the surrender value as of the date of the determination of the so-called net cost. **5**

net debt The total of all debt after deducting such items as sinking funds.

net earnings The amount of the gross income less the operating expenses and any other expenses and before payment of any dividends. **31, 36**

net free or net borrowed reserves Excess reserves less member bank borrowings from Federal Reserve Banks. The resulting difference is called net free when positive, and net borrowed when negative. **56**

net income In general, synonymous with net earnings, but considered a broader and better term; the balance remaining, after deducting from the gross income all operating expense, maintenance, taxes and losses pertaining to operating properties, excepting interest or other financial charges on borrowed or other capital. **54**

net interest See "pure interest."

net lease A lease where, in addition to the rental stipulated, the lessee assumes payment of all property charges such as taxes, insurance and maintenance. **54**

net national debt National debt less such amounts held in United States trust accounts.

net national product A measure of the aggregate market value of all goods and services which do not replace worn-out, dam-

224

aged or obsolete capital goods, and which are produced by the economy within a given period of time. Thus, it equals gross national product less capital consumption allowances. **7**

net option A written instrument which grants the right to purchase property at a specified price to the owner. **5**

net price The price paid after all deductions such as discounts, rebates, allowances and kickbacks.

net profit The actual profit realized by a business over a specific period of time, or for an individual transaction or sale, after deducting all costs from gross receipts.

net sales Sales minus discounts, allowances, and returns. **38**

net worth The excess of the assets of an individual or an enterprise over all his or its liabilities. **33**

net yield The return obtained from an investment after deduction of costs and losses involved in procuring and managing the investment. **33**

neutral money A plan whereby various commodities could be exchanged for a fixed amount of money, the objective being the elimination of price level fluctuations.

New Deal The popular designation for the political policies and administration of the late President of the United States, Franklin D. Roosevelt.

new issue A stock or bond sold by a corporation for the first time. Proceeds may be used to retire outstanding securities of the company, for new plants or equipment, or for additional working capital. **2**

New York Curb Exchange Former title of the American Stock Exchange. **44**

New York Stock Exchange The major security exchange in the world. It is an unincorporated association in which membership is limited in number and may be obtained only upon acceptance by a membership committee. Such membership is called "a seat." See "stock exchanges."

next of kin The person or persons in the nearest degree of blood relationship to a person.

no-limit order Means the opposite of a limit order; in other words, it is a market order because it has no stipulation as to prices. May be either a buy or sell order. **44**

no-load fund A mutual fund which has no sales organization but whose sponsor sells shares directly to the public for little or no commission (load charge). **44**

nominal account In bookkeeping, a ledger account which is closed out when the books are balanced.

nominal interest rate The contractual interest rate shown on the face and in the body of a bond, and representing the amount of interest to be paid, in contrast with the effective interest rate. **29**

nominalist An individual who holds that "money" is limited to the standard money defined by a government. Most economists today consider money to be inclusive not only of the currency in circulation but also of deposits which are subject to demand withdrawal.

nominal price See "nominal quote." It may also be a token price.

nominal quote The probable price of a security, based upon an evaluation of previous prices of the security or of similar securities.

nominal yield The amount of interest stated on an instrument's face. The amount of dividend stated on the face of the stock (if preferred).

nonassessable stock A type of security which cannot be assessed in the event of insolvency or failure, *i.e.,* it is fully paid for. Most stocks are of this nature, thus the holder cannot be assessed. **44**

non compos mentis Not of sound mind. A term that includes all forms of mental unsoundness and incompetence.

nonconforming use Any building or land lawfully occupied by a use at the time of the passage of a zoning resolution or subsequent amendments thereto, which does not conform after the passage of the resolution or amendments thereto, with all the regulations of the district in which said building or land is situated. **10**

noncupative will An oral will made by a person on his deathbed or by one who is conscious of the possibility of meeting death in the near future. It is declared in the presence of at least two witnesses and later reduced to writing and offered for probate in the manner prescribed by statute. **30**

nonforfeiture options Options available to an insured after policy values have been established. **42**

non-interest-bearing note A note on which the maker is not required to pay interest. **16**

nonoperating income An increase in the income of a business that is derived from gains through the financial control of the business rather than through sales or other operations of the business. It is also known as financial income, nonrecurring income, or other income.

nonpar item Item for which the drawee bank will not remit to a collecting bank without deducting an exchange charge.   **25**

nonprofit institutions Enterprises set up to do some useful service and seek no profit; colleges, schools, churches, also such foundations established to better business relationships and understanding with and by the public, etc.   **59**

nonrecourse A situation in which the holder of an instrument does not have the legal right to compel a prior endorser or drawer to pay the amount of the negotiable instrument if it is dishonored. This may be because of a prior endorsement having the term "nonrecourse" as part of the endorsement. Or it may be because the holder is not "in due course."

nonwaiver agreement Assent by the insured that investigation and determination of the value of the claim by the insurance company does not constitute an admission that the insurance company has assumed liability.   **5**

no-par value Having no face value.   **16**

normal price That price which will balance the supply and demand for a product for an extended period of time and to which the price will tend to return upon fluctuation up or down. Sometimes called the equilibrium price.

nostro account The name applied to an accounting record of an account maintained by one bank with another.   **1**

nostro overdraft The designation on a bank's statement that it has sold more foreign bills of exchange than it has purchased, and thus the domestic bank owes funds to foreign banks in the amount of the nostro (our) overdraft.

notary public A quasi-public official appointed by a state governor or other appointing authority to perform designated duties, such as attesting signatures on documents and administering oaths.   **25**

note A written promise to pay a definite sum of money on demand or at a specified time.   **38**

notes payable An account in the ledger showing the liability for notes given by the business.   **38**

notes receivable Promissory notes received by the business from its customers.   **16**

nuisance tax A levy or duty which provides less revenue than the value of the time needed to compute and pay the tax.

nuncuperative will See "noncupative will."

O

objective value The price which an economic good can command in terms of other goods in the market.   33

obligation An amount of money or contracted performance one is morally or legally bound to pay or carry out.   59

obligee One to whom an obligation is owed, such as a bondholder.   30

obligor One who has an obligation to discharge, such as a corporation which issues bonds.   30

obsolescence The decrease in value caused by changes in models and new inventions that render previous versions or models out of date.

obsolete No longer in use. Outdated.   38

occupational level The degree of vocational skill, such as laborer, foreman, semiprofessional, professional, or other intermediate classifications.

occupation tax A privilege tax for engaging in a covered line of business activity. Plumbers, barbers, and most professions have to pay such a tax as a license to engage in the designated activity.

occupied 1) Presently in possession or use.
2) Applied to a building, shall be construed as though followed by the words "or intended, arranged or designed to be occupied."   11

occurrence A continuance or repeated exposure to conditions which result in injury. A clause frequently found under a personal liability policy; *e.g.*, all damages which arise out of the same general conditions are considered as arising from one occurrence. A leaky gas heater in a home might cause illness over a period of days without the person exposed to it being completely overcome at any one time. Such illness would be described as due to one occurrence under terms of a personal liability policy.   52

odd lot An amount of stock less than the established 100-share unit or 10-share unit of trading: From 1 to 99 shares for the great majority of issues, 1 to 9 for so-called inactive stocks. See "round lot" and "inactive stock." **2**

odd-lot dealer A broker or a dealer who assembles orders to buy or sell smaller quantities of a security than the normal trading unit and who consolidates such orders into a round-lot transaction. **40**

off-board This term may refer to transactions over-the-counter in unlisted securities, or, in a special situation, to a transaction involving a block of listed shares which was not executed on a national securities exchange. See "over-the-counter" and "secondary distribution." **2**

offer 1) To present for acceptance or refusal.
2) The price at which a seller will sell.

offering price See "asked price."

official exchange rate The rate at which the monetary authority of a nation will exchange its currency for the currency of another nation.

officer's check Same as cashier's check. **25**

oligopoly A condition of partial monopoly in which there are so few sellers of a product or service that each may affect the price and market, and in view of this, can judge the probable impact of his actions on the other sellers.

oligopsony A condition of partial monopoly in which there are so few buyers of a product or service that each may affect the price and market, and in view of this, can judge the probable impact of his actions on the other buyers.

one-hundred-percent reserve A banking system which would be substituted for the fractional reserve system. Commercial banks would be required to maintain reserves of the entire amount of their deposits and thus could not make loans with any funds except those available from paid-in capital and surplus. Loans would be made by some other agency or financial institution such as an investment bank.

one-name paper Single-name paper. Straight paper. An instrument which is signed by only one party, individual, or firm as distinguished from obligations which have two or more obligors.

one-thousand-hour clause A provision of the Fair Labor Standards Act which limits a worker covered under the Act to no more than one thousand hours of work during a single 26-week period.

on margin Securities which have been purchased by a customer who borrowed part of the purchase price from the broker, *i.e.,* they are not fully paid for. **44**

open account Credit (usually unsecured) extended to an individual, firm, corporation, or other legal entity based on an estimate of the general ability to pay, as distinguished from credit extended that is supported by a note, mortgage, or other formal written evidence of indebtedness. **1**

open certificate An insurance policy under which the rates and policy provisions may be changed. Fraternal insurance companies are required by law to issue this type of certificate. **5**

open competition A trade designation for the practice of firms in an industry of exchanging trade data such as prices, backlog of orders, past-due accounts, orders, production rate, etc.

open credit See "open account."

open-door policy A policy whereby citizens and goods of foreign nations receive the same treatment as domestic citizens and goods.

open-end contract The contract of a supplier to furnish all the required designated material to a purchaser for a stated period of time, even though the total volume is not known at the time the contract is signed.

open-end investment company A company, popularly known as a "mutual fund," which stands ready to redeem its shares at any time, usually at the prevailing net asset value per share. With rare exceptions, such companies also continuously offer new shares to investors. **14**

open-end investment trust An investment trust in which the trustee, by the terms of the trust, is authorized to invest in shares of stock other than those in the trust at the time of the inception of the trust or of the participation in the trust. **22**

opening The time or price at which trading begins in a commodity or security. Some orders to buy or sell are to be executed at the "opening."

opening entry 1) In accounting and bookkeeping, an entry that is made in the general journal to record the assets, liabilities, and proprietorship of a new business at the time the business is organized, or of a going concern at the time a new set of books is opened.

2) The first entry that is made in opening a new set of books. It is recorded in the general journal and presents a complete record of the assets, the liabilities, and the proprietorship as of the date of the entry. **16**

opening price The price of the first transaction in the security during the day is termed the opening price and constitutes one of the important quotations carried in financial publications. See "opening" and "opening range."

opening range Commodities, unlike securities, are often traded at several prices at the opening or close of the market. Buying or selling orders at the opening might be filled at any point in such a price range for the commodity. **9**

open interest In a contract market, it is the total position on one side of the market shown by all clearing brokers at any given time. In any one delivery month the short interest equals the long interest; in other words, the total number of contracts sold equals the total number bought. **9**

open letter of credit An open letter has no restrictions on the presenting of documents such as bills of lading against drafts, and is paid simply on a valid draft. See "letter of credit."

open market A highly competitive and broad market without limitations as to the qualifications of either the purchaser or seller.

open-market operations The actions of the Federal Reserve Bank of New York in carrying out the instructions of the Federal Open Market Committee to buy and sell government securities as one of the major tools of monetary policy. In most cases, bills are bought or sold for the accounts of the twelve Federal Reserve Banks. Buying creates excess reserves and eases the interest-rate structure. Selling government securities reduces reserves and firms interest rates.

open-market paper Short-term, high-grade promissory notes sold in the open market.

open mortgage A past-due mortgage which is being held by the mortgagee without requiring refinancing or the execution of an extension agreement. **33**

open order An order to buy or sell a security at a specified price. An open order remains in effect until executed or canceled by the customer. **2**

open-price system The practice of one or more companies in an industry keeping the other producers informed about the prices and trends of their products.

open shop A shop in which union membership is neither required as a condition of securing, nor of retaining employment. **12**

open stock Goods in show windows, on display, or on shelves. **5**

open-to-buy The amount which a store buyer may spend for merchandise during a given period of time, such as a month.

open trade A transaction which has not yet been closed. **44**

open union A labor union which does not restrict membership by any discriminatory devices such as by establishing bloodline relationship to existing members, high initiation fees, or race.

operating cost Cost of maintenance, utilities, office supplies, salaries, and such, required to keep a business or organization running. **38**

operating expense All expenses incurred in the normal operation of a business or other organization. **31, 36**

operating profit For purposes of marketing, gross margin (gross profit), less operating expenses (including salaries of managers, whether proprietors or employees), fixed plant and equipment cost, and sometimes interest on invested capital. **13**

operating ratio The ratio of the operating expenses to the operating revenues. **19**

operating statement A tabulation of data, generally of a financial nature, such as income and outgo for a stated period such as a week, month, or year.

opportunity cost A concept of cost which includes not only the amount paid out but also the amount of income lost as the cost of a course of action.

optimum population The population which can produce the greatest per capita output with a given amount of land, capital, and technology.

option The right to buy something at a certain price within a certain time. **38**

optional dividend A dividend in which the shareholder has the right of choice of a cash dividend or a stock dividend.

order Has several meanings. 1) A written instruction or commission to do something such as buy, sell, negotiate, or supply. 2) A direction from a proper court of jurisdiction.

232

3) Regulation.

order bill of lading A special form of bill of lading that is used in C.O.D. freight shipments. It is negotiable, and is good only to the person in whose favor it is drawn or the person to whom it is endorsed. **22**

ordinary interest Interest computed on the basis of 360 days to the year—12 months of 30 days each. **44**

ordinary rent The periodic payment for the use of such capital goods as machinery or land.

ordinary stock Common or equity stock.

original cost All costs associated with the acquisition of a fixed asset necessary to place it in effective use. **2&**

original-issue stock Those shares which were initially issued at the time the corporation was formed and are part of the starting capitalization.

other expense An expense not considered to be one of the regular operating expenses of a business or other organization. **16**

other income A financial gain derived from unusual sources, not regular routine operation transactions of a business, or not from an individual's usual source of income.

outlaw strikes Work stoppages which lack the approval of the national or international union and usually violate either a collective agreement or the union constitution. **12**

outlay That which is laid out or expended; cost. **38**

out-of-pocket costs Costs which are paid out or owed in cash.

outside broker An investment broker who does not belong to the local board or exchange.

outside market Means over-the-counter, or a market where unlisted securities are traded. **44**

over-and-short account An account carried in the general ledger. Overages and shortages from all sources, and their nature, are posted to this account, which is also termed a "suspense" or "differences" account in banks. At the end of the fiscal period, this account is closed out to profit and loss, and becomes either an increase or a decrease to the undivided profits account in the general ledger. **1**

overbought An opinion as to price levels. May refer to a security which has had a sharp rise, or to the market as a whole after a period of vigorous buying, which, it may be argued, has left prices "too high." See "technical position." **2**

overcapitalized 1) A corporation whose capital is valued at less than the property which secures it.

2) A corporation whose assets exceed the need of the business. The business has too much capacity for the market for its production. Since these two meanings of the same term vary so much, care must be taken to be sure of the context. See "watered stock."

overcertification The certification by a bank of a customer's check in those cases where the collected balance in the customer's account is less than the amount of the check.

overdraft 1) The amount by which checks, drafts, or other demands for payment on the treasury or on a bank exceed the amount of the credit against which they are drawn.

2) The amount by which requisitions, purchase orders, or audited vouchers exceed the appropriation or other credit to which they are chargeable.   **29**

overdraw See "overdraft."

overextension 1) Credit received or extended beyond the debtor's ability to pay.

2) The condition where a dealer in securities obligates himself for an amount beyond his borrowing power or ability to pay.

3) The expansion of buildings, equipment, etc., by a business concern which is in excess of its present or prospective future needs.   **1**

overhead Expenses, such as rent or insurance, which are not included in the actual running and operating of a business, organization, or other enterprise.

overissue In reference to investment trading, an amount in excess of the authorized or ordered amount.

overlapping debt The proportionate share of the debts of local government units located wholly or in part within the limits of the reporting government which must be borne by property within such government.   **29**

overlying mortgage A junior mortgage which is subject to the claim of a senior mortgage which has priority of claim.

overproduction A supply of goods greater than can be sold within a reasonable time at a price sufficient to keep a business or industry producing the product.

override A commission paid to managerial personnel in addition to their basic compensation.   **38**

oversavings 1) A situation where there are more liquid assets than can be profitably invested.

2) When capital-savings have been used to produce more goods than can be profitably sold.

oversold An opinion—the reverse of overbought. A single security or a market which, it is believed, has declined to an unreasonable level. See "technical position." **2**

oversubscription The situation in which, for a given issue of securities, more orders have been received than can be filled.

over-the-counter A term for the method of trading when securities are not listed on a recognized securities exchange and when transactions are made either by a broker acting directly on behalf of the buyer and seller or directly by a dealer. **40**

overtime Hours worked in excess of the maximum regular number of hours fixed by statute or collective agreement. **12**

ownership certificate A form furnished by the Collector of Internal Revenue for the filing of information as to the ownership of bonds containing a tax-free covenant. An ownership certificate must accompany the deposit of coupons from such bonds. **34**

ownership utility The feeling of satisfaction in possessing things. Since most things are acquired by work, exchange, or purchase, one would not acquire something unless it provided greater satisfaction or ownership utility than that which was used to acquire it.

P

pacesetter An individual worker in a business, generally manufacturing piecework, who is used as a guide to the rate of output that may be obtained. Since he is generally faster and more skilled, his production may be used as a goal for those less productive.

packaged mortgage plan A mortgage plan that permits the borrower to include as part of the mortgaged real estate such household equipment as refrigerators, ranges, and home laundries, thus bringing these articles under the lien of the mortgage. **33**

packing list The document which is included with goods

shipped, which includes a description of the type and number of items but generally not the prices.

paid-in capital Capital contributed by stockholders and credited to accounts other than capital stock. **21**

paid-in surplus That amount of surplus which was not earned but contributed to the corporation.

paid-up additions Units of single premium insurance purchased with participating policy dividends under one of the customary dividend options. **5**

paid-up stock Capital stock upon which the initial purchaser from the issuing corporation has paid in goods, services, or money an amount at least as much as the par value.

panic That part of a business cycle characterized by a very sharp drop in prices and general confidence in the economy and a high increase in business failures.

paper money Those pieces of paper which a sovereign designates to be money.

paper profit An unrealized profit on a security still held which would become realized profit if sold immediately. Paper profits become realized profits only when the security is sold.

paper rate A published railroad transport rate under which no traffic moves. **19**

par Technically, 100 percent; full value.

parallel standards A monetary system in which two or more metals are coined but in which there is no exchange ratio between the metals.

Pareto's Law A generalization which states that regardless of the form of a nation's institutional structure its income distribution will be the same.

par exchange rate The rate or price in gold, designated by the International Monetary Fund, in cooperation with a nation's monetary authorities, at which that currency may be exchanged for the currency of another member nation of the IMF whose currency is computed on the same basis. The nations need not be on a gold standard for in this case only gold is used as the common denominator for all the IMF members' currency.

par items Items for which a drawee bank will remit to another bank without charge. **25**

parity 1) The relationship of one foreign currency to another as indicated by their exchange value in gold or silver.

236

2) The relationship of agricultural prices in covered commodities, such as wheat and corn, to a base period of prices which farmers had to pay. The base period is used to measure the increase in prices for the commodities which the farmer purchases.

par list A list (issued by the Federal Reserve System) of banks which will remit in full for items payable to them.   **25**

parol evidence Testimony or evidence which is oral, as contrasted to written or documentary evidence.   **22**

partial limitation clause A provision in an insurance policy for the payment of the total loss when a loss is more than a specified amount.   **51, 52**

partial monopoly A condition of partial monopoly in which there are so few sellers of a product or service that each may affect the price and market and, in view of this, can judge the probable impact of his actions on the other sellers.

participation certificate An instrument that evidences a proportionate interest in a security or group of securities held by a trustee for the benefit of a group of investors.   **33**

participation loan Limitations have been set up by banking laws whereby banks are not permitted to lend more than a fixed percent of their capital and surplus to any one borrower. (In most states, this fixed percent is approximately 10%.) This limitation causes banks to invite other banks to participate in making a large loan. If the financial background and credit position of the borrower warrants the large loan, several banks may each lend a portion of the amount to the borrower. The participating banks work together in handling the loan, and work out a joint agreement as to the liquidation program of the loan, since some of the banks may wish to be paid off ahead of other banks.   **1**

partition A division of property held jointly or in common. It may be effected by consent of parties or by compulsion of law.   **35**

partnership An association of two or more persons for the conduct of an enterprise other than in corporate form. The rights, duties, and responsibilities of the people so associated may be covered by a partnership agreement or, if not, they are determined by law.   **22**

partnership certificate A certificate filed with a bank showing the interest of each partner in a business enterprise operating as a partnership. **1**

part-paid stock A stock on which part of the amount owed the corporation has not been paid.

party wall A dividing wall erected upon and over a line separating two adjoining properties and in which the owners of the respective parcels have common rights to its use. **54**

par value The principal or nominal value appearing on a bond, note, coupon, or other instrument calling for the payment of money. **25**

par-value stock Stock that has been assigned a definite value and the value is printed on the stock certificates. **16**

passbook A book issued to an inventor, saver, or borrower, which evidences his investment and subsequent additions or withdrawals in the case of a saver, and records the payments made in the case of a borrower. **31, 36**

passed dividend Omission of a regular or scheduled dividend. **2**

passive trade balance A trade deficit; an unfavorable balance of trade.

passive trust A trust in which the trustee has no active duties to perform being merely a titleholder; the same as bare, dry, or naked trust; opposed to an active trust. **30**

patent 1) A special license issued by the federal government that insures to an inventor the exclusive right to manufacture his invention for a period of seventeen years. **16**

2) The title deed by which the United States or a state conveys its lands. **5**

patent office That agency of the government which is in charge of records, granting of patents, and determining who is correct where conflicts regarding priority arise.

paternalism The actions of a company or a government in providing social-welfare benefits for workers or citizens.

pattern bargaining Collective bargaining in which the union tries to apply identical terms, conditions, or demands to a number of employers in an industry although the employers act individually rather than as a group. **12**

pawnbroker The businessman who will lend on items which are pledged as security for the loan. He is generally licensed by the local political subdivision and must report to police periodically those items which are pawned. If the loan is not repaid within the statute of limitations for such loans, the pawn-broker may sell the security to compensate for nonpayment.

pay 1) To remit; to give money or some other medium of exchange for goods delivered or services rendered.

2) To pay a check in cash, as when a check is paid by the paying teller.

3) To charge a check against a customer's account, as in the case of a check coming through the clearings.

payee The person or firm to whom a promissory note or a check is payable. **16**

payer The party primarily responsible for the payment of the amount owed as evidenced by a given negotiable instrument. **1**

payment bill A bill which is presented for payment rather than acceptance.

payroll taxes Taxes based on the wages and salaries of employees. They are also known as employment taxes. **16**

pecuniary exchange The use of money for purchasing things as compared with barter which does not use money.

pegged price 1) The agreed, customary, or legal price at which any commodity has been fixed.

2) A price level for a particular security at which buying support nearly always develops and prevents a decline—thus "pegging" the price. **44**

pendente lite During the continuance of a suit at law or in equity. **22**

Pennsylvania rule A rule that requires credit of extraordinary dividends received in trust on the basis of the source of such dividends; to income if declared from earnings of the corporation during the life of the trust, and to principal if from earnings accumulated before commencement of the trust. **22**

penny stocks Low-priced issues, often highly speculative, selling at less than $1 a share. Frequently used as a term of disparagement, although a few penny stocks have developed into investment-caliber issues. **2**

pension A regular allowance made to someone who has worked a certain number of years, attained a certain age, suffered some injury, retired, etc. **38**

pension plan An arrangement evidenced by a written agreement providing for the accumulation of funds from a corporation, or its employees, or both, to be used for monthly or other periodic payments to employees of the corporation after their retirement. **22**

pension pool A system for the payment of pension to workers in a limited geographic area in which subscribing employers all contribute according to some formula to a common fund or pool for their employees' pensions. In the event that any employee transfers from one of the subscribing employer's firm to another subscribing employer's firm, he has not lost any of the pension rights.

peppercorn rent A nominal rent, paid in order to give formal recognition to the landlord's position.

per capita A term expressing the result of dividing stated sums by the applicable number of people (population figures), thereby relating the sums to an amount per person, such as the proportion of a community's total debt per person. **40**

percentage lease A lease providing for payment of rent based on a percentage of the gross sales or the sales over a fixed amount. **22**

per-contra item In bookkeeping, a ledger account which exactly offsets some other ledger account.

per diem Per day.

perfect competition The market situation where no one trader can materially affect the market for a product.

peril Cause of a possible loss. Perils include such things as fires, windstorms, explosions, damage suits, robbery, and accidents. **50, 51, 52**

peril point That level below which a reduction in customs duty on imported goods would injure a domestic industry.

period of digestion A period immediately following the issuance of a large or a new security offering during which sales are being effected to more or less permanent investors. **40**

perjury Willful utterance of a false statement under oath. **38**

permissive-wage adjustment System authorizing the opening of negotiations for new wage rates at stated intervals during the life of a union contract, or when either party can demonstrate a significant change in factors such as prevailing wages, price of product, etc. **12**

permit A document giving the right to perform some action.

perpetual inventory (Book inventories) Records maintained for a manufacturing business so that they show a continuous inventory of such items as raw materials, goods in process, and finished goods. **16**

perpetuity Duration without limitation as to time. See "rule against perpetuities." **30**

per procuration The signature of a principal made by his agent. The agent instead of having power of attorney is given limited authority by the principal. The words "per procuration" call attention to the limitation, and the holder of the instrument is within his rights in requesting a statement in which the authority for the signature is given.

perquisite Any incidental gain or profit from work beyond monetary wages. Meals or clothing furnished an employee are examples of such benefits.

person An individual, partnership, association, joint stock company, trust, or corporation. **63**

personal account An account carried in the name of an individual or business.

personal check A check drawn by an individual on his personal account. **1**

personal credit That credit which an individual possesses as differentiated from credit of a firm, partnership, or corporation.

personal distribution The division of the total income of individuals among themselves.

personal finance company A personal loan company which lends individuals relatively modest amounts of money at rates of interest which are generally higher than bank rates.

personal holding company A device used by individuals for tax minimization. The Internal Revenue Code defines the conditions under which a corporation is considered to be a personal holding company and thus subject to special surtaxes.

personal income 1) Income earned or received by an individual. 2) National income, less various kinds of income not actually received by individuals (*i.e.,* undistributed corporate profits, corporate taxes, contributions for social insurance), plus certain receipts which do not arise from production (*i.e.,* transfer payments and government interest). **7**

personal property The rights, powers, and privileges a person has in movable things both corporeal (as furniture and jewelry) and incorporeal (as stocks and bonds). **31, 36**

personal property floater An insurance policy with broad coverage for personal property either at home or away. Contractual coverage of insured's personal effects against loss or theft.   **5**

personal property tax A tax on personal property such as home furnishings, jewelry, securities, and bank balances but not real estate.

personal representative A general term applicable to both executor and administrator.   **22**

personal saving The difference between disposable personal income and personal consumption expenditures. Personal saving includes the changes in cash and deposits, security holdings, indebtedness, reserves of life insurance companies and mutual savings institutions, the net investment of unincorporated enterprises and the acquisition of real property net of depreciation. Personal saving includes saving by individuals, nonprofit institutions, and private pension, health, welfare and trust funds.   **7**

personal selling Oral presentation in a conversation with one or more prospective customers for the purpose of making sales.   **13**

personal surety A person who agrees to be financially responsible for the debt of another person.   **16**

personalty Personal property.   **30**

personnel People employed in a business or other occupation.   **38**

per stirpes (by the branch) A term used in the distribution of property; distribution to persons as members of a family (per stirpes), and not as individuals (per capita). Two or more children of the same parent take per stirpes when together they take what the parent, if living, would take. For example, "I give my estate to my son A and to my grandsons C, D and E (the sons of my deceased son B). My grandsons are to take per stirpes." C, D and E take, as the sons of B (not as individuals), each receiving one-sixth of the estate (one-third of the one-half to which B would be entitled if living), while A receives one-half of the estate. Taking per stirpes is also known as taking by right of representation.   **22**

petty cash A sum of money, either in the form of currency or a special bank deposit, set aside for the purpose of making change or immediate payments of comparatively small amounts. See "imprest fund."   **29**

physical distribution Moving and handling products from the point of storage to the point of consumption or use.   **20**

physical inventory To take account of stock by actually hand-counting and listing all merchandise on hand.   **38**

physical value A term erroneously used to designate an estimate of reproduction or replacement cost, or the estimated value of physical assets as distinct from nonphysical assets.   **54**

picketing Union's patrolling alongside the premises of a business to organize the workers, to gain recognition as a bargaining agent, or to publicize a labor dispute with the owner or with some other firm with which the owner deals.   **12**

pictorial graph A graph that makes use of pictures, drawings, or cartoons to make the figures or proportions more interesting.   **16**

piece-rate plan A form of incentive plan whereby direct labor is paid a standard amount for each piece produced. See "direct labor."   **28**

piecework A means of paying workers by the number of items the worker processes during a period of time such as hour, day, or week.

piggyback trucking Transporting loaded truck trailers to distant points on railroad flatcars, rather than by pulling them over the highways by tractors.   **12**

pilferage Any petty thievery or the theft of a portion of property such as theft of a tire from an automobile.   **52**

pit The trading point in some exchanges.

place utility That added value gained by having a product where it is used or consumed.

plagiarism Literary or artistic theft; representing someone else's work as one's own.   **38**

plaintiff Individual who brings a lawsuit against a defendant.   **5**

plane of living Level of living. The material benefits which an individual or society possesses. Standard of living.

plant The building and equipment used by a business, usually a manufacturing concern.

plat A map or plan of an identified area of land.   **33**

pledge 1) To place something as security; guarantee.
2) The transference of property, such as the cash value of a life insurance policy, to a creditor as security for a debt.   **5**

plottage increment The increase or appreciation of the unit value resulting from the joining together of smaller lots, parcels, or land units into one large single ownership, the resulting total value being larger than the individual unit values. **54**

plutocracy A government or society in which the wealthy have control.

point In the case of shares of stock, a point means $1. If General Motors shares rise 3 points, each share has risen $3. In the case of bonds, a point means $10, since a bond is quoted as a percentage of $1,000. A bond which rises 3 points gains 3 percent of $1,000, or $30 in value. An advance from 87 to 90 would mean an advance in dollar value from $870 to $900 for each $1,000 bond. In the case of market averages, the word point means merely that and no more. If, for example, the Dow-Jones industrial average rises from 470.25 to 471.25, it has risen a point. A point in the averages, however, is not equivalent to $1. See "average." **2**

point-and-figure charting A technique for graphically plotting price changes in relation to previous price changes. The "point" refers to the price unit chosen for the security or commodity. Each such price change is indicated by a figure or mark such as an "X." The result appears as a line of varying vertical dimensions made up of "X's." These charts are used by market analysts as a means of judging the price action of the item being charted.

point of ideal proportions That theoretical balance of the capital, land, labor, and entrepreneurial ability in a business which would provide the greatest profit.

point of indifference That theoretical balance of capital, land, labor, and entrepreneurial ability in a business where one additional unit of any of the productive factors would just equal the probable return from such factor. At this point the business manager is indifferent in increasing his volume because his profit will not increase.

policy 1) A plan of action; a way of doing things.
2) A written agreement about insurance. **38**

policyholder The person insured or the one having control of the policy. Usually, but not necessarily, the insured. **42**

policy loan A loan made by an insurance company to a policyholder on the security of the cash value of his policy. **53**

policy reserves The funds that an insurance company holds specifically for the fulfillment of its policy obligations. Reserves are so calculated that, together with the future premiums and interest earnings, they will enable the company to pay all future claims. **53, 58**

policy value Amount of cash available to the insured on surrender of the policy. **42**

political economy A term, still used extensively in Europe for the subject-matter area; known as economics in the United States.

poll tax A head tax or capitation tax formerly associated with the payment required in some states before one could vote. It might, however, be tied to some other privilege.

pool A combination of resources, or funds for some common purpose or benefit. **38**

portal claims Wage claims for time spent on incidental activities before or after the regular working period. **12**

Portal-to-Portal Act Federal statute limiting employees' Wage-Hour Law suits based on "portal" claims. **12**

portal-to-portal pay Payment for time spent in traveling to and from the entrance to the employer's premises and the work area.

Port Authority The agency authorized by a state, states, or federal government which is empowered to regulate, plan, and finance traffic through a port.

port differential In commerce, the difference between through rates on the same class or commodity to or from competing ports, from or to the same point. **19**

portfolio Holdings of securities by an individual or institution. A portfolio may contain bonds, preferred stocks, and common stocks of various types of enterprises. **2**

port of entry Any seaport, airport, or place where customs duties are collected.

possession The right to exclusive occupancy and use of real property. **33**

possession utility See "ownership utility."

postal savings That service by the Post Office Department of many nations which permits deposit savings accounts to be made by individuals and for them to receive interest on maximum amounts within the limitations established.

postal savings certificates Those papers evidencing deposits in United States postal savings accounts which are not negotiable except to the named individual. The postal savings program was terminated in 1967.

postaudit An audit made after the transactions to be audited have taken place and have been recorded or have been approved for recording by designated officials, if such approval is required. See "preaudit." 29

postdate To date an instrument a time after that on which it is made. 38

posting The process of transferring journal entries to the ledger. 16

potential demand A loose term signifying an estimation of how much demand would or will exist for something at some time in the future. It is generally based on projection of economic trends and relationships.

potential stock The difference between the total authorized capital stock and the actually issued stock.

poverty The level of living at which an individual has so little of the necessities of life that his ability to retain physical efficiency has declined.

power in trust A power which the donee (the trustee) is under a duty to exercise in favor of the beneficiary of the trust. 22

power of alienation The power to assign, transfer, or otherwise dispose of property. 22

power of attorney A written document authorizing a named person to perform certain acts in place of the signer. It is usually acknowledged before a public officer or witness and is void on the death of the signer. 31, 36

preaudit An examination for the purpose of determining the propriety of proposed financial transactions and of financial transactions which have already taken place but have not yet been recorded, or, if such approval is required, before the approval of the financial transactions by designated officials for recording. There is frequently confusion between the audit as a whole and the auditing of individual transactions. For example, if we speak of an audit as a whole, then an independent auditor may be said to be performing a postaudit, since most of the transactions whose propriety he examines have already been approved for recording. The independent auditor may, however, also have to deal with transactions which have not been approved for recording (for example, accrued salaries and wages) but in speaking of an audit as a whole we may ignore these and say that the audit under consideration is a postaudit. On the other hand, if the audit of individual transactions is involved, the independent auditor, in the case illustrated, would be performing a postaudit with respect to most of the transactions, but a preaudit with respect to some of them. Sometimes the term "preaudit" is used as a synonym for "internal audit" (*q.v.*) but such usage is not recommended. See "postaudit." **29**

precatory words Expressions in a will praying or requesting (but not directing) that a thing be done or not done. **22**

preclusive buying The purchase of goods and services, not for the purpose of one's own normal use, but rather for the purpose of preventing someone else from buying them.

predatory price-cutting The competitive device of selling merchandise or a service below purchase price or cost of production. This term does not include the sale at below-cost prices of seasonal or perishable merchandise. **13**

preemptive rights A prior right or privilege, such as the right of a stockholder to be offered the privilege of buying additional shares before the stock is offered to others. **22**

prefabricated 1) A wall or other unit fabricated prior to erection or installation on a building or structure foundation. **11** 2) The manufacturing of a modular unit or standard item which permits the manufactured part to be assembled at some other site, rather than fully manufactured there.

preference share Preferred stock. See "preferred stock."

preferential duty A customs duty that varies when levied on similar items because of the country of origin, type of labor used to make the product, or some other reason.

preferential shop A business which has a labor-relations policy of favoring union members over nonunion employees.

preferred creditor A creditor whose claim takes legal preference over the claim of another (such as government taxes over the amount owed to an individual). **1**

preferred stock A class of stock with a claim on the company's earnings before payment may be made on the common stock and usually entitled to priority over the common stock and usually entitled to dividends at a specified rate—when declared by the board of directors and before payment of a dividend on the common stock—depending upon the terms of the issue. See "preferred stock, cumulative" and "preferred stock, participating." 2

preferred stock, callable Can be called in for payment at a stated price. 55

preferred stock, cumulative A stock having a provision that if one or more dividends are omitted, the omitted dividends must be paid up before dividends may be paid on the company's common stock. 2

preferred stock, participating A preferred stock which is entitled to its stated dividend and, also, to additional dividends on a specified basis upon payment of dividends on the common stock. 2

preferred stock, prior A preferred stock which usually takes precedence over other preferreds issued by the same company. 2

premium 1) A consideration (price) paid for a contract of insurance.
2) A fee charged for the granting of a loan. 31, 36
3) The amount by which a security is priced over par. A $1,000 bond with a market price of $1,050 has a premium of $50. 49

premium discount plan A plan available in some rating jurisdictions providing for a percentage reduction on premium dependent upon the size of the premium. In workmen's compensation insurance it is recognized that the proportionate cost of issuing and servicing a policy is less as the premium increases. The premium discount plan gives the policyholder the benefit of this reduction. 52

premium for risk The net return on an investment after the "pure interest" for that type of investment has been deducted from the gross income. See "pure interest."

premium loan A policy loan made for the purpose of paying premiums. 53

premium on securities The amount by which a security (a bond or a share of stock) is bought or sold for more than its face or par value; opposed to discount on securities. 22

premium pay A rate of pay, higher than that paid for normal working hours, that is given as compensation for work performed during inconvenient hours or uncomfortable conditions.

premium rate 1) The price per unit of insurance.

2) In security trading, it is the premium which must be paid to borrow stocks for a short sale when the stocks are not selling flat.

premium stock A stock which lends at a premium, *i.e.,* an amount has been charged for loaning it to someone who borrowed it to make delivery on a short sale. Also may denote an above-average, superior stock; an established leader. **44**

prepaid charge plan An accumulation plan under which the major deductions for selling charges are made during the first year or two of the program. Investor must complete program in order to minimize purchasing expenses. **3**

prepaid expense An expenditure, often recurrent, for benefits as yet not received. Unexpired insurance is a prepaid expense from the policyholder's point of view. **5**

prepaid transportation charges Transportation charges paid at the shipping point by the person who is sending the shipment. **16**

prepayment penalty A special charge, provided for in a mortgage contract, which may be collected from the mortgagor if he repays all or a part of the loan in advance of the due date. **33**

prerefunding A refunding in which the securities eligible for conversion mature in not more than one year. **47**

prescription A title to property or means of obtaining title based upon uninterrupted possession.

presentation A legal term used in connection with negotiable instruments. The act of presentation technically means the actual delivery of a negotiable instrument by a holder in due course to the drawee for acceptance, or to the maker for payment. Upon presentation, the holder in due course requests acceptance of a draft, or requests payment of the instrument from the maker of a note, check, etc. See "negotiable." **1**

present beneficiary See "immediate beneficiary."

present value 1) The current value of something, taking into account depreciation, appreciation, wear and tear, etc.
2) The discounted value of a certain sum due and payable at a certain specified future date. **1**

price The amount, in the current medium of exchange, which is asked or received in exchange for an economic good. **33**

price-consumption curve An indifference curve which shows the various amounts of two goods which will be purchased if the ratio between their prices is varied.

price controls The restrictions on price increases by some agency such as the Office of Price Stabilization or Office of Price Administration. Both of these agencies were emergency activities caused by war.

price discrimination The charging of different prices for a good or service to similar customers.

priced out of the market A market situation in which the price asked for a product has eliminated many potential buyers and thus the volume of sales and profits has declined.

price-earnings ratio The price of a stock divided by its earnings per share.

price-fixing or **stabilization** Holding prices at a certain level. Often attempted by governments, but generally illegal if attempted by private firms.

price index A statistical device for showing the percentage change in the price of a thing or a group of things from the base period which is assigned the value of one hundred.

price leadership A situation in which a major producer of a product establishes a price and other producers in the same field adopt that price as their own.

price level A relative position in the scale of prices as determined by a comparison of prices (of labor, materials, capital, etc.), as of one time with prices as of other times.   **54**

price loco The price at the location where the product or service was purchased.

price spread See "markup."

price supports Any of many ways to keep prices from falling below some preconceived level. Agricultural prices in the United States are in many cases supported by such devices as subsidies, loans, government purchases, soil banks, and school lunch programs.

price system An economy in which goods and services are produced for profit and the amounts produced and consumed are determined by price.

pricing Deciding what prices to charge.   **38**

prima facie At first view. Prima facie evidence is such as in law sufficient to establish a fact, unless rebutted.   **5**

primary beneficiary See "immediate beneficiary."

primary boycott The action by a union to prevent the handling, purchase, or use of a product of an employer with whom the union has a dispute.

primary deposit A deposit in a bank which is created by an inflow of cash or checks as compared with a deposit created by the commercial bank making a loan and crediting the account of the borrower with a deposit for the amount of the loan. The latter is a derivative deposit. However, a derivative deposit, when withdrawn by check may become a primary deposit in the receiving bank.

primary distribution Also called primary offering. The original sale of a company's securities. See "investment banking" and "secondary distribution." **2**

primary industries Those which take their materials directly from natural resources: mining, agriculture, trapping, or fishing. **38**

primary money Standard money.

primary reserves Those assets of a bank, consisting of cash and balances on deposit with other banks, which are immediately available for the payment of liabilities. **33**

prime bill of exchange A draft or trade acceptance which states on the face of the instrument that it was created through a business transaction involving the movement of goods. **1**

prime cost A direct cost; an operating cost; a running cost; a cost which fluctuates directly with the volume of production, such as the cost of the raw material.

prime maker The party (or parties) who signs his name to a negotiable instrument and who becomes the original primary responsible party for its payment. See "liability, direct." **1**

prime rate The minimum interest rate on bank loans as set by commercial banks and granted to only top business borrowers. The rate is influenced by the size of the loan, larger loans receiving better rates; and by general business conditions, geographical area, availability of reserves, etc. **44**

primogeniture The right of the eldest son to inherit such things as real estate or title to the exclusion of other children in the family.

principal 1) The sum of money stated in a contract, an account, or a financial instrument as distinguished from the sum actually to be paid; in other words, the amount of a loan or debt exclusive of interest.

2) A person who is primarily liable on an obligation.

3) A person who appoints another person to act for him as agent. **33**

priority Legal preference. **5**

priority system A technique for distributing a limited supply of goods among the members of the society on some basis other than complete reliance on price sovereignty. In periods of emergency, where supplies are abnormally limited, it may be deemed more socially desirable to have a distribution of scarce products based on allocation. Ration books, ration stamps, and similar devices are used in the consumer area. Certificates of necessity and quotas may be used in the production area.

prior stock A preferred stock.

prison labor Work done by convicts. **12**

private bank An unincorporated institution which is owned and operated by an individual or a partnership. It may or may not be subject to supervision by the banking authorities, depending on the laws of the particular state in which it is located. **25**

private brands Brands sponsored by merchants or agents as distinguished from those sponsored by manufacturers or producers. **13**

private carrier An individual contract carrier as compared to a common or public carrier. **5**

private corporation A corporation founded and operated for purposes of making money for the stockholders of the company.

private debt The monetary amount owed by the people and businesses of a nation and not including the amount owed by the governmental units, federal, state, or local.

private enterprise Those profit-seeking activities carried out by private individuals in any business form. Activities of government agencies, even if producing profits, do not come under the heading of private enterprise.

private property That which is individually owned. The right of an individual or firm to use and dispose of goods or things within the normal police powers of a government.

private trust 1) A trust created for the benefit of a designated beneficiary or designated beneficiaries; as a trust for the benefit of the settlor's or the testator's wife and children; opposed to a charitable (or public) trust.

2) A trust created under a declaration of trust or under a trust

252

agreement; as a living trust or an insurance trust; opposed to a trust coming under the immediate supervision of a court. See "court trust." **22**

private-wire house A brokerage firm that leases telegraph wires to various cities, especially financial and commodity centers.

privilege Synonymous to a stock-option contract, such as a call or put, which permits one of the parties to exercise some right or privilege stated in the contract during the specified time period. **44**

privilege tax See "occupation tax."

privity Exists where heirs, executors, and certain others succeed to the rights of a contract. This permits them to have the same rights as the original party. Privity may be a factor in action of negligence. **5**

probability The likelihood that a future event will take place. **5**

probate court A court having jurisdiction of the proof of wills, the settlement of estates and, usually, of guardianships. In some states it is the district court. **5**

probate of will Formal proof before the proper officer or court that the instrument offered is the last will of the decedent, as it purports and is alleged to be. **30**

probationary employee A worker hired with the understanding that he may be discharged with or without cause during an initial trial period. **12**

proceeds A very general term used to designate the total amount realized or received in any transaction, whether it be a sale, an issue of stock, the collection of receivables, a donation, or the borrowing of money. **17**

process effects That increase in consumer expenditures which has come about because of an increase in governmental expenditures.

produce exchange 1) A spot market for such items as perishable agricultural products.

2) A contract market in which futures contracts are bought and sold for products of agriculture.

producers' capital See "instrumental capital."

producers' cooperative marketing That type of cooperative marketing which involves primarily the sale of goods or services of the associated producing membership. **13**

producers' goods See "capital goods."

production The creation of something capable of satisfying a need.

production factors Measurements such as time series and economic indexes which provide data on productivity.

production function A curve or schedule which shows how total quantity of a product will vary with changing proportions of factors of production such as labor and machinery.

productivity That which a man or machine produces within a stated period of time. It may also be expressed as an increase in the rate of production from one period to another.

productivity theory That attempt to explain wage rates in terms of the value or productivity of work performed.

profit The excess of the selling price over all costs and expenses incurred in making the sale. The reward to the entrepreneur for the risks assumed by him in the establishment, operation, and management of a given enterprise or undertaking. See "entrepreneur."   1

profit and loss account 1) Account transferred from accounts receivable to separate ledger.

2) Amount deducted from accounts receivable balance.

3) An account deemed to be uncollectible, or an account which is a certain number of months past due, becomes eligible for transfer to the "profit and loss account" ledger.   26

profit and loss statement See "income statement."

profit-sharing plan An arrangement between an employer and his employees by which employees are to receive a fixed share of all or part of the profits.   12

profit taking 1) Selling to take a profit.

2) The process of converting paper profits into cash.   2

progressive taxation Any tax which has the rate increase as the item that is subject to tax increases in size or amount. The income tax, federal or state, is an example of a progressive tax.

prohibited risk A line of insurance which an insurance company will not insure under any condition due to an unusually high risk.

proletariat Workers, unskilled and semiskilled. Wage earners.

promissory note An unconditional written promise to pay a fixed amount of money at a definite time. It is signed by the person or persons agreeing to make the payment.   16

promoter An individual who, acting as a middleman, brings together the various needed factors of a venture in business, especially as they are associated with a new firm.

proof of loss In insurance, a written statement complying with certain conditions made by the insured and given to the insurance company. Its purpose is to place before the company sufficient information concerning the loss to enable it to determine its liability under the policy or bond. **50, 52**

propensity to consume The relationship between total income and the total of consumer expenditures. The propensity thus is expressed as a percentage of consumer expenditures divided by income.

propensity to invest That proportion or percentage of national income which is invested in new capital formation.

propensity to save That proportion or percentage of national income which is not used for consumption. It is derived by subtracting consumption from income and dividing the result by income.

property That which one owns; the possession or possessions of a particular owner. **38**

property account In bookkeeping, a real account. An account that is not closed out when a balance is taken but is continued to the next accounting period.

property tax A general property tax. A levy by a governmental unit on any asset. The asset may be real, such as land and buildings, or it may be personal such as deposits or securities.

proportionality, law of An economic concept which states that in any act of production there is an optimum point of production by using the correct proportions of land, labor, capital, and management. Also known as law of variable proportions.

proportional taxation A tax levy designed to apply the same rate of taxation to the property subject to the tax. Thus, a property valued at twice the amount of another property would pay the same rate which would result in a monetary amount of twice the tax on the second property.

proprietary corporation A nonoperating parent company of a nonoperating controlling company.

proprietorship The owner of the business; ownership. **38**

proprietory accounts Those accounts which show actual financial condition and operations such as actual assets, liabilities, reserves, surplus, revenues and expenditures, as distinguished from budgetary accounts. **29**

pro rata In proportion to the total amount. **31, 36**

pro rata distribution clause In a fire insurance policy, it provides that the amount of insurance written shall apply to each building or location in that proportion which the value of each building or location bears to the total value of the described property. **52**

pro rata liability clause Provides that the insurance company is liable for not more than the proportion of loss which the amount insured under the policy bears to all insurance policies covering the loss. **52**

pro rata rate A premium rate charged for a short term, at the same proportion of the rate for a longer term as the short term bears to the longer term. **51**

prospectus 1) An outline or plan of a proposed enterprise or undertaking.

2) A brief description of a property for sale or lease, usually including basic specifications.

3) A detailed statement issued by a company prior to the sale of new or additional securities, giving a full description of facts and information as required by the Securities and Exchange Commission. **40**

prosperity That phase of the business cycle in which production in the general economy is at a high level.

protectionism The practice of protecting a nation's industries from foreign competition.

protective tariff A customs duty schedule which permits domestic producers of the scheduled items to be able to profitably sell and continue to produce without fear of the competition of imported similar products.

protest A written statement by a notary public, or other authorized person, under seal for the purpose of giving formal notice to parties secondarily liable that an instrument has been dishonored, either by refusal to accept or by refusal to make payment. **25**

proxy A person authorized to act for another. **35**

prudent investment cost The amount arrived at in valuation of a business or property which considers original cost of the property but deducts from that amount those expenses or frills which a prudent man would not accept.

prudent man rule An investment standard. In some states, the law requires that a fiduciary, such as a trustee, may invest the fund's money only in a list of securities designated by the state —the so-called legal list. In other states, the trustee may invest in a security if it is one which a prudent man of discretion and intelligence, who is seeking a reasonable income and preservation of capital, would buy. **2**

psychic income The nonmonetary return from activity. While all people may obtain a feeling of satisfaction from their work, certain activities such as teaching, preaching, the creative arts, and social work are considered to provide great psychic income to those engaged in such fields. In part, this is used to explain why people will do such things when they could earn more in other activities.

psychological theory of the cycle A theory which attributes the rise and fall of the business cycle to varying degrees of optimism and pessimism on the part of the business community.

public administrator A county officer whose main official duty is to settle the estates of persons who die intestate. **22**

public carrier Individual or company offering to transport people or merchandise for a fee. Such public or common carriers are required by law to accept shipments from all who request and pay for their services. **5**

public corporation Any corporation formed by and for a governmental agency to help in the conducting of public activities.

public credit The credit of a government or subdivision of a government as distinguished from the private credit of private firms or individuals.

public debt That total or subtotal of the debt of any or all governments, federal, state, or local.

public domain 1) The portion of the land owned by the government.
2) That situation in which the period of copyright or patent has passed and anyone may freely use or reproduce the thing patented or copyrighted.

public finance Those financial activities which are associated with any phase of government. Taxes, customs, public debt, public expenditures, and related fields all comprise public finance.

public good Those economic goods or services which the government, federal, state, or local, makes available without direct costs to its citizens. It would include such things as public roads, public health programs, public libraries, public parks, and education.

Public Housing Administration That part of the United States Housing and Home Finance Agency which is concerned with the provision of financing and legislation on the national level for local public housing.

publicity The process of securing public notice.   **38**

public lands See "public domain."

public ownership The control and ownership of some productive facility for providing some good or service to the citizens of a community or nation by an agency of government. Public ownership is not uncommon in the public utility fields.

public property That property which is owned by other than the individual or individuals or private corporations; that is, property whose ownership is vested in the community.   **54**

public relations The systematic development of favorable contacts with the public.   **31**

public revenue Any income received by the government such as from taxes, customs, franchises, or services.

Public Service Commission That state agency which establishes rates and supervises public-utility corporations.

public-service corporation See "public utility."

public space Any area where the public may freely enter in the normal course of business and during business hours. A private establishment such as a store or bank has a space for the public and customers to transact their business. Such an area is called public space.

public trust The same as a charitable trust; opposed to a private trust.   **22**

public utility In the generally accepted sense, privately owned (as opposed to publicly owned) corporations engaged in public-service enterprises supplying electricity, gas, telephone, water, and other services.   **40**

public warehouse Those storage facilities which are available to the general public as distinguished from private warehouses which are for the exclusive use of one firm.

public works The activities of governmental agencies in providing public improvements such as roads, parks, sewers, and other physical structures as compared with services.

pump priming The expenditure of governmental funds, generally during periods of depression, for the purpose of creating jobs and demand for material which in turn will cause recovery.

purchase A term applicable to every method of acquiring property except by descent—that is, by right of blood, or by charitable gift.

purchase money mortgage A mortgage given by the purchaser to the seller as security for the payment of a part of the purchase price of property.   **33**

purchase order A document which authorizes the delivery of specified merchandise or the rendering of certain services and the making of a charge for them.   **29**

purchasing power The capacity to purchase possessed by an individual buyer, a group of buyers, or the aggregate of the buyers in an area or a market.   **13**

purchasing power of the dollar A measurement of the quantity (not quality) of goods and services that a dollar will buy compared with the amount that it could buy in some base period. It is obtained by taking the reciprocal of a price index, usually the consumers' price index.   **7**

pure competition The market situation where no one trader can materially affect the market price of a product.

pure interest A theoretical concept that excludes all costs for risk and overhead from the cost paid for capital. See "consols."

push money (pm) Commissions paid retail clerks to encourage disposal of certain items; a form of incentive premium.   **12**

put A contract to have the option to sell a security within a stated time and amount to the drawer of the option. It is the opposite of a call. See "call."

pyramiding Has two major meanings: 1) A situation where a series of holding companies own stock in related holding or operating companies. Generally, the holding is for control and speculative profit and does not serve as an improvement in the operating efficiency of the individual companies.
2) The use of the increased value of a purchased security above the margin requirement is used as the collateral to purchase additional securities, also on margin. In turn, if these increase in price over the margin required, additional purchases are made. It tends to magnify profits in a bull market and magnify losses in a bear market.

Q

qualified acceptance In reality, a counteroffer to another's original offer. To be binding, original acceptance must be unqualified. Since a condition or qualification is made by one party the other must accept the qualification completely before the contract has both offer and acceptance. If changes are made, then an entirely new offer is being presented for approval or rejection.

qualified endorsement Use of such words or terms as "without recourse" preceding the endorsement which serves as a limitation of the warranties of the one making the endorsement.

qualified report A report with exceptions or inadequate facts so that full credence should not be given to the finding. A credit report on an applicant for insurance may qualify some of the findings.   5

quantity theory of money The belief that prices are related directly to the quantity of money in circulation. As the quantity of money increases, prices increase; as the money in circulation decreases prices also decrease. Modern economists add additional factors to the equation of exchange and various formulas express the idea.

quarter stock Stock with a par value of twenty-five dollars per share.

quasi contract 1) An obligation similar in character to that of a contract, but which arises not from an agreement between the parties but from some relationship between them, or from a voluntary act by one or more of them. For example, the management of the affairs of another without authority, or the management of a common property without authority.   22
2) Situation imposed by law to prevent unjust enrichment or injustice and not dependent on agreement of the parties to the contract.   5

quasi corporation A political subdivision such as an unincorporated town that operates in the manner of an incorporated municipality.

quasi-public corporation An incorporated organization that is privately operated but in which some general interest of the public is evident.   5

quickie strikes Work stoppages called without advance notice, usually because of some employer practice resented by the employees or the local union, and usually not authorized by the national or international union.   **12**

quick ratio The ratio between the quick assets and the current liabilities; an indication of the ability of a business to pay all of its current liabilities quickly in cash.   **16**

quieting title Removing a cloud from a title by a proper action in court.   **5**

quitclaim deed A deed by which the owner of real estate conveys to another whatever title or interest he has to the property, but which makes no representation that the property is free from encumbrances, except those created by the owner himself.   **31, 36**

quitrent A rent paid by a freeholder or copyholder for release from some service otherwise required by him.

quorum The minimum number of persons necessary to transact business of a corporation, legislative body, assembly, etc.   **35**

quota sample The division of a statistical universe into groups and then taking a sample of these groups in the same proportion these groups have to the total.

R

rack jobber A wholesaler serving retail stores, especially supermarkets; offers a complete service in the merchandising of certain items of nonfood departments—housewares, toiletries, toys, and soft goods—thus relieving the store of inventory as well as merchandising activities; selects, assembles, prices, and delivers merchandise, and arranges and maintains the display on the shelves or racks on the dealer's floors; sells principally on a consignment basis but frequently on other terms.   **24**

rack rent A very high contract rent for a property which equals or exceeds the economic rent of the property.

Railway Labor Act Federal statute recognizing the right of collective bargaining in the railroad and airline industries.   **12**

raised check One on which the amount has been fraudulently increased.   **25**

rally A brisk rise following a decline in the general price level of the stock market, or in an individual stock.   **2**

range 1) The discrepancy between the highest and lowest values in a sample.

2) In the land laws of the United States, a strip of land six miles wide, running north and south, marked off by government survey. **5**

rate That fixed relationship between two series of data. Such as a 6% rate of interest on a loan, or a wage rate of two dollars per hour, or a tax rate of one dollar of tax for every hundred dollars of valuation.

rate base Those factors such as cost of plant, equipment, labor, rent, capital charges and other costs which are included in a consideration for establishing a rate. The rate base permits the businessman to obtain a fair and reasonable return.

rate of exchange The ratio at which foreign currency exchanges for a domestic currency. See "foreign exchange."

rate of return 1) The yield obtainable on a security based on its purchase price or its current market price. This may be the amortized yield to maturity on a bond or the current income return.

2) The income earned by a public utility company on its property or capital investment, expressed as a percentage. **40**

rate regulation The establishment of a rate or a maximum or minimum range of rate fluctuation by some authoritative body such as a Public Utility Commission.

rate war A destructive type of competition in which the various sellers of a good or service progressively decrease their prices even below their costs for the purposes of driving their competitors out of business.

ratification Confirmation of a contract or act done by oneself or by one's agent. **35**

rating 1) The evaluation of the moral or other risk of an individual or organization.

2) The making of insurance, freight, or other rates or charges.

rating bureau Organization which prepares insurance studies and these rates are used by members. It classifies risk and promulgates rates, usually on the basis of statistical data compiled by the bureau or of inspection of risks made by it. **51**

rating, experience Determination of the insurance premium rate for an individual risk partially or wholly on the basis of that risk's own experience. **51**

ratio chart A logarithmic or semilogarithmic graphic device to show rates of changes in data rather than absolute variations in data.

rationalization Administrative techniques and policies which increase productivity.

rationing of exchange A system which requires exporters to sell all foreign exchange to the government for domestic currency. The government then sells foreign exchange to those importers engaged in approved activities.

raw materials Articles that are either changed in form or united with other articles in a manufacturing business to become a part of the finished products of the factory. **16**

real account See "property account."

real estate The right, title or interest that a person has in real property, as distinguished from the property itself, which is the subject matter of the interest. **30**

real estate tax That tax or amount of money levied by taxing authority against the ownership of real estate for purposes of financing the functioning of the government. **5**

real investment Capital formation. The production or creation of new capital.

realistic method The inductive method of logical reasoning from observed data which permits a hypothesis.

realization The act or process of converting an asset or the total assets of an individual or business into cash. **1**

realized profit or loss A profit or loss resulting from the sale or other disposal of a security, as distinguished from a paper profit or loss. **40**

real money Money, the composition of which contains one or more metals having intrinsic value, as distinguished from representative money such as currency issued by a realm, and checks, drafts, etc., issued by legal entities in society. **1**

real property Land, buildings, and other improvements to property that may legally be classified as real, in contrast to personal. **33**

real wages Wages in terms of goods and services that money wages will buy. **12**

recapitalization Any change in the existing capital structure of a corporation. This may involve changing the value of stock, issuing new stocks or bonds, or calling in bonds or callable preferred.

recapture clause A clause in an agreement providing for retaking or recovering possession. As used in percentage leases, to take a portion of earnings or profits above a fixed amount of rent. **54**

recapture of earnings See "recapture clause."

receivable An asset in the form of an amount which is due from a borrower.

receiver A person appointed, ordinarily by a court of equity jurisdiction, to receive and hold in trust, money or other property which is the subject of litigation, pending the suit, as in case of a person incompetent to manage his property, or of the dissolution and winding up of a partnership or a corporation. **35**

receiver's certificate A note issued by a receiver for the purpose of obtaining working capital to keep a distressed corporation in operation. The note is generally for a short term and given a priority over other open-book accounts. The exact priority is determined by authority of the court.

receivership The status of a carrier's property while in charge of a receiver appointed by a court of equity. See "trusteeship." **19**

recession That phase of a business cycle characterized by a reduction in the level of production and employment from the previous phase.

reciprocal business An order to buy or sell securities given by one person or firm to another in return for a more or less equivalent order, or business favor, previously granted. Quite often, brokerage firms will have a correspondent relationship with another firm which may be a member of a particular stock exchange, and orders brought in may be repaid by another type of business in return. **44**

reciprocal exchange An unincorporated association organized to write insurance for its members. Members are both insurers and policyholders. Each member is liable for his proportionate share of total liabilities but may be assessed for additional funds if they are needed. **52**

reciprocal law State laws providing for equal privileges to all alien insurers as accorded domestic insurers in alien states. See "retaliatory law." **42**

reciprocity Equality between citizens and businesses of two countries with respect to commercial privileges in trade, tariffs, taxation, and related governmental restrictions.

reclamation 1) A negotiable instrument such as a check or note which has incorrectly been posted through a clearinghouse and is now to be corrected or reclaimed.

2) The process of making a heretofore unproductive asset such as eroded land productive by restoring through terracing and good land management.

recognition Employer acceptance of a union as the exclusive bargaining representative for the employees in the bargaining unit.   12

reconciliation 1) Bringing into agreement or harmony.

2) Adjusting amounts which should be equal.   38

reconversion The administrative and tool changes necessary to permit a business, industry, or economy to produce a different style or type of product or service.

recordation In connection with a mortgage, the recording of the fact that a lien has been created against certain property, described in the mortgage, such entry usually being made in the appropriate public record of the county or other jurisdiction in which the particular property is located.   22

record date The day designated by a corporation for the determination of holders entitled to a dividend, previously declared.   22

recourse The right to require performance of an obligation by an indorser, assignor, or other prior holder of an instrument.   33

recovery 1) That phase of a business cycle characterized by improvement in the level of business. Recovery is generally preceded by recession or depression but precedes prosperity.

2) Money or other valuables that an insurance company obtains from subrogation, salvage, or reinsurance.   5

redeemable stock A preferred stock which is callable.

redemption The liquidation of an indebtedness whether on maturity or prior to maturity, such as the retirement of a bond issue prior to its maturity date.   1

redemption agent A firm which redeems obligations. These obligations may be securities, mutilated currency, trading stamps, or similar claims.

redemption fund A fund created for the purpose of retiring an obligation maturing serially, or purchasing them as they become available.   1

redemption price The price at which a bond may be redeemed before maturity, at the option of the issuing company. Redemption value also applies to the price the company must pay to call in certain types of preferred stock. See "preferred stock, callable." **2**

red herring An advance or preliminary prospectus which gives the details of an expected offering of corporate securities. A statement in red ink stamped on the prospectus indicates the issue cannot be sold until the Securities and Exchange Commission finishes the process of registering and clearing it for sale. **44**

rediscount The process by which a Federal Reserve or other bank discounts for a member or customer bank the notes, drafts, or acceptances which the member or customer bank has already discounted for its customers. The rediscounted paper itself. **25**

rediscount rate The interest rate charged by one of the twelve Federal Reserve Banks to a member bank on eligible commercial paper which the member bank has used as collateral for a loan.

redraft A cross bill. When a check or other bill of exchange which has been presented for payment and is dishonored, and as a result is protested, the holder of the instrument may draw a bill of exchange for the original amount of the obligation plus the cost of the notary and other protest expenses. This new instrument is known as a redraft or cross bill.

reexport A product which has been imported into a foreign trade zone of a country and then is exported in relatively the same basic form.

referee 1) A person appointed in court proceedings for the judicial settlement of a trustee's accounts to conduct hearings with the interested parties and report his findings to the court. **22**
2) A medical examiner who, in addition to the regular duties, also secures special underwriting reports. **42**

refinancing The payment of indebtedness with funds obtained through the creation of a new obligation or obligations. **33**

reflation An increase or decrease in the quantity of money by action of the monetary authorities in an attempt to return to a previous level of prices.

reformation of contract Proof in a court of equity that a contract does not state the true intentions of both parties will permit reformation of the contract to correct the contract. **5**

refunding The refinancing of an indebtedness on or before its maturity in order to reduce the fixed interest charge or to reduce the amount of fixed payment, due to the inability to conveniently liquidate an indebtedness when it matures.   1

register A record for the consecutive entry of a certain class of events, documents, or transactions, with a proper notation of all the required particulars.   29

register check The title given to a check used in parts of the United States in lieu of cashier's checks or bank drafts.   1

registered mail The United States Post Office Department will insure up to a maximum of $1,000 mail sent registered. If the value is higher than $1,000, it may be insured with insurance companies that provide that service.   5

registered representative Present name for the older term "customer's man." The registered representative is an employee of a stock exchange member firm, registered with the exchange as having passed certain tests and met certain requirements, authorized to serve the public customers of his firm. Also known as "customer's broker."   2

registrar In connection with stock, the agent which affixes its signature to each stock certificate issued, the object being the prevention of overinsurance. In connection with bonds, the agent which maintains the record of ownership of registered bonds.   22

registration statement A statement which sets forth certain facts as prescribed by statute and by rules and regulations issued thereunder, and which (subject to certain exceptions) must be filed with the Securities and Exchange Commission prior to a public offering of new securities.   22

regressive supply A market condition in which, as the price of something declines, a larger quantity is supplied.

regressive tax A tax designed so that the rate goes down as the value of the thing taxed goes up. A tax which will fall proportionately more on the poor than on the rich. A tax on food would be regressive because poor people spend a larger proportion of their income on food than the wealthy.

regular-way delivery Unless otherwise specified, securities (other than government's) sold on the New York Stock Exchange are to be delivered to the buying broker by the selling broker and payment made to the selling broker by the buying broker on the fourth business day after the transaction. Regular-way delivery for government bonds is the following business day. See "delivery" and "transfer." **2**

rehypothecate To transfer to another a note which is secured by the hypothecation of property. **25**

reinstatement Restoration of an insurance policy to full force and effect upon presentation of evidence of insurability satisfactory to the company, together with payment of premiums due. For life policies, an additional charge for interest may be made. See "automatic reinstatement clause." **42**

reinsurance Insurance for the insurer. A portion or all of a risk is transferred from the issuing company to a reinsurer to prevent undue fluctuations in death claims. The insured, being covered under the standard terms of the issuing company, deals directly with the original insurer and is in no way affected by a reinsuring agreement. See "retrocession" and "share agreements." **42**

reinsurance, assumption Transfer of a full insurance risk because of the insolvency or discontinuance of the original insurance company. **42**

reinsurance carrier The reinsurer. A second insurance company assuming liability for all or a portion of a risk by transfer. **42**

reinsurance, catastrophe Agreement whereby a reinsuring company assumes defined losses above a stated amount that result from a catastrophe. **5**

reinsurance, excess Reinsurance against loss in an amount in excess of a stipulated primary amount. **5**

reinsurance, share Acceptance by a reinsurer of a share of the risk or risks of the reinsured, the two companies sharing all losses and expenses as agreed. **51**

reinsurance treaty Contract by which one insurer agrees to reinsure risks written by the other, subject to conditions of the contract. **42**

reinsured An insurer whose risks are reinsured by a reinsurer. **51**

reinsurer See "reinsurance carrier."

release 1) A written statement that an obligation has been satisfied.

2) The giving up of a claim by the person entitled to it, to the person against whom the claim exists. **31, 36**

release of mortgage The act of releasing or relinquishing the claim against property established by a mortgage. The instrument by which such a release is effected. **33**

remainder The estate in property created simultaneously with other estates, such as a life estate, by a single grant and consisting of the rights and interests contingent upon and remaining after the termination of the other estate. **5**

remainderman The person who is entitled to an estate after the prior estate has expired. Originally the term applied, and in many states still does apply, to real property only. **30**

remargining The act of putting up additional margin against a loan. When securities have dropped in price, brokers may require their customers who have margin accounts to provide additional collateral either in the form of other securities or of cash.

remonetize To reinstate as standard, lawful money—a type of money which had been demonetized.

rent The return in money, labor, or chattel provisions which are given by the renter to the owner of the land in compensation for the use or right of use of the real estate. **5**

rent control Control by a government agency of the amount to be charged as rent. **54**

reopening clause Clause in a collective bargaining agreement providing for reopening negotiations as to wage rates, etc., during the term of the agreement. **12**

reorganization The changing of the capital structure of a corporation which is in distress financially under the appropriate legislation such as the National Bankruptcy Act. The objective is to remove the cause of the failure, make a fair settlement with the creditors, and permit the corporation to stay in business.

repatriation The liquidation of foreign investments and return of the proceeds to the nation of the investor. In a broader sense, it means the return to one's own country of either persons or things.

replacement cost The cost as of a certain date of a property which can render similar service (but need not necessarily be of the same structural form) as the property to be replaced. See "reproduction cost." **29**

replacement demand The demand for goods which is attributable to similar goods being consumed, worn-out, or obsolete.

replevin The writ by which, or the action in which, personal property wrongfully taken is returned to the rightful owner. **35**

reporting pay Guaranteed payment to employees who report for work at their usual time and find no work to do.

repossession Legal procedure where seller or financer of goods on installment basis repossesses goods because of failure of purchaser to fulfill agreement. **26**

representative goods Those evidences of ownership of wealth such as notes, bonds, stocks, and money are considered to be representative goods.

representative moneys Those paper moneys which have full standard money backing or are freely redeemable in the standard such as gold or silver.

repressive taxation A tax system which tends to discourage new capital formation or production.

reproduction cost Normal cost of the exact duplication of a property as of a certain date. **5**

repudiation The intentional and willful refusal to pay a debt in whole or in part. The term usually refers to the willful act of a government or a subdivision thereof. **1**

repurchase agreement An agreement by one individual or firm to buy back, under certain terms, the thing which it originally sold to the second party of the transaction.

required reserves Those liquid assets state-chartered banks are required to maintain by the state Superintendent of Banking and which member banks are required to maintain by the Federal Reserve authorities.

requisition A written demand or request, usually from one department in a firm or organization to the purchasing officer or to another department, for specified articles or services. **29**

resale price agreement A contract between a producer and a seller whereby the seller agrees to not price the subject product below a certain minimum level.

rescind To cancel a contract or order so that both parties may be put, as far as possible, in the same position as before making the contract. **35**

research and development Applying the processes, operations, and techniques of science and technology to create products, processes, and services which may benefit an enterprise. **20**

reservation price In auctions some products are conditionally offered with a reservation price which means that the initial bid must be at least that high or the auctioneer will withdraw the item.

reserve 1) A portion of the earnings which has been set aside to take care of any possible losses in the conduct of the business or organization. **31, 36**

2) Funds which are set aside by an insurance company for the purpose of meeting obligations as they fall due. A liability set up by an insurer for a particular purpose. **51, 52**

3) A portion of a bank's funds which has been set aside for the purpose of assuring its ability to meet its liabilities to depositors in cash. Minimum reserves to be maintained against demand and time deposits are usually specified by banking law. See "legal reserve." **25**

reserve city bank A member bank of the Federal Reserve System which is located in cities designated by the Federal Reserve Act, as amended, as reserve cities. Banks are divided for reserve requirements by the Act into two classes, reserve city banks and country banks.

reserve for bad debts Same as allowance for bad debts; the amount recorded on the books that represents the estimated reduction in the value of the accounts receivable because of estimated and anticipated losses on bad debts from uncollectible accounts. **16**

reserve for depreciation Same as allowance for depreciation; the accumulated estimated decrease in the value of a fixed asset because of depreciation; the total depreciation that has been recorded for a fixed asset since the time the asset was put into service. **16**

reserve ratio The proportion of deposit liability which a bank keeps as reserves. The ratio required by member banks of the Federal Reserve System varies by type of deposit, time, or demand, and by location of bank in country or reserve city. It is in the form of deposits with the regional Federal Reserve Bank and a minor amount may be vault cash.

residence employee An employee whose duties are incidental to the ownership, maintenance, or use of personal residential premises and to the personal, rather than the business activities of his employer. **51, 52**

residuary legatee A person to whom is given the remainder of testator's personal property after all other legacies have been satisfied. **22**

resistance points Those points or areas of price fluctuation at which a security or security average comes to a resistance or stop prior to moving in a direction.

respondentia Is to cargo what bottomry is to hulls. A combination of moneylending and insurance found in early marine insurance policies.   **5**

resting order In investment trading, one which, if an order to buy, is limited to a price below the market, or which, if an order to sell, is limited to a price above the market. The order may be open or good until canceled.   **9**

restoration premium The premium charged to restore an insurance policy or bond to its original value after payment of a loss.   **50, 51**

restraint of trade Activities which interfere with the regular marketing process. Generally, the illegal restraint of trade is prohibited by the Sherman Antitrust Act.

restrictive endorsement An endorsement on a negotiable instrument which limits its negotiability.

resulting trust A trust which results in law from the acts of the parties, regardless of whether they intend to create a trust, as when a person disposes of property under circumstances which raise an inference that he does not intend that the person taking or holding the property shall have the beneficial interest in it; to be distinguished from an express trust and a constructive trust.   **22**

retail Dealing with the final consumer of goods or service involved; handling sales in small quantities and amounts.   **59**

retailer A person or firm engaged in selling merchandise for personal, household, or farm consumption, and rendering services incidental to the sale of the merchandise.   **24**

retail method of inventory Basing inventory values on retail rather than wholesale price of each item.   **38**

retained earnings That part of the net profits of a corporation which has not been paid out as dividends.

retaliatory customs duty A duty that discriminates against imports from a specific nation on the basis or reason that that nation discriminates against the first nation in some way.

retaliatory law State law imposing requirements on all alien companies equal to those imposed on domestic companies operating in alien states. See "reciprocal law."   **42**

retention policy An insurance contract in which the insured agrees to pay all losses up to a specified amount in consideration of a lower premium. This policy is legal only in certain states. Certain states permit a retention class insurance policy to be sold. Under such a policy the insured pays 50% of the usual premium. When the total loss reaches this figure, the insured then has full coverage for all losses above that figure.   **52**

retroactive restoration 1) Reinstatement of a bond or policy to its original face value after a loss has been paid, for the purposes of providing payment should prior losses be discovered at a future date.

2) Automatic restoration of the original amount of an insurance contract or bond, after payment of loss, to cover prior undiscovered as well as future losses not connected with the one previously paid.   **50, 51, 52**

retrocession Transfer of a part of an insurance risk by a first reinsurer to a second. See "reinsurance."   **42**

retrocessionaire A reinsurer that accepts a retrocession.   **51**

return See "yield."

returns to scale Refers to the rate of change of output when increasing amounts of the factors of production are used.

revaluation The revaluation or restoration of purchasing power to an inflated currency.

revenue Revenue results from the sale of goods and the rendering of services, and is measured by the charge made to customers, clients, or tenants for goods and services furnished to them. It also includes gains from the sale or exchange of assets (other than stock in trade), interest and dividends earned on investments, and other increases in the owner's equity except those arising from capital contributions and capital adjustments.   **17**

revenue expenditures Those expenditures that do not increase the value of the fixed assets but that are necessary to maintain the assets in an efficient operating condition.   **16**

revenue stamps (documentary stamps) Adhesive stamps issued by the federal or a state government, which must be purchased and affixed, in amounts provided by law, to documents or instruments representing original issues, sales, and transfers of stocks and bonds, deeds of conveyances, and certain types of foreign insurance policies.   **22**

reverse split Also called a split down; the opposite of a stock split. The number of outstanding shares of a corporation is reduced, and the market price of these remaining shares is increased. **44**

reversing entries General journal entries made at the beginning of a new fiscal period to reverse the adjusting entries that were recorded at the end of the preceding period. **16**

reversion The interest in an estate remaining in the grantor after a particular interest, less than the whole estate, has been granted by the owner to another person; to be distinguished from remainder. The reversion remains in the grantor; the remainder goes to some grantee. **22**

revocable letter of credit A letter of credit which may be canceled.

revolving fund A fund provided to carry out a cycle of operations. The amounts expended from the fund are restored thereto either from earnings from operations, or from transfers by other funds, so that the original capital of the fund is kept intact. See "imprest fund" and "working capital fund." **29**

revolving letter of credit A letter of credit issued for a specific amount which renews itself for the same amount over a given period. Usually the unused renewable portion of the credit is cumulative, so long as drafts are drawn before the expiration of the credit. **1**

Ricardian theory of rent Theory that held that differences in rent resulted from differences in the productivity of land.

rider A document or form containing special provisions that are not contained in the policy contract. Such forms are to be added or attached to the policy. **51, 52**

right-of-way The term has two significances: 1) As a privilege to pass or cross, it is an easement over another's land.
2) It is also used to describe that strip of land which railroad companies use for a roadbed, or as dedicated to public use for roadway, walk or other way. **54**

rights 1) The legal privileges, protections, and options available to all people by a government and its laws.
2) The privilege extended by an issuer to existing security holders to subscribe to new or additional securities, usually at a price below the current market and in a fixed relationship to the amount of securities owned by each holder. **40**

right-to-work law State law prohibiting union shop, closed shop, or any other union-security arrangement which requires employees to join a union as a condition of retaining employment. **12**

riparian Pertaining to, or living on, the bank of a river, a lake, or of a tidewater; specifically, the use of lands lying between the high-water mark and the low-water mark. Local legal regulations determine the extent of the riparian right of the upland owner. **54**

risk 1) That which is insured.
2) Chance of loss. **42**

risk capital 1) Venture capital.
2) That proportion of a total capitalization which is not secured by a lien or mortgage.
3) Common stock in a new enterprise.

Robinson-Patman Act Passed in 1936. Prohibits firms engaged in interstate commerce from charging different buyers different prices for the same good unless there is a difference in cost.

rollback A governmental attempt to reduce a price to some previous level either through verbal request to manufacturers or distributors to lower their profit margins, or by a subsidy or tax rebate.

rolling stock That property of a railroad that is on wheels, such as freight cars, locomotives, and other rolling equipment.

roll over The procedure of repeated investment of the proceeds of short-term securities upon maturity. **22**

rotating shift An assignment of a worker in a plant that is operating on more than one shift, in such a way that he does not continually work in one shift, but spends a relatively equal amount of time in a week or month on all the shifts.

roundabout production See "indirect production."

round lot A unit of trading or a multiple thereof. On the New York Stock Exchange, the unit of trading is generally 100 shares in stocks, and $1,000 par value in the case of bonds. **2**

round turn The offsetting sale or purchase to a previous purchase or sale, thus completing the transaction and resulting in a profit or loss.

royalty 1) Agreements by which an author, musician, or inventor receives a certain payment on each copy of his work which is sold.
2) A payment reserved by the grantor of a patent, lease of a mine, oil property, or similar right and payable proportion-

ately to the use made of the right or output by the grantee. **22**

rubricated account A term applied by bankers to any "earmarked" account. **1**

rule against perpetuities A rule of common law that makes void any estate or interest in property so limited that it will not take effect or vest within a period measured by a life or lives in being at the time of the creation of the estate plus twenty-one years. In many states, the rule has been modified by statute. In some states, it is known as the rule against remoteness of vesting. **30**

rule of reason Interpretation of a rule or law in which consideration of the reasonableness of a situation or act is taken into the basis of judgment.

run The action by a large number of people doing the same thing. A run on a bank is caused by an abnormally large number of withdrawals. A run on a product or commodity may be caused by some scare, such as war or strike.

runaway inflation A very sharp increase in the general price level. The severe inflation becomes part of an inflationary spiral in which higher prices lead to demands for higher wages, which in turn leads to higher prices.

runaway shop A plant transferred to destroy union effectiveness, and to evade bargaining duties. **12**

running costs See "direct cost," "operating cost," "prime cost," and "variable cost."

running with the land Affecting the land and the successive owners thereof; usually spoken of a covenant or an easement. **5**

S

sabotage Malicious destruction, waste, or damage of an employer's property or equipment, or the obstruction and interference with normal operations, typically during an industrial dispute or strike.

safe deposit box A metal container kept under lock and key in a section of a bank's vault for customer use. The boxes are kept in small compartments, each with a separate lock. These boxes are rented with the compartment to depositors and customers

276

for an annual rental. Each customer has an individual key to the safe deposit box that he rents. The bank also has a separate key to each box. The box cannot be opened unless both keys are used, the customer's key opening one set of tumblers, and the bank's key opening another set to release the lock.   1

afekeeping A service rendered by banks, especially banks in large metropolitan areas, where securities and valuables of all types and descriptions are protected in the vaults of the bank for the customer for a service fee.   1

alary A fixed compensation periodically paid to a person by an employer for regular work or services.

ales The amount of goods and services sold.   38

ales budget An estimate of the probable dollar sales and probable selling costs for a specified period.   13

ales charge The amount charged in connection with the issuance of shares of a mutual fund and their distribution to the public. It is added to the net asset value per share in the determination of the offering price.   14

ales forecast An estimate of dollar or unit sales for a specified future period under a proposed marketing plan or program. The forecast may be for a specified item or the entire line; it may be for a market as a whole or for any portion thereof.   24

ales management The planning, direction, and control of personal selling, including recruiting, selecting, training, equipping, assigning, routing, supervising, paying, and motivating as these tasks apply to the personal sales force.   13

ales potential The share of a market potential which a company expects to achieve.   13

ales quota A statement of the amount of sales that each salesman, supervisor, and branch manager is expected to complete during a future fiscal period.   16

ales tax A tax on sales that the seller collects from customers and pays to the state or federal government.   16

alvage 1) The recovery reducing the amount of loss. As a verb, meaning to save endangered property and to enhance the value of damaged property.
2) In marine insurance it means the cost of saving property exposed to a peril.
3) In suretyship it is that which is recovered from the principal or an indemnitor to offset in whole, or in part, the loss and

expense paid by a surety in satisfying its obligation under a bond. **50, 52**

salvage value The value attached to a fixed asset at the time it is retired from service.

sample A part or thing which is used as evidence of the quality of a whole.

sandwich lease A leasehold in which the interest of the sublessor is inserted between the fee owner and the user of the property. The owner A of a fee simple leases to B, who in turn leases to C. The interest of A may be called the leased fee; that of B the sandwich lease, and that of C the leasehold. **54**

satiety, law of See "diminishing utility."

satisfaction of judgment Legal procedure followed when debtor pays amount of judgment, together with interest and costs. "Satisfaction of judgment" is then entered on records of Court of Record. **26**

saturation point That point in the securities market when the supply of stocks begins to exceed the demand. This coincides with the peak of a market cycle. **44**

savings Money, or goods and other valuable property set aside from earnings, investments, etc., left over after the costs of living have been met. **59**

savings and loan association A financial corporation organized under state or federal statute for the primary purpose of selling shares to individuals, the proceeds of which are largely invested in home mortgages. The return to the investor is in the form of a dividend on shares, and not as interest on deposits. **34**

savings bank A corporation chartered by the state to receive savings deposits, primarily from people of moderate means. It invests those deposits for the most part in securities (bonds) and real estate mortgages. **25**

Say's law Classical economic statement that overproduction is not possible since people produce things to sell, in order that they may purchase other goods, and thus demand is created from supply.

scab A union term generally applied to a worker who refuses to join co-workers in a strike. Sometimes applied to members of a nonstriking union who pass through a striking union's picket line. **12**

scaling A technique of trading in commodities or securities by placing orders for purchase or sale at intervals of price, rather than placing the order in full at the market or at a price.

calping A speculative attempt to obtain a quick profit by purchase of a security at an initial offering price with the expectation that the issue, being oversubscribed, will then advance in price at which time the security may then be sold. In some cases, the sale will be consummated by the scalper before he is required to pay for his purchase. Thus, no capital was tied up or little capital in terms of the total transactions. Scalping is also found on commodity exchanges where the scalper buys and sells during the trading day in equal amounts, so that at the end of the trading period he has no position—either long or short.

carcity value The rate of worth of a thing which is fixed in supply.

catter diagram A graph method of determining the degree of correlation between two variables, one horizontal and the other vertical. One variable is plotted on the y-axis and the other on the x-axis. The closer the plotted points come to forming a straight line, the higher is the degree of correlation.

chedule 1) In business, a schedule refers to some systematic plan for future production or action tied to stated periods of time.
2) In economics, a schedule refers to a systematic recording of the amount, supply, rate, or other measurement of one factor which will be utilized, supplied, demanded, or otherwise developed in terms of some other factor.
3) An enumeration of various properties covered by an insurance policy. A system for computing rates.

cheduled property In insurance, the listing of a specific dollar amount against each item covered by one insurance policy.   **5**

crap The material residue left from certain manufacturing operations. The term scrap is frequently erroneously applied to spoilage. See "spoilage."   **28**

crip Any temporary document which entitles the holder or bearer to receive stock or a fractional share of stock in a corporation, cash, or some other article of value upon demand, or at some specified future date.   **1**

crip dividend A type of dividend issued by a corporation to its stockholders entitling the holder or bearer to receive cash, stock or a fractional share of stock, or one or more units of the product manufactured, upon presentation, or at a specified future date. **1**

script certificate A document representing a fractional share of stock. See "scrip dividend."

seal In law, any impression, device, sign, or mark which is recognized by judicial decision or by statute law making the instrument on which it is placed enforceable at law. **25**

sealed bid A technique for submitting an offer to buy or perform something. All interested parties are invited to submit (in a sealed envelope) their bid to buy or perform something, such as a construction of a building or other type of work. The bids are all opened at one time and the most attractive bid is accepted.

seasonal adjustment Allowance made in monthly or other periodical data for seasonal fluctuations. **19**

seasonal fluctuation The tendency for certain economic factors to increase or diminish each year in a relatively predictable way tied to seasons of the year.

seasonal risk An insured property that is only used for part of the year. A summer cottage at the shore, or a vegetable-packing plant are examples of seasonal risks. **5**

seasonal unemployment That unemployment which results from the operations of the seasons.

seasoned securities Securities with a well-recognized reputation that are generally accepted by the investing public. **40**

seat A traditional figure of speech for a membership on a securities or commodity exchange. Price and admission requirements vary. **2**

secondary boycott Refusal to deal with a neutral party in a labor dispute, usually accompanied by a demand that he bring pressure upon the employer involved in the dispute to accede to the boycotter's terms. **12**

secondary distribution Also known as a secondary offering. The redistribution of a block of stock sometime after it has been sold by the issuing company. **2**

secondary picketing The picketing by union members of an employer with whom the union has no direct relations in an effort to force that employer to stop dealing with another employer with whom the union does have a dispute.

secondary reserves Those assets of a bank that are convertible into cash on short notice by sale in the open market or by rediscount. **33**

secondary strike A strike called against one employer with a view to influencing another. See "strike." **12**

section of land One of the portions of one square mile each, or 640 acres, into which the public lands of the United States are divided; one thirty-sixth part of a township. Much of this public land has been sold to individuals, or homesteaded. **54**

secular stagnation The long-term period in which there has been little or no rate of economic growth and a relative equilibrium at substantially less than full employment.

secular trend A long-term irregular trend, as compared with a seasonal variation or business cycle movement.

secured creditor An individual or firm that has a claim on the debtor's assets in the form of definite collateral such as a real estate mortgage on the debtor's land.

secured loan Loans that are made certain of payment by the pledging of valuable property to be forfeited in case of default. **59**

securities Literally, things given, deposited, or pledged to assure the fulfillment of an obligation. In this narrow sense a mortgage is security; but the term is now generally used in a broader sense to include stocks as well as bonds, notes, and other evidences of indebtedness. **22**

Securities and Exchange Commission Established by Congress to help protect investors. The Securities and Exchange Commission (SEC) administers the Securities Act of 1933, the Securities Exchange Act of 1934, the Trust Indenture Act, the Investment Company Act, the Investment Adviser's Act, and the Public Utility Holding Company Act. **2**

security capital That proportion of a total capitalization which is relatively secured by a lien or mortgage. The rest of the capitalization consists of risk capital.

security exchange See "stock exchange."

segregated appropriation See "itemized appropriation."

seigniorage The difference between the value of bullion such as gold or silver, and the face value of the same metal when it has been coined, less the actual cost of coining.

seisin Frequently spelled seizin. Possession whether of land or chattels; the possession of a freehold estate in land by one having the title thereto. The act of delivery of the land to the new freeholder. **5**

selective selling The policy of selling only to dealers and distributors who meet the seller's requirements, such as size of orders, volume of purchases, profitability, or area, or type of operations. **13**

self-interest Greater consideration for one's own interest than for the interest of others.

self-liquidating loan A short-term commercial loan, usually supported by a lien on a given product or commodities, which is liquidated from the proceeds of the sale of the product or commodities. See "floor-plan financing." **1**

seller's market A market in which goods are scarce so that buyers compete among themselves to obtain supplies. **38**

seller's surplus That amount which is the difference between the price a seller receives and the lowest price he would accept.

selling against the box A method of protecting a paper profit. Let's say you own 100 shares of XYZ which has advanced in price, and you think the price may decline. So you sell 100 shares short, borrowing 100 shares to make delivery. You retain in your security box the 100 shares which you own. If XYZ declines, the profit on your short sale is exactly offset by the loss in the market value of the stock you own. If XYZ advances, the loss on your short sale is exactly offset by the profit in the market value of the stock you have retained. You can close out your short sale by buying 100 shares to return to the person from whom you borrowed, or you can send him the 100 shares which you own. See "hedge" and "short sale." **2**

selling group A combination of securities dealers operating under the leadership of a syndicate department of an underwriting firm, and participating in the public sale of an issue of securities. **44**

selling short See "short sale."

semiskilled labor Persons whose work requires manipulative ability of a high order, but is limited to a well-defined work routine.

senior interest A participation senior or ahead of another participation. **5**

seniority System granting preference in security, promotions, authority, and rewards to employees in accordance with their length of service. **12**

senior lien The lien which has prior claim before other liens.

senior securities Securities having a prior claim on assets and earnings; usually bonds and preferred stocks as contrasted with common stocks.   **40**

sequestered account In bookkeeping and accounting, a term used to describe an account that has been impounded under due process of law. Since disbursement of such an account is subject to court action, the account is usually set up in a separate control. See "attached account."   **1**

service business Business that does things for you, rather than sells you goods. Examples of services include the public utilities, such as telephone, transportation, etc., as well as such trades as laundry, dry cleaning, maintenance and repair work, etc.   **38**

service wholesaler A merchant middleman who sells to retailers and other merchants and/or to industrial, institutional, and commercial users but who does not sell in significant amounts to ultimate consumers.   **13**

servicing 1) The extra obligations or related functions performed by the seller of a good or service, regarding his product.

2) In connection with bonded indebtedness, the payment by the obligor of the interest and principal as they become due. In mortgage financing, the performance by the mortgagee or his agent of the many services which must be taken care of while the mortgage is held by the institution, such as searching of title, billing, collection of interest and principal payments, reinspections and reappraisals of the real property, readjustment of the terms of the mortgage contract when necessary, tax follow-up work, etc.   **34**

settlement 1) An agreement between two or more parties regarding a matter of mutual interest.

2) The winding up and distribution of an estate by an executor or an administrator; to be distinguished from the administration of an estate by a trustee or a guardian.

3) A property arrangement, as between a husband and wife, or a parent and child, frequently involving a trust.   **22**

settlement option Provides that an insurance company has the choice of settling a claim in more than one way, such as with money or the same type of property.

settlor A person who creates a trust, such as a living trust, to become operative during his lifetime; also called donor, grantor, and trustor. Compare testator. **30**

severance pay Generally a lump-sum payment made to a worker whose employment is permanently ended for causes beyond the worker's control by an employer, and which is in addition to any back wages or salary due the worker. **12**

severance tax That levy made for removing natural resources such as oil, wood, shell, coal, or minerals.

shading The act of granting a small reduction in price or terms.

shape-up Practice of having job applicants, usually in casual employment, congregate in a central location where the union, the employer, or both, select the individuals who are to work on the available jobs.

share agreements Method for reinsuring jumbo health and accident risks, to permit reinsurers to participate in as much of the business as possible in order to get a spread of risk. **42**

sharecropper See "share tenant."

shareholder Coowners of specific percentages of the whole. **59**

shares The equal interests into which the capital stock of a corporation is divided, the ownership usually being evidenced by certificates called stock certificates. **34**

share tenant (sharecropper) One who tills the soil owned by another and who receives payment for his labor, services, and effort, in form of a given stipulated share of the crop or crops he produces. **1**

sheriff's deed An instrument drawn under order of court to convey title to property sold to satisfy a judgment at law. **54**

sheriff's sale A sale of real or personal property made by a sheriff or other like ministerial officer, in obedience to an execution or other similar mandate of the court. **5**

Sherman Antitrust Act Federal legislation which declares illegal every contract, combination, or conspiracy, in restraint of normal trade.

shift differential A premium wage, sometimes based on a percentage, sometimes a flat sum, paid workers on other than the day shift to compensate them for their inconvenient working hours. **12**

shifting taxation The ability of an individual or firm which is taxed to transfer the incidence of the tax to some other person or body.

shop chairman Union steward usually chosen by the department stewards to serve as chairman over all the stewards in the plant and to deal with higher management representatives in adjusting grievances. **12**

shop steward Union man ordinarily elected to represent workers in a particular shop or department. He collects dues, solicits for new members, announces meetings, and receives, investigates, and attempts the adjustment of grievances. **12**

short In finance, one who has sold commodities or securities that he does not own at the time of the sale. He sells in expectation of buying them back at a lower price.

short covering Buying stock to return stock previously borrowed to make delivery on a short sale. **2**

short-form credit report Type of credit bureau report. Usually combining certain features of oral report and written report in abbreviated form. **26**

short hundredweight (sh cwt) 100 avoirdupois pounds. **37**

short interest The total of the short sales in a security or a commodity or on an exchange which are outstanding. Typically, short-interest figures are released by exchanges on a weekly basis.

short line In transportation, that carrier or combination of carriers having the shortest mileage via an authorized route between two points. **19**

short position Stocks sold short and not covered as of a particular date. **2**

short run 1) In manufacturing, a short, one-time job.
2) A period which will vary from situation to situation. In a business it is the time within which a company can change price or production with a given fixed plant, but not change the size of its plant or terminate operations.

short sale In investment trading, a short sale is made by instructing one's broker to sell a stock which one does not own. In order to do this, the broker borrows the shares to be sold, and the seller hopes to be able to buy them back at a lower price in order to profit. Eventually, the short seller must purchase the shares sold short in order to replace the stock borrowed. **55**

short-term debt Notes, drafts, acceptances, or other similar evidences of indebtedness payable on demand or which, by their terms, are payable within one year or less from the date of issuance. **21**

shrinkage 1) Contraction in size, volume, weight, or texture of a product caused by exposure to the elements or handling.
2) The tendency for the dollar to buy less and less all the time. This is commonly referred to as the "shrinking dollar."

sight bill of exchange Any bill of exchange that becomes due and payable when presented by the holder to the party upon whom it is drawn. See "draft." **1**

sight draft A commercial draft payable upon presentation. **16**

silent partner One who is known to the public as a member of the firm but who does not take an active part in the management of the business. **16**

silver certificates United States paper money which was in circulation until 1967. The certificates were redeemable for silver.

simple interest The interest arising from the principal sum only. **5**

single-capital-structure company Company having only one class of security outstanding. **3**

single entry An accounting system which does not use double-entry bookkeeping techniques. A Boston ledger, for example, uses the single-entry system.

single-name paper A note for which only one legal entity—the maker—is obligated to make payment at maturity. A legal distinction exists in single-name paper, in that if the obligation is incurred for one purpose, or one common interest, the paper may have more than one maker or endorser, and still be termed single-name paper. **1**

single standard Monometallism, a monetary system in which one metal, generally gold, is given free and unlimited coinage.

single tax A concept of one tax which would provide all the revenue for government.

sinking fund An accumulation of amounts set aside periodically by municipalities or corporations, which will be sufficient to satisfy a debt, such as a bond issue, at maturity. See "amortization." **22**

sinking-fund depreciation method A plan for depreciating fixed assets through the medium of establishing an actual cash fund in the hands of a trustee to be used for subsequent replacement of the assets. **28**

sit-down strike A strike in which the workers refuse to work but stay inside the employer's factory. **12**

site 1) The area on which anything is, has been, or is to be located. **38**

2) A location or plot of ground delineated for a specific purpose or function. **54**

3) Lands made suitable for building purposes by dividing into lots, laying out streets, and the like. **54**

sixty-day notice 1) The notice that, under the Taft-Hartley Act, must be given by either party to a collective bargaining agreement when desiring to reopen or terminate it. No strike or lockout may be begun during this sixty days. **12**

2) Notice required to be given to the Internal Revenue Department in those cases where the decedent's gross taxable estate exceeds or may exceed the exemption under the federal estate tax law. **22**

size of the market In the securities business, this term describes the number of round lots bid for at the highest price showing on the specialist's book, and the total number being offered for sale simultaneously at the lowest price quoted, at any specific moment. An answer to a request for the size of the market might be "4 and 2," which means that four hundred shares have been bid for at the highest price, and two hundred shares are offered at the lowest price on the book. **44**

skewness Refers to a distribution curve which is not symmetrical.

skilled labor Persons working at a craft who possess thorough and comprehensive knowledge of the process and can exercise independent judgment, usually having a high degree of manual dexterity.

slander Malicious speaking of false and defamatory words concerning another, whereby he is injured. Liability for slander is a risk of newspapers, magazines, radio, and television. **5**

sleeper An item, individual, or security which has not displayed any unusual characteristics but which is believed to be undervalued, and that increase in its value or productivity should develop in the near future.

sliding scale Wage rates automatically adjusted to changes of the selling price of the commodity. **12**

sliding-scale tariff A customs duty tied to a formula so that the duties fluctuate in some relationship to the prevailing price of the import.

slowdown A concerted and sustained refusal by working men to produce at the normal production rate. **12**

slum clearance The tearing down of old, unsafe structures. If done by private enterprise, generally for profit and better utilization of the site. If done by a governmental agency, slum clearance, generally public housing or other public purpose, is the reason.

small business There are many different definitions depending upon the source of the term. The Small Business Administration, the Census Bureau, the National Industrial Conference Board, the Investment Bankers' Association and others have defined the term with somewhat different characteristics. Some definitions permit as many as 500 employees to work for a small business. Others use sales of less than 200,000 dollars a year. Others use relative size in an industry. Still others consider public financing and corporations that are not closed to indicate a business that is not small. For exact meaning, one must know the source using the term and even the time since the Small Business Administration has modified its original definition.

smuggle Taking goods or persons into or out of a nation without obtaining permission to do so, or without payment of duties, or purchasing travel tickets from the carrier.

socialism The political and economic system in which the government owns and operates production facilities.

Social Security Act Federal legislation providing social insurance on a national scale. **5**

social security tax A general term used to refer to any tax imposed under the terms of the Social Security Act; a tax assessed against certain workers and their employers under the terms of the Social Security Act. **16**

soft money Has three different meanings—the context will indicate which one to use. A situation in which interest rates are low and loans are easy to arrange. A paper rather than metallic currency. A nation's currency which is not desired by foreigners in lieu of a "hard" currency which may be domestic or other foreign currency.

Soil Bank A governmental attempt to help solve the problem of oversupply of agricultural commodities by paying the farmer-owner to plant trees or grasses in place of crops.

soldiering A slowdown and deliberate attempt to not produce or work at a normal level or rate.

sole proprietorship Ownership by one person of an entire business. **35**

solidarism A political-economic system in which the government provides many social goods such as public housing, insurance, and medical services for low-income groups. The funds for such activities are to be provided by the wealthy in the form of high inheritance taxes and sharply progressive taxation.

solvent Condition in which assets exceed liabilities. Condition in which debtor is able to pay his debts as they mature.

special agent Individual representing his company in an exclusive territory. He supervises certain agents of the company and the operations of his company.

special assessment A tax levied against certain real estate owners to pay for public improvements that are assumed to specifically benefit their property. **5**

special-assessment bond Bonds payable from the proceeds of special assessments. **29**

special deposit A fund established for the payment of interest, dividends, or other debts, or to insure the performance of contracts, and other deposits of a special nature as distinguished from sinking funds. **19**

special depositary A bank authorized by the United States Treasury to receive as deposits the proceeds of sales of government bonds.

special endorsement A negotiable instrument made out to the order of John Jones, for example, would have a special endorsement if he endorsed it with the words "Pay to the order of Frank Brown" and then signed it "John Jones." This is an unqualified endorsement which limits the negotiability to Frank Brown or his order.

special-interest account A term used by some commercial banks to apply to a deposit of savings (time deposit) when the state law restricts the use of the term savings account to exclusively savings institutions. **25**

special issues Securities issued by the Treasury for investment of reserves of government trust funds and for certain payments to veterans. **7**

specialist A member of a stock exchange who assumes two responsibilities: First, to maintain an orderly market, insofar as reasonably practicable, in the stocks in which he is registered as a specialist. In order to maintain an orderly market, the specialist must be prepared to buy or sell for his own account, to a reasonable degree, when there is a temporary disparity between supply and demand. Second, the specialist acts as a broker's broker. When a commission broker on the exchange floor receives a limit order, say, to buy at $50 a stock then selling at $60—he cannot wait at the particular post where the stock is traded until the price reaches the specified level. So he leaves the order with the specialist, who will try to execute it in the market if and when the stock declines to the specified price. At all times the specialist must put his customers' interests above his own. There are about 350 specialists on the New York Stock Exchange. **2**

specialist's book Also called simply, the book. It is composed of orders that have come to the specialist in a security on the stock-exchange floor at prices limited to other than the prevailing market price. The orders are kept in a book, to be executed at such time as the market price reaches their limitations. A specialist will have a book on each security in which he specializes, standing ready to accept orders from brokers who are unable to execute them. **44**

specialization of labor See "division of labor."

specialized capital goods Those capital goods which have use in limited roles of production. The term is one of degree. Some tools are more specialized than others. Some buildings are more specialized in their use than others.

specialized management trust An investment company whose investment policy is confined to securities of businesses found in one industry such as oils, electronics, or aircraft.

special-privilege monopoly That monopoly which results from a governmental policy favoring a specific company.

special stock That stock which is issued for a special, and probably not recurring, purpose.

specialty goods Those consumers' goods on which a significant group of buyers characteristically insist and for which they are willing to make a special purchasing effort. These goods do not have a general consumer-appeal. **13**

specialty shop A retail store that makes its appeal on the basis of a restricted class of shopping goods. **13**

specification A detailed description of a thing, specifically about any work to be done, building, etc. **38**

specific duty That customs levy based upon certain physical characteristics of goods subject to the duty.

specific legacy A gift, by will, of a specific article of personal property, such as a watch. **30**

speed-up A system designed to increase worker productivity. **12**

spending unit A family, a group of individuals, or, in some cases, an individual that spends as a unit. Income generally is pooled, meals eaten together, and the property is considered for their joint use, and is possessed by the unit.

spendthrift trust A trust in which the interest of a beneficiary cannot be assigned or disposed of by him, or attached, or otherwise reached by his creditors. **30**

spin-off Division of a corporate business into two or more companies by the original corporation transferring certain of the properties to another corporation formed for that purpose, and then distributing the new corporation's stock to the original corporation's stockholders in proportion to their holdings. See "split-off" and "split-up."

split The division of the outstanding shares of a corporation into a larger number of shares. **2**

split-off Division of a corporate business into two or more companies by the original corporation transferring certain of the corporate properties to another corporation formed for that purpose. The original stockholders turn in part of their old stock in exchange for the new stock. See "spin-off" and "split-up."

split opening That situation on a commodity or security exchange in which a security or a commodity has simultaneous opening prices which are spread, or different. This can occur when a number of traders at a trading post break up into groups and the sales take place in two groups at the same time but at different prices.

split order An order to buy or to sell a given commodity or security which, because of the large size of the transaction, might cause a material price fluctuation, is "split" or executed in smaller units over a period of time.

split shift A term for a regular daily work period which is divided into two or more parts, rather than being continuous.

split-up 1) Division of a corporate business into two or more companies by the original corporation transferring all of the property to two or more new corporations formed for that purpose, and then exchanging the old stock of the original corporation for the stock of the new corporations. In most cases the original corporation would then go out of business. 2) Split-up also may be used to refer to the division of the number of existing shares into a larger number, such as a two-for-one stock split. See "spin-off" and "split-off."

spoilage Production which does not meet dimensional or quality standards. Rejects. See "scrap."   **28**

spot In commodity trading and foreign exchange, this term indicates ready delivery as compared with some future time.

spot price The selling price of the physical commodity.

spread 1) The difference between the bid and asked price.
2) The use of both a put and a call on a specific security.
3) The purchase of one futures contract and the simultaneous sale of the same commodity, but in a different month, with both the sale and purchase remaining open until one of the contracts matures.

squatter's right The right at common law created by the occupancy of land for long and undisturbed use, but without legal title.   **54**

stabilization Action by government, labor, or business to reduce fluctuations.

stabilization fund Fund established in 1934, as a result of the devaluation of the dollar, with two billion dollars to stabilize exchange values of the United States dollar, to deal in such things as foreign exchange and gold, and to invest in direct obligations of the United States Government. Under the Bretton Woods Agreement much of the assets of the fund were used to contribute to the International Bank for Reconstruction and Development and the International Monetary Fund. See "World Bank."

stabilized dollar Plan proposed by Fisher of Yale to provide constant purchasing power for the dollar by making it into a commodity standard by means of changing the weight of the gold content of the dollar, in order to compensate for the changing prices.

stable money Money which does not fluctuate much in purchasing power. One of the goals of the Federal Reserve authorities is to maintain a stable level of prices.

staggered election An election of a board of directors in which only part of the board stands for election in any one year.

stagnation Condition of an economy, business, industry, security, or commodity in which activity and volume has dropped substantially from previous levels.

stagnation thesis Keynesian economic concept that mature economies tend to drop in their rate of growth of production for several reasons such as oversaving, decline in population rate of growth, or loss of geographic frontiers.

stale check One that has been held an unreasonably long time after issue before being presented for payment to the bank on which it is drawn. **25**

stamp tax A tax on legal documents, certificates, and papers which requires that revenue stamps be affixed to the documents to indicate that payment of the tax has been made.

Standard and Poor's Corporation A leading organization in the field of financial service which provides corporate information such as dividend, stock and bond reports as well as other pertinent records. **44**

Standard and Poor's 500-Stock Price Index A popular gauge of stock market movements as computed by Standard & Poor's Corporation from the price action of 425 leading industrial issues, 25 railroads, and 50 utilities. The average market prices of these stocks during 1941–43 are used as the base period, and the Index shows the relationship with today's average prices. **44**

standard bullion Bullion which is composed of the same proportions of metals and the same degree of purity as the standard gold and silver coins, and thus is ready for coinage without further refining.

standard cost A predetermined cost of product expected to be attained during the period to which it applies, based upon average efficiency in use of materials, average of expected prices for the period, and normal hours of operation over the period. Used as the basis for judging efficiency and for determining net profit. **19**

standard-cost system A method of operating cost accounts whereby quantity variations and price variations from standard costs of production are recorded for each element by periods. **19**

standardization The determination of basic limits or grades in the form of specifications to which manufactured goods must conform, and classes into which the products of agriculture and the extractive industries may be sorted. **13**

standard money Primary money. A monetary unit which is made of the standard such as gold. A coin which is worth as much as its face value—if used as a commodity or medium of exchange.

standard of living Those luxuries and necessities which an individual or class of people generally possess or use.

standstill agreement That agreement between a debtor and his creditor or creditors under which new conditions of a loan or loans are reached. In most cases this will involve a postponement of payments, and may also include a reduction in the principal due. Such agreements are the result of adverse economic developments in which the debtor obviously cannot meet the terms of the loan, and the creditor or creditors recognize that it is to their and the debtor's best interest to accept terms which have some probability of being met rather than possessing a claim of a debtor in default.

state bank A corporation organized under the general banking law of a state and authorized to do a commercial banking business—that is, receive deposits subject to check, and make loans. It usually performs a variety of other functions as well. In a broader sense, a state bank is any bank chartered by the state. **25**

stated value The value given to a corporation's stock and carried on the books if there is no assigned par value. **44**

statement 1) An account; a list of bills due, sent periodically to customers.

2) A report sent, usually monthly, to a depositor in a bank or a debtor of a business firm. **38**

statement of condition A financial picture of an association or business which shows the amount and character of its assets, liabilities, and reserves as of a certain date; also known as the balance sheet. **31, 36**

state-use system A technique for using prison labor for the production of things which will not interfere with the private business in the state.

static economy An economy which is at equilibrium. That is, the forces of supply and demand which are equated by price are such that little change in production or demand is created.

statism A situation in which the central government acquires increasing power in the economy by controls, planning, and nationalization.

statute A law established by the act of the legislature. **5**

statute of frauds A statute, first enacted in England in 1677, designed to prevent many fraudulent practices by requiring proof of a specific kind, usually in writing, of the important transactions of business, declaring that no action shall be brought or that no contract shall be allowed to be good when the transaction is not so evidenced. **22**

statute of limitations The periods fixed by statute within which suits must be brought if legal redress is to be obtained. At the expiration of these periods, suits are forever barred. Periods vary in the several states and within a state according to the rights to be enforced. **25**

statutes of wills Statutes (the first one passed in 1541) providing that no will shall be valid, and no devise or bequest shall be valid, unless the will is in writing, signed and attested in the manner provided by the statute. **30**

sterilized gold A technique for preventing newly imported gold from expanding the credit base of a nation. One method of gold sterilization is to have the Treasury of the United States pay for the gold with a draft on a commercial bank in which it has an account, rather than drawing upon the Federal Reserve System and then issuing gold certificates. This reduces the multiple expansion potential, and sterilizes or prevents normal inflation which would usually result.

sterling That which has a standard of fineness or value such as established by the government of Great Britain for silver or gold or bank notes.

sterling area Those nations since 1939 which have been closely tied to the British pound and the monetary policies of the British Empire.

sterling bloc See "sterling area."

steward Union employee in plant or department who represents other employees in handling grievances, and who sees that terms specified in the contract are complied with. Also called committeeman.

stock Supply of goods and merchandise in store for sale. Shares of ownership in a corporation which pay dividends, or share in the profits. **38**

stock-bonus trust A trust established by a corporation to enable its employees to receive benefits in the form of the corporation's stock as a reward for meritorious service, seniority, or as a means of sharing in the profits of the enterprise. **30**

stockbroker An individual or firm engaged in the business of buying and selling securities for others.

stock certificate The printed evidence of a stockholder's ownership in a corporation. **16**

stock dividend This is a dividend which consists of additional shares, rather than a money dividend.

stock exchange An association of brokers and dealers engaged in the business of buying and selling securities. The place where such brokers and dealers meet to do their trading. **25**

stock insurance company Association of persons formed for the purpose of issuing insurance coverage on the lives of others. **42**

stock-option contract A negotiable instrument, also called a "paper" or "privilege," which gives the purchaser the right to buy (call) or sell (put) the number of shares of stock designated in the contract at a fixed price within a stated period of time. **44**

stockpile A quantity of essential products originally obtained to meet inventory requirements.

stock rights See "rights" and "warrant."

stock split The division of shares of stock of a corporation among its present stockholders which goes to increase the number of outstanding shares, but does not increase the capitalization of the company. **22**

stock-transfer tax The federal and/or state tax on sale or transfer and, in some cases, loan of stock.

stock warrants See "rights" and "warrant."

stock watering The act of issuing stock in exchange for overvalued assets. In effect, this dilutes the equity of those owners who were issued stock for properly valued assets.

stop-limit order In investment trading, a form of a stop order from a client to his stockbroker, by which a specific price limit is set. Any price below this will not be accepted if it is a sell order, or any price above this will not be accepted if this is a buy order. **44**

stop-loss order or **stop order** An order issued by a client to his stockbroker entered to buy or sell specific securities when the market reaches a specified point.

stop-payment order An order issued by a depositor to his bank instructing it to refuse payment of the check or checks specified in the order. **25**

stop price In investment trading, that price where a client's stop order to his broker becomes a market order.

store credit Credit granted by merchants to consumers for the purchase of goods.

stores requisition A special form showing an itemized list of raw materials to be withdrawn from the storeroom for use in the factory. **16**

straddle 1) The simultaneous purchase of options to buy and sell a specific security.

2) The exercising of both a put and a call in the same security.

3) In commodities, the simultaneous sale of one futures month with the purchase of the same commodity in a different month.

straight bill of lading A bill of lading which states a specific person to whom the goods should be delivered and which is not negotiable.

straight letter of credit An irrevocable letter of credit which has been confirmed. See "letter of credit."

straight-line method A method of accounting for depreciation which spreads the depreciation charges uniformly over the estimated service life of the property. **19**

straight-term mortgage loan A mortgage loan granted for a fixed term of years, the entire loan becoming due at the end of that time. **33**

strategic materials See "critical materials."

street broker An over-the-counter broker as distinguished from a broker who is a member of an exchange.

street certificate A security or stock certificate which has been made out to a broker, and which the broker has endorsed, so that it is negotiable and thus may be transferred to others.

stretch-out 1) Actions by workers to try to extend the period of their employment by taking longer than is customary to do a job.

2) An increase in the work load of an employee by an employer without any added payment.

strike A concerted and sustained refusal by workingmen to perform some or all of the services for which they were hired.   **12**

strikebreakers Workers hired during a strike primarily for the purpose of defeating the strike.   **12**

strike suit A legal action brought mostly for nuisance value. See "ex gratia payment."   **5**

strike vote A vote conducted among employees in the bargaining unit on the question of whether they should go out on strike.   **12**

striking price In investment trading, the fixed price at which a stock may be bought in a call contract, or sold in a put contract.   **44**

stringency The condition in the money market characterized by difficulty in obtaining credit and increasing rates of interest.

struck-work clause Collective bargaining agreement clause which permits employees to work on materials coming from a strike-bound plant.   **12**

subject bid A bid which is not firm, but rather exploratory, in the expectation that it may induce an offer which will permit negotiation.

subjective value The value which an individual may place upon goods for his own purposes, which may differ from their general or usual value.   **33**

subject offer An offer which is not firm but rather exploratory, in the expectation that it may induce a bid which will permit additional negotiation on price.

subpoena A writ or order commanding by law the person named in it to appear and testify in a legal proceeding.   **38**

subrogation The substitution of one person in the place of another with reference to a lawful claim or right.   **33**

subscriber One who agrees in writing to purchase certain securities offerings such as a certain number of shares of designated stock of a given corporation, or a certain number of bonds of a given stipulated (par) value.   **1**

subscription The offer to purchase a certain offering, as a certain number of shares of stipulated stock or bonds, for a stipulated amount of money. Such offer is not binding unless accepted by

298

the proper authorized representatives of the issuing firm or corporation. See "subscriber." **1**

subscription price The offering price at which new or additional security issues of a corporation may be purchased. **44**

subscription rights A privilege to the stockholders of a corporation to purchase proportionate amounts of a new issue of securities, at an established price, usually below the current market price; also, the negotiable certificate evidencing such privilege. **21**

subsidiary account One of a group of related accounts which support in detail the debit and credit summaries recorded in a controlling account. **29**

subsidiary coins Any coin with the denomination of less than one dollar, including minor coins such as nickels or cents.

subsidiary company A company which is under the control of another company. Generally this is accomplished by the ownership of sufficient shares of the subsidiary to direct policy.

subsidiary ledger A separate ledger containing detailed information that is summarized in a controlling account in the general ledger. **16**

subsidy A grant of money from a government or other organization to a person or industrial plan considered beneficial to the public.

subsistence That amount of the necessities of life just adequate to keep one alive.

subsistence law of wages See "brazen law of wages."

substitution, law of Economic concept that if one product or service may be readily exchanged or substituted for another the prices of the two must be relatively close.

subvention A grant. **29**

succession The act or fact of a person's becoming entitled to property of a deceased person, whether by operation of law upon his dying intestate, or by taking under his will. **22**

succession tax 1) A tax upon the transmission of property by a deceased person, in which case it will be charged upon the whole estate, regardless of the manner in which it is to be distributed, in which case it is called a probate or estate tax. 2) The more common form of a tax on the privilege of taking property by will or by inheritance or by succession in any other form upon the death of the owner, and in such case it is imposed upon each legacy or distributive share of the estate as it is received. **22**

sue-and-labor clause Provision of marine policy that requires the insured to attempt salvage. The insurance company pays not only the claim but also the salvage expenses. **5**

summarizing entry An entry in journal form that is written below the footings in a columnar journal to show that the debits and the credits are equal. **16**

summons A written order commanding a defendant to appear in court and answer to the charge of the plaintiff. **35**

sum-of-the-digits depreciation method A plan for depreciating fixed assets based on the theory that the greatest depreciation should be taken during the early life of the asset, and the least depreciation taken during the final years. The annual charge is determined by adding together the number of years of remaining life and using this figure as the denominator of a fraction. For example, 10 years, 1 to 10 added together equals 55. The numerator is represented by the remaining life— $10/55 — 9/55 — 8/55$, etc. This plan is purely theoretical and seldom encountered. **28**

sumptuary laws Those laws designed to stop or reduce the consumption of socially harmful products.

sunk costs A fixed expense that probably cannot be recovered without total liquidation. A building, well, road, foundation, special jigs or dies all represent sunk costs.

superette Retail store somewhat smaller than a supermarket providing most of the same basic functions.

supermarket Large retail store typically having at least such departments as meat, produce, dairy, and grocery, operating on a cash-and-carry technique.

superseniority Seniority superior to, and not based upon, length of service; often granted to union officers. **12**

supersession A form of economic obsolescence, sometimes called the element of inadequacy, resulting from an inadequate improvement to land. **5**

supplementary costs Those fixed, indirect, or overhead expenses of a business activity which do not vary with the volume of activity.

supply and demand, law of The theory that the price of a product fluctuates in the same direction as demand and in the opposite direction of the supply.

support the market In investment trading, the entering of buy orders at or slightly below the prevailing market level to support and stabilize the existing prices and promote a rise in prices if possible. **44**

surcharge (noun) An amount which the fiduciary is required by court decree to make good because of negligence or other failure of duty. The term is also used as a verb, as, the court surcharged the trustee. **22**

surety One who promises to answer for a debt or obligation to a third person on behalf of a second person. **35**

suretyship All forms of obligations to pay the debt or default of another. The function of being a surety. **50, 51**

surplus 1) Supply of a commodity above requirements. **9** 2) The accumulated profits of past periods left invested in a business. In a bank it represents the amount paid in by the stockholders in addition to their capital stock subscriptions when the bank is organized and amounts (not available for dividends) added to capital from earnings. **25**

surplus reserve A reserve representing the segregation of surplus for specified purposes. An example is a reserve for inventories. **29**

surrender charge Small fee charged upon discontinuance of an insurance policy within the first years. Net values are shown in policies and rate manual. **42**

surrender value (cash surrender value) A term used in insurance designating the progressive increase in the percentage of, or the amount of the total life insurance in force that will be paid to the policyholder when he elects to surrender his policy and receive such proportionate part. The cash surrender value of a policy is the amount frequently used to determine the amount of money that will be loaned against the policy. **1**

surrogate A probate judge.

surtax An extra tax on something already taxed. **38**

suspend trading In investment trading, an action which can be taken if there is evidence that an orderly market may be threatened because of some unusual event. Might be invoked if there is a sudden influx of buy or sell orders, and continued so long as necessary. **44**

suspense account A bookkeeping account which carries charges or credits temporarily, pending the determination of the proper account or accounts to which they are to be posted.   **29**

sweating 1) To reduce the metallic content of gold coins so that the coin can later be used and the gold dust can be recovered. 2) To employ people in a sweatshop.

sweatshop A factory which has poor physical working conditions such as inadequate lighting, lack of sanitation, unsafe machinery, and bad ventilation.

sweetheart contract Term of derision for an agreement negotiated by an employer and a union granting concessions to the employer or the union, the usual purpose being to keep a rival union out.   **12**

swing time Time employee lunches, or is unemployed, during his tour of duty.   **39**

symmetallism 1) A monetary system in which the paper currency is redeemable in two or more metals which are paid in a fixed and proportionate combination.
2) A standard coin which is a combination of two or more precious metals.

sympathetic strike Concerted work stoppage by employees of Employer A to express sympathy for striking employees of Employer B, and to exert indirect pressure on B.   **12**

syndicalism An economic system in which the workers of each industry exert control over it.

syndicate A combination of people or firms formed to carry out some project requiring large resources of capital.   **38**

T

tabular standard of value A theoretical monetary standard in which a price index of representative commodities would be used. A unit of value would be represented by a given quantity of each of the component commodities.

tacit collusion Conspiracy without evidence except from the results. In cases of oligopoly when one buyer or seller takes an action such as changing a bid or asked price and the same action is promptly taken by another in a consistent pattern, courts of law may hold that tacit collusion exists.

Taft-Hartley Act Federal statute which amends the National

Labor Relations Act to regulate some union activities, authorizes damage suits for collective bargaining violations and certain strikes and boycotts, and sets up procedures for trying to settle "national emergency strikes." **12**

take-home pay The amount of wages or salary left to the worker after taxes, any insurance, and other deductions have been taken out. **59**

talon That portion of a debt instrument which remains on an unmatured bond after the interest coupons which were attached have been presented. The talon is then exchanged for a new certificate with coupons.

tangible property Property which can be touched or realized with the senses, such as a chair; opposed to intangible property, such as an insurance policy. **22**

tap line A short railroad line usually owned or controlled by the industries which it serves and "tapping" (connecting with) a trunk line.

tare weight As applied to a carload, weight of the car exclusive of its contents.

tariff 1) Duties imposed on exports and imports. **38**
2) A published schedule showing the rates, fares, charges, classification of freight, rules and regulations applying to the various kinds of transportation and incidental services. **19**

tariff for revenue A tariff not designed for protection of domestic manufacturers but to obtain taxes for the government.

tariff union See "customs union."

tax 1) To assess or determine judicially the amount of levy for the support of certain government functions for public purposes.
2) A charge or burden, usually pecuniary, laid upon persons or property for public purposes.
3) A forced contribution of wealth to meet the public needs of a government. **54**

tax abatement Amount of tax abated; deduction; decrease rebate, especially of a tax or burden improperly laid. The act of abating such tax or burden. **54**

taxable estate The gross estate of a citizen or resident less allowable administrative expenses, indebtedness, taxes, losses, transfers for public, charitable, and religious uses, transfers to a surviving spouse, and the specific exemption of $60,000. **7**

tax anticipation notes Notes (sometimes called "warrants") issued in anticipation of collection of taxes, usually retirable only from tax collections, and frequently only from the proceeds of the tax levy whose collection they anticipate. 29

tax assessment The placing of a value on real or personal property for tax purposes.

tax avoidance The use of legal means to minimize one's taxes.

tax base The thing or right upon which the computation of a tax is determined.

tax collector That elected or appointed government official who is responsible for the collection of those taxes within his area of responsibility. In addition, certain administrative functions are also performed.

tax commission That elected or appointed group on a local, state, or national level charged with administration of specific types of taxes.

Tax Court of the United States Special federal court which deals only with internal revenue cases.

tax deed A deed issued by a public authority as a result of a tax sale of the property. 5

tax dodge Any legal or illegal attempt to avoid taxes.

tax evasion The use of illegal means to reduce one's taxes.

tax exemption The excuse or freedom and immunity from tax, or a portion of a tax.

tax farming Practice whereby a government sells its tax claims to a private collector.

tax foreclosure Seizure of property, because of unpaid taxes, by the duly authorized officials of the public authority empowered to tax. 5

tax limit The maximum rate or amount of general property tax which a local government may levy. 29

taxpayer 1) One who pays taxes.
2) A building erected for the primary purpose of producing revenues to meet the taxes on the land. When the land has ripened, the taxpayer is demolished and a more substantial structure put up in its place. Thus the building and property with the "taxpayer" is producing some return, generally enough to pay the taxes. 54

tax rate The amount of tax stated in terms of a unit of the tax base; for example, 25 mills per dollar of assessed valuation. 29

tax roll The official list showing the amount of taxes levied against each taxpayer or property. **29**

tax sale The sale of property, sometimes at auction, for nonpayment of taxes. **38**

tax selling The practice of effecting securities that will realize a capital gain or loss which is desired as an offset to the losses or gains realized in the same tax period. The purpose of this practice is to minimize the tax impact of the seller's capital transactions during a tax period. **40**

tax sharing That condition in which more than one governmental level or division divide tax receipts among themselves.

tax title The title by which one holds lands purchased at a tax sale. **54**

Taylor differential piece-rate system An incentive plan for paying direct labor based on a modified piece-rate plan. The worker is paid at one rate for each piece produced up to a standard production per hour, and at a higher rate on each piece if he exceeds his standard. Due to wage-and-hour legislation, a minimum guarantee is generally associated with this plan. See "direct labor" and "piece-rate plan." **28**

technical position A term applied to the various internal factors affecting the market, opposed to external forces such as earnings, dividends, political considerations and general economic conditions. Some internal factors considered in appraising the market's technical position include the size of the short interest, whether the market has had a sustained advance or decline without interruption, a sharp advance or decline on small volume, and the amount of credit in use in the market. See "overbought" and "oversold." **2**

technician Also called a chartist because his analysis of a particular security or market is based primarily upon the technical, or chart-formation, aspect of the changes taking place. **44**

technocracy The political proposal for the establishment of a social and economic system in which technology, rather than the price system would determine production. This would keep productive capacity operating at capacity and everyone would enjoy a higher standard of living. The proposal during the mid-1930's had some support from people who considered the price mechanism had failed.

technological unemployment Job loss caused by changes in production methods or the installation of labor-saving devices. **12**

technology The application of sciences, especially to engineering, administration, and production, in the use of machines to increase productivity.

teller A bank representative who, in one capacity or another, transacts over-the-counter business with customers. **25**

teller's check A check drawn by a bank on another (drawee) bank and signed by a teller or tellers of the drawer bank. Teller's checks are used in payment of withdrawal orders and, in lieu of savings bank money orders, are sometimes sold to depositors in exchange for cash. **34**

temporary admission See "admission temporaire."

temporary national economic committee investigation Study by a Congressional committee with particular reference to monopoly power in the United States. **5**

tenancy The holding of real property by any form of title. **22**

tenancy at will A tenancy in which the tenant holds the property at the will or pleasure of the grantor. **30**

tenancy by the entirety Tenancy by a husband and wife in such a manner that, except in concert with the other, neither husband nor wife has a disposable interest in the property during the lifetime of the other. Upon the death of either, the property goes to the survivor. To be distinguished from joint tenancy and tenancy in common. **22**

tenancy for years A tenancy for a definite period of time—for example, a year or ninety-nine years. It cannot be terminated by either party alone, except at the expiration of the time agreed upon. **30**

tenancy in common The holding of property by two or more persons in such a manner that each has an undivided interest which, upon his death, passes as such to his heirs or devisees and not to the survivor or survivors; the same as an estate in common; to be distinguished from joint tenancy and tenancy by the entirety. **30**

tenant One who holds or possesses real estate by any kind of title, either in fee, for life, for years, or at will. In a more limited and popular sense, a tenant is one who has the temporary use of real estate which belongs to another. **5**

tender The unconditional offer of payment by a debtor to the creditor of the amount owed.

terminal wage That amount paid to an employee upon his dismissal.

term issue A bond issue that matures as a whole in a single future year. See "bond, serial."   **40**

term loan A loan scheduled to run for more than one year and usually repayable in annual or more frequent payments. Term loan should be differentiated from term issue and serial issue.   **40**

terms of trade Those discounts from the list price which may be taken if payment is made within a stated period, such as ten days from the date of delivery.

testament Under the early English law, a term that referred to the disposition of personal property by will. The words "and testament" are no longer necessary since a will now relates to both real and personal property.   **22**

testamentary capacity Mental capacity to make a valid will. **22**

testamentary disposition The disposition of property by deed, will, or otherwise in such a manner that it shall not take effect unless or until the grantor dies.   **22**

testamentary trust A trust established by the terms of a will.   **30**

testate Having made and left a valid will; opposed to intestate.   **30**

testator A deceased person who left a will setting forth the disposition of his wealth (total assets).   **1**

thin market A market in which there are comparatively few bids to buy, or offers to sell, or both. The phrase may apply to a single security or to the entire stock market.   **2**

third market Trading in the over-the-counter market of securities listed on an exchange.   **45**

through bill of lading That type of bill of lading which is used in the event that more than one carrier will be handling a shipment so that processing of documents is minimized at the intermediate connecting stations. See "bill of lading."

ticker The instrument which prints prices and volume of security transactions in cities and towns throughout the United States within minutes after each trade on the floor.   **2**

tickler Any record or file established to serve as a reminder of action to be taken on a fixed future date. It is always arranged in the order of dates on which such action is to be taken. **22**

tied-in sale A sale that is conditioned upon the purchaser also purchasing a specific item to qualify for purchasing a different item.

tied loan A loan in which the granting of the loan is conditioned (tied) to the borrower using the proceeds for a very specific purchase from a named supplier.

tight credit That condition in an economy in which credit accommodations are difficult to obtain and in which interest rates tend to increase.

tight money See "tight credit."

till money Money set aside for use by a teller at his window as distinguished from money in the vault, on deposit in other banks, etc.   1

time-and-motion study Analysis of the motions and measurements of the time an average worker needs to perform a given job.

time bill A bill of exchange that has a fixed or determinable date of payment as contrasted with a sight or demand bill.

time deposit A deposit from which the customer has the right to withdraw funds at a specified date thirty or more days after the date of deposit, or from which, if the bank so requires, the customer may withdraw funds only by giving the bank written notice thirty days or more in advance of the contemplated withdrawal.   33

time draft A draft that is payable at a fixed or determinable future time.   25

time loan A loan that is payable at some specified future date.   25

time-off plan System under which an employee who works overtime in some week of the pay period is given a sufficient number of hours off during some other week in the same pay period to offset the overtime week so that the usual wage for the pay period covers the total pay, including overtime, due the worker for each separate work week.   12

time series Data of measurement of something, in which time is the independent variable.

time utility That value added to a good or service by time. Many products, especially agricultural products, by being stored, gain time utility.

timework Work where wages are based on the time it takes to do the job rather than by the piece.   12

title The right to ownership of property. Evidence or proof of ownership. **33**

token coins Those coins which have a commodity value less than their face value. Coins which if smelted down and sold for metal would not sell as metal for as much as the amount at which they circulate as money.

tolerance That fractional allowance of variation from a given standard.

toll As used today, it is a charge for the use of some facility of a fairly public nature such as a toll bridge, a toll road, or a toll tunnel. Many years ago the term was applied to a rent paid at a market or fair.

tonnage The contents of a vessel or ship in which 100 cubic feet is computed as one registered ton. The tax on a vessel, computed on its cubic contents, is also called tonnage.

tontine A reverse form of life insurance that did not pay on any deaths of the insured until they lived through the tontine period. The few that were then alive thus shared the very high benefit. In Europe it had various applications as a gambling device. In the United States the tontine insurance was a modification of the original, and the insurance company put a stated amount of gross receipts of premiums into a special tontine fund to be paid only to those living at the end of the stated period. This type of insurance is not available now and was disapproved by the Armstrong Investigation. **5**

top out The gradual leveling off of market prices after an extended upward climb. Also may refer to a temporary peak in the market or in a particular stock which is unlikely to be surpassed in the near future. **44**

Torrens certificate A certificate issued by a public official, known as a registrar of titles, establishing an indefeasible title in an indicated owner. **33**

Torrens Registration System of registration of land title as opposed to registration or recording of evidence of such title. The originator of the system was Sir Richard Torrens, 1814–1884, reformer of Australian Land Laws. **22**

tort A wrong arising independently of a contract; a private wrong as distinguished from a crime. **35**

total and permanent disability Complete inability to work with little prospect of improvement or recovery. **42**

total loss The complete destroying or ruining of a property. A claim of sufficient size to require settlement of the maximum amount of insurance on the covered property.   5

total reserves Member bank deposits with Federal Reserve Banks plus member bank vault cash. The sum required and excess reserves.   56

total utility A theoretical total of the sum of all the utility, time, place, quantity, possession, etc., which a quantity of a good would have considering the diminishing utility of a quantity of goods.

Totten trust Trust created by deposit of one's own money in his own name as trustee for another. Title is vested in the record owner (trustee), who during his life holds it on a revocable trust for the named beneficiary. At the death of the depositor a presumption arises that an absolute trust was created as to the balance on hand at the death of the depositor.   22

trade The buying, selling, or exchanging of commodities either by wholesale or by retail, within a country or between countries.   38

trade acceptance A written promise drawn by the seller of merchandise at the time of sale and signed by the purchaser.   16

trade agreement See "labor agreement."

trade association Businesses in the same line of work promoting their common interest.   38

trade barriers Those restrictions or regulations which tend to reduce the freedom of movement of products and services from one area to another.

trade channel The path of distribution of goods from producer to consumer.

trade cycle British expression for business cycle. See "business cycle."

trade deficit An adverse balance of trade. A passive trade balance.

trade discount The deduction from the list price.   16

trade gap The difference between the larger amount of imports of merchandise and the lesser amount of exports of merchandise in a given period.

trade-in The part of a sale represented by trading an old product for a new product, as contrasted to the part of the sale completed by payment of money.   59

trademark Symbol identifying a business or product.   38

trade monopoly See "monopoly."

trade name The name by which a product is known in commercial circles.   **38**

trader One who buys and sells. In investment trading, one who transacts for his own account for short-term profit.   **2**

trade union Generally the members of such a union are limited to a specific occupation or trade. See "labor union."

trading area 1) A district whose boundaries are usually determined by the economical buying or selling range for a commodity or group of related commodities from a center of distribution.

2) The "pit" or "floor" of a stock or commodity exchange.   **13**

trading limit In most North American commodity contract markets there is a maximum price change permitted for a single session. These limits vary in the different commodity markets. After prices have advanced or declined to the permissible daily limits, trading automatically ceases unless, of course, offers appear at the permissible upper-trading limit, or, on the other hand, bids appear at the permissible lower limit.   **9**

trading post One of eighteen horseshoe-shaped trading locations on the floor of the New York Stock Exchange at which stocks assigned to that location are bought and sold. About 75 stocks are traded at each post.   **2**

trading stamps A sales-promotion device in which the purchaser is given stamps in some relationship to his purchases at no additional cost to the retail price. When enough stamps have been acquired, generally in the form of books, they may be exchanged for merchandise listed in the catalog of the organization sponsoring the trading stamps.

train-mile The movement of a train the distance of one mile.   **19**

transactions tax A turnover or sales tax.

transfer The passage of property or rights, with title, from one person to another.   **38**

transfer agent A bank, a trust company, or an individual appointed by a corporation to see that all the requirements are met in connection with the transfer of its stock.   **25**

transfer books Ledgers required to be kept by the county auditor, showing all transfers of real estate within the county. **5**

transfer in contemplation of death A transfer of property by gift made in apprehension of death arising from some existing

311

bodily condition or impending peril, and not the general expectation of eventual decease commonly entertained by all persons. **22**

transfer payments Payments to individuals by government and business for which no goods or services are currently rendered. **7**

transfer tax A tax imposed upon the transfer of ownership of stocks and bonds, usually paid by affixing, and canceling, stamps to the certificates or other documents evidencing the transfer of ownership. **22**

transit items Cash items which are payable outside the town or city of the bank receiving them for credit to customers' accounts. **25**

transit number A key to the name and location of a drawee bank under the national numerical system. **25**

transit rate A transportation rate restricted in its application to traffic which has been or will be milled, stored, or otherwise specially treated in transit. **19**

transplacement (or **slide**) An error caused by moving all the digits of an amount to the right or the left without changing the order of the digits. **16**

Transportation Act of 1920 Approved February 28, 1920. Provided for the termination of federal control, enacted provisions relating to the settlement of disputes between carriers and their employees, and made important amendments to the Interstate Commerce Act. **19**

Transportation Act of 1940 Approved September 18, 1940. Provides for declaration of a national transportation policy, regulation of water carriers in interstate and foreign commerce, establishment of a board of investigation and research to investigate the various modes of transportation, government to pay full rates on certain traffic, and various amendments to the Interstate Commerce Act. **19**

transposition An error caused by the interchanging of digits in an amount, such as writing "61" instead of "16." **16**

trap car A railroad car used within terminal limits for assembling and distributing, as a carload, less than carload shipments to or from private sidings of industries. Sometimes referred to as a ferry car. The meaning varies with railways and regions. **19**

traveler's checks Special checks supplied by banks and other companies at small cost for the use of travelers. **25**

traveler's letter of credit A letter addressed by a bank to its correspondent banks either in the same country or in foreign countries, authorizing the person named in the letter to draw drafts on the correspondent banks to the extent of the credit specified. The person in whose favor the letter of credit is issued deposits with the issuing bank a sum of money equal to the total amount of the credit plus the bank's charges for this service. **25**

treasurer's check See "cashier's check."

treasury bills Noncoupon obligations; sold at discount through competitive bidding; generally having original maturities of three months, and one year. **49**

treasury certificates of indebtedness Obligations which usually mature in 9 to 12 months from date of issue. **4**

treasury notes Coupon obligations having original maturities of from one to five years. **49**

treasury stock Stock that has been issued and that is later reacquired by the corporation. **11**

trend 1) The general course or prevailing tendency of something.
2) In economics, the direction prices or other indicators are taking.

trial balance The proof of the equality of the debits and the credits in the ledger. **16**

triangular trade Trade between three nations in which a rough balance exists. However, balance does not exist between any two in a direct sense, without the trade between them and the third nation.

true interest See "pure interest" and "net interest."

trunk line A transportation line operating over an extensive territory. **19**

trust An arrangement by which an individual or a corporation as trustee holds the title to property for the benefit of one or more persons, usually under the terms of a will or a written agreement. **25**

trust administrator A person in the employment of a trust institution who handles trust accounts in the sense of having direct contacts and dealings with trust customers and beneficiaries. **22**

trust company A corporation, one of whose stated objectives is to engage in trust business. **22**

trust deed A written agreement, under seal, conveying property (usually real but sometimes personal property) from the owner to a trustee for the accomplishment of the objectives set forth in the agreement. **33**

trustee One to whom property is legally committed in trust. **3**

trustee in bankruptcy A qualified person elected by the creditors to take charge of the property of the bankrupt. **35**

trusteeship The status of bankrupt property which has been taken over.

trust fund Technically, only money held in trust; but frequently applied to all the property held in trust in a given account. **22**

trust indenture An instrument in writing which contains a description of all property originally placed in the trust, the agreement as to the rights of the trustee in administering the property, the rights of all beneficiaries named, along with their proportionate share in the trust, the duration of the trusteeship, the distribution of income from the trust principal to the life-tenants, and the distribution of the trust property of the remaindermen at the termination of the trust. **1**

trust inter vivos See "voluntary trust" and "living trust."

trustor A person who creates a trust; a broad term which includes both settlor and testator. **30**

trust receipt A formal receipt issued by a trustee for property held in trust; used in certain commercial transactions. **30**

trust under will A trust created by a valid will, to become operative only on the death of the testator; the same as a testamentary trust and opposed to a living trust. **30**

turn The completed transaction of a purchase and sale of a commodity or a security. It may be a long purchase followed by a sale, or a short sale followed by a long purchase. The last transaction completes the "turn."

turnover 1) The volume of business in a security or the entire market. **2**

2) Number of employees who are separated from the payroll. **12**

3) The ratio obtained by dividing sales for a period such as a month or year by some related figure such as accounts receivables, capital, or inventory. To be clearly understood the term

314

"turnover" should in addition have reference to the time and item which has turned over.

turnover tax See "sales tax."

twisting Practice of inducing any insurance policyholder to lapse or cancel a policy for the purpose of replacing such policy with another to the detriment of the policyholder. The practice is considered to be unethical as well as illegal.　**50**

two-dollar broker Members on the floor of the New York Stock Exchange who execute orders for other brokers having more business at that time than they can handle themselves, or for firms who do not have their Exchange member-partner on the floor. The term derives from the time when these members received $2 per hundred shares for executing such orders. The fee is paid by the broker, and today it varies with the price of the stock. See "commission broker."　**2**

two-name paper Notes on which two persons are liable for payment.　**25**

two-year rule National Labor Relations Board rule holding the first two years of a collective bargaining agreement to be a reasonable period during which rival claims to representation will not be considered.　**12**

tying contract Any contract which forbids the buyer or the lessee to transact business with competitors of the supplier.

U

ultimate consumer One who buys and/or uses goods or services to satisfy personal or household wants rather than for resale or use in business, institutional, or industrial operations.　**13**

ultra vires An act beyond the powers legally granted a corporation.　**5**

unclassified stores Material purchased for special or unusual reasons and which will probably not be reordered.　**28**

uncollected cash items Checks in the process of collection for which payment has not yet been received from the banks on which the checks are drawn.　**4**

unconfirmed letter of credit A letter of credit in which the issuing bank has processed all the necessary documents and advised the financial institution upon which the letter is drawn, but the institution has not confirmed, acknowledged, and accepted the advice of the letter. See "letter of credit."

underdeveloped country A state or nation which has the potential for greater productivity but which has a real per capita income below the average of Western nations.

underemployment equilibrium A condition in which the price and production level is steady in an economy but substantial numbers of the labor force are not gainfully employed.

underlying mortgage A mortgage which has priority over some other mortgage.

under the rule When a member of an exchange does not complete delivery of a security in terms of the rules of the exchange, the security is purchased by an official of the exchange who makes the delivery under the rule.

underwriter 1) In insurance, the individual whose duty it is to determine the acceptability of insurance risks. A person whose duty it is to select risks for insurance and to determine in what amounts, and on what terms, the insurance company will accept the risks. **51, 52**

2) One who arranges for the distribution and sale of a large block of securities and who assumes responsibility for paying the net purchase price to the seller at a predetermined price. In most instances, the underwriter deals in a new issue and with the issuing company. **40**

underwriting profit That portion of the earnings of an insurance company that comes from the function of underwriting. It is found by deducting incurred losses and expenses from earned premiums. It excludes the earnings from investments either in the form of income from securities or sale of securities at a profit. **51**

undistributed profits See "earned surplus."

undistributed-profits tax A federal tax levied on companies with large amounts of undistributed profits for which there is no valid business reason.

undue influence The influence which one person exerts over another person to the point where the latter is prevented from exercising his own free will. **22**

unearned discount Interest collected but not yet earned. **25**

unearned income See "deferred credits."

unearned increment The increase in the value of property that can be attributed to changing social or economic conditions beyond the control of the titleholder as distinguished from that increase in value that can be attributed to the improvements made or additions added by the efforts of the titleholder. 1

unearned premium In insurance, that part of the original insurance premium paid in advance and not yet earned by the insurance company, and therefore due the policyholder if the policy should be canceled. **50, 52**

unearned premium reserve The fund set aside by an insurance company to provide for the payment of unearned premiums on canceled policies. **51, 52**

uneconomic Any production or service which has higher costs than the values produced.

unencumbered An asset owned which is free from all claims made by, or granted to, another. 1

unencumbered property Property that is free and clear of assessments, liens, easements, claims, and exceptions of all kinds. See "encumbrance." 38

unfair labor practices Those employer or union activities that are classed as unfair by federal or state labor relations acts. 12

unfair trade practices Those actions by a business or industry designed to increase the profits which violate a high code of ethics. These would include such actions as bribing a competitor's employees, short weight, false product description, misleading advertising, etc.

unfavorable balance of payments A condition in which the monetary value of exports of goods and services is less than the monetary value of imports of goods and services for a stated period of time. These services would include such things as earnings on foreign investments, insurance, and shipping fees. The portion or difference in the balance is generally made up by export of gold or the acquisition of claims against the country by foreigners.

unfavorable balance of trade A condition in which the monetary value of exports of merchandise is less than the monetary value of imports of merchandise for a stated period of time.

unfunded debt Debt which is short-term and not represented by formal securities such as bonds. See "floating debt."

unilateral agreement An obligation which is binding on only one party to the agreement.

317

unilinear tariff See "general tariff."

union Formal organization of workers formed primarily for the purpose of dealing collectively with their employer on matters pertaining to their employment.

union certification The recognition by an authorized governmental agency that a particular union has complied with the legal provisions to be considered as the rightful bargaining agent for employees of a firm.

union label Recognized imprint on a product indicating the item was made under union conditions. **12**

union registration Filing by unions with the Secretary of Labor of the descriptions of their internal organization and procedures, the copies of their constitutions and bylaws, and the annual financial reports required by the Taft-Hartley Act as a first step before unions may pursue their rights under that statute. **12**

union security clause Provision in union contract that fixes the position of the union in the plant and its relation to the workers and their jobs. **12**

union shop Form of union security under which an employer may hire nonunion workers who must, however, become members after they are employed as a condition of retaining their employee status. **12**

unissued stock That portion of the authorized capital stock of a corporation which is not outstanding or issued.

unit bank A single independent bank which conducts all its operations at one office. **25**

unit cost A term used in cost accounting to denote the cost of producing a unit of product or rendering a unit of service. **29**

universe The total from which a sample is taken.

unlimited mortgage A mortgage with an open-end. This permits the borrower to finance under a single mortgage rather than being forced to issue several. While the mortgage has an open-end, it generally has certain restrictions such as the ratio of debt instruments to the total value of the assets securing the debt.

unlisted securities The opposite of listed securities. See "listed securities" and "over-the-counter." **40**

unlisted trading privileges On some exchanges a stock may be traded at the request of a member without any prior application being made by the company itself. The company has no agreement to conform with standards of the exchange. Companies admitted to unlisted trading privileges prior to enactment of the Securities Exchange Act of 1934 are not subject to the rules and regulations under that Act. Today, admission of a stock to unlisted trading privileges requires the Securities and Exchange Commission's approval of an application filed by the exchange. The information in the application must be made available by the exchange to the public. No unlisted stocks are traded on the New York Stock Exchange.   2

unload The sale of securities or commodities in expectation of a price decline.

unparted bullion Bullion which contains base metals in addition to the precious metal.

unproductive consumption The process of consumption by individuals who are not productive. The ill, the institutionalized, and those in prisons, in most cases, are examples of unproductive consumption.

unqualified certificate An auditor's certificate which contains no qualifications or exceptions.   29

unrealized profits The existence of paper profits which have not yet been made actual.   44

unregistered exchanges Those small-volume stock exchanges which have been exempted from complying with the registration requirements of the Securities and Exchange Commission.

unsatisfied judgment funds A fund created by state law in several states. Reimbursement is made to persons having claims arising out of automobile accidents who have been unable to collect from the party responsible for the accident because the party is not insured or is financially not in a position to pay.   5

unsecured creditor A general creditor such as the tradesman who sold the merchandise to the debtor on open-book account. His claim is subordinate to the claim of a creditor who has priority because of such features as a mortgage or other security.

unsecured loan A loan made by a bank, based upon credit information on the borrower and his integrity, to repay his obligations. The loan is not secured by collateral, but is made on the signature of the borrower.   1

unvalued stock Stock which has no par or stated value. The term is a misnomer since it must have value to be bought and sold, but the unvalued reference is to the value which the issuer of the stock carries it on the books. The trend in recent years is away from unvalued or no-par stock because it is generally taxed as if it had a value of $100 par.

usance 1) That period of time, which varies from country to country, in which foreign bills may be presented for payment. It does not include the days of grace.

2) An income from wealth. Interest which money earns.

3) Employment.

use tax That tax, imposed in several states for the purpose of putting on the same tax basis products which are bought in another state to avoid the first state's sales tax.

use value That value determined on the basis of the amount paid for the actual use of a property as compared with the holding of a property out of use.   **5**

usury Lending money over the legal rate of interest.   **38**

utility For business usage see "public utility." In an economic sense, it is that quality of anything which will satisfy a human want.

utility or other-enterprise fund A fund established to finance the construction, operation, and maintenance of municipally owned utilities, such as gas, water, and light plants, transportation facilities, and other self-supporting enterprises such as airports and housing projects.   **29**

utility theory of value The oversimplified explanation of value which directly relates value to the utility of goods and services.

utilization factor The ratio of an average electric-power load (kilowatts) over a designated period of time to the net capability in the same period of time. This ratio represents the average use made of the net capability of equipment over a specific period of time.   **21**

V

valorization The action of some influential body such as a governmental agency which arbitrarily sets a price on a good or service. The price may be, but probably is not, a price which the free workings of the market would determine.

valuation Appraised or estimated worth. **42**

value 1) Value in use . . . The worth of any economic wealth, product, service, etc., to one possessing it. Many things not for sale have great value in use, which may at times be described roughly in dollar terms.

2) Value in exchange . . . The worth of anything in the marketplace—"Price" represents value as agreed to in an actual sale. **59**

value added The selling price of produced goods less the cost of the raw material used in production.

value date In accounting and bookkeeping for banks, the date on which an entry made on an account is considered effective. The value date has no relation to the entry date, since it is based on the collection or payment of items which may be received from a depositor, or sent to a depository bank. Its use is generally associated with foreign accounts maintained with, or by, a bank. **1**

valued policy An insurance policy which provides that a special amount shall be paid in event of a total loss of the property. **50, 52**

valued-policy law State law requiring an insurance company to pay the total face amount of a policy in the event that the insured has a total loss. **5**

variable cost That prime cost which fluctuates with the level of production. See "direct cost."

variable proportions, law of See "proportionality, law of."

variety store A retail store that handles a wide assortment of goods usually of a low or limited price. **13**

velocity of circulation The rate at which money and those substitutes such as checks are transferred from one holder to the next.

vendee The person who purchases, or agrees to purchase, an item of property or service. **22**

vendor (vender) The person who sells, or agrees to sell, an item of property or service. **22**

vendor's lien An equitable lien which a vendor of property or services has thereon for the unpaid purchase money. **5**

venture capital See "risk capital."

venue The place or county where a suit is brought. **35**

vertical expansion 1) The establishment of facilities to permit a firm to expand its business from the basic raw material, through processing and manufacturing and distribution to the sale to ultimate consumer. Vertical expansion may start at any level of activity, be it production or distribution. The main feature is that control is maintained by one firm at all the levels. Naturally, there are degrees of less than full vertical expansion.
2) The consolidation of companies involved in similar product areas.

vertical integration Ownership or control of the various levels of production and distribution for a class of merchandise generally from raw material to the ultimate consumer.

vertical union A union which represents workers of different skills and occupations but with a common industry.

vested Placed firmly in the possession of a person or persons; fixed.   **38**

vested interest An immediate, fixed interest in real or personal property although the right of possession and enjoyment may be postponed until some future date, or until the happening of some event; to be distinguished from a contingent interest.   **22**

vested remainder A fixed interest in real property, with the right of possession and enjoyment postponed until the termination of the prior estate; to be distinguished from a contingent remainder.   **22**

vice-consul The United States Foreign Service officer, under the Consul, located in a foreign nation who represents the American tourists, businessmen, and the traveling nationals of the United States.

vice propre An inherent characteristic that may cause loss of value. See "inherent vice."   **51**

visible items of trade Those exports and imports of recorded goods, but not including the invisible items of insurance and shipping, paid by or to foreigners.

vis major An act of God. An accident for which no one is responsible.   **5**

vital statistics Generally, those statistics pertaining to deaths, births, population, and similar areas.

voidable contract A valid contract that may be rescinded by one

322

of the parties due to such grounds as fraud, duress, insanity, incompetency, or minority.   **5**

voluntary bankruptcy That state of insolvency of an individual, corporation, or other legal entity in which the debtor has petitioned a competent court and been judged insolvent and has had his property assigned for the benefit of his creditors.

voluntary plan A type of accumulation plan for investment on a regular basis but without any total-time period or ultimate investment amount specified. The sales charge is applicable individually to each purchase made.   **14**

voluntary trust A trust created by the voluntary act of the settlor and not conditioned upon his death; the same as a living trust; to be distinguished from a trust under will or testamentary trust.   **30**

voting stock Stock in a corporation in which the holders are entitled to vote for the directors.   **44**

voting trust A device whereby the owner of shares turns over the control of the stock to a trustee who exchanges a voting trust certificate for the stock. The certificate gives the holder all the rights he previously had as to dividends and equity, but transfers the right to vote to the trustee for a stated period of time. At the end of that time the trust may be dissolved and the shares reexchanged for the trust certificates or the trust may be renewed.

voucher A document which evidences the propriety of transactions and usually indicates the accounts in which they are to be recorded.   **29**

voucher check A check that contains on its face a brief summary of the voucher to show the purpose for which the check is issued.   **16**

voucher register A special book of original entry in which all the vouchers of a business using the voucher system are recorded.   **16**

voucher system A system which calls for the preparation of vouchers for all transactions involving payments, and for the recording of such vouchers in a special book of original entry known as a voucher register in the order in which payment is approved.   **29**

W

wage Payment for services rendered, especially the pay for workers by hour, day, week, or month.

wage and salary stabilization Statutorily backed program for holding wages and salaries as closely as possible to existing levels as an anti-inflation measure. Also referred to as wage and price control.   **12**

wage differentials Different rates of pay for the same general type of work, the variations resulting from differences in conditions under which the work is done, differences in performance standards, and differences in the types of workers.   **12**

wage dividend That additional payment to employees beyond their regular wages which represents a sharing with the stockholders of a corporation of the earnings of the business.

wage fund theory A theory that wages could not be increased unless the number of workers employed decreased, or that there was an increase in the amount of capital investment.

wage leadership The stimulus given the wage pattern in an area or industry by a wage settlement by an important employer.

wage plan Any system by which a worker's compensation is determined.

wage-price spiral A situation in a period of inflation in which the granting of higher wages is followed by the manufacturer increasing his prices, which in turn leads to increases in the cost of living, followed by escalator-clause increases in wages and demands from nonescalator-clause workers for higher wages. The spiral lasts as long as a sellers' market lasts but tapers off when a buyers' market returns.

Wages and Hours Act See "Fair Labor Standards Act."

Wagner Act Federal statute, originally known as the Wagner Act and now a part of the Taft-Hartley Act, which guarantees to employees in industries affecting interstate commerce the right to self-organization, to bargain collectively, and to engage in concerted activities.   **12**

waiver The voluntary relinquishment of a right, privilege, or advantage. The document by which the relinquishment is evidenced.   **22**

waiver of premium A provision that under certain conditions an insurance policy will be kept in full force by the insurance company without the payment of premiums. It is used most often as a total and permanent disability benefit and may be available in certain other cases. **53**

walking delegate An officer of a local union who handles the local union's affairs.

walkout A workers' strike against an employer or employers.

Wall Street The geographic area of the financial district of New York City which includes most of the major banks, insurance companies, exchanges, and other financial institutions located not only on Wall Street but also in the surrounding area.

Walsh-Healey Public Contracts Act Federal statute fixing wage, hour, and working conditions for most federal supply contracts in excess of $10,000. **12**

war clause A clause in an insurance contract relieving the insurer of liability, or reducing its liability, for loss caused by war. **51**

ward A person who by reason of minority, mental incompetence, or other incapacity is under the protection of the court either directly or through a guardian, committee, curator, conservator, or tutor. **22**

war economy The changes in an economy from peacetime practices to a sharp increase in governmental intervention in the form of controls, rationing, and production for the war effort rather than the peacetime production of consumer goods.

warehouse certificate See "warehouse receipt."

warehouse loans Loans, generally made by a bank on the collateral of warehouse receipts, which are evidence of material which is stored in a public warehouse.

warehouse receipt A receipt for goods stored in a warehouse and an agreement between the warehouseman and the person storing the goods. By its terms the warehouseman promises to keep the goods safely and to redeliver them upon the surrender of the receipt, properly indorsed, and payment of the storage charges. The receipt is also evidence that the owner or holder has title to the stored goods. **25**

warrant 1) Warrants are evidences of indebtedness incurred by legal entities, and which will be duly redeemed for cash or check when presented to the drawee of the warrant. **1**
2) An option to buy a specified number of shares of the issuing company's stock at a specified price. The warrant may be valid for a limited period of time only, or it may be valid

permanently.   **3**

3) An official paper, ordered by the proper government official, giving authority to arrest.

4) To guarantee; authorize; justify.

warranty A pledge that a certain matter is true; statements of a seller that goods sold are of a certain quality; a legal guarantee.   **35**

In insurance, assertions or undertakings on the part of the insured to the strict and literal truth of all statements made.   **42**

warranty deed A deed conveying real property containing the usual covenants of warranty of title.   **22**

wash sale An illegal security manipulation where a security is bought and sold by the same interest to give the impression of market activity and price rise. This may be done by using different brokers and instructing one to buy and the other to sell at the same time.

waste 1) Material which is lost in a manufacturing process or which has no appreciable recovery value.   **28**

2) Spoil or destruction of real property done or permitted by the tenant in possession to the prejudice of the heir or owner of the remainder or reversion.   **22**

wasting trust A trust composed of property which is gradually being consumed.   **22**

watered stock When the actual value of the assets behind the stock is less than its par value.   **38**

water rights A property consisting of the rights to a water supply.   **54**

waybill A record prepared at the point of shipment showing the origin, destination, consignee and consignor for a shipment.   **38**

Webb-Pomerene Act Law which permits insurance combinations for purposes of foreign trade that would not be permitted in domestic trade.   **5**

weighted average inventory plan A method of inventory valuation whereby the unit cost is arrived at by dividing the total cost of the inventory by the number of units. This "weights" the unit cost toward the cost of those units which make up a larger portion of the inventory.

welfare economics Those economic policies and actions taken by any governmental agency which have as their primary goal improvement of social conditions.

welfare state A condition in which welfare economics has become dominant and, as a result, many areas of free enterprise have disappeared.

Wheeler-Lea Act Amendment to the Federal Trade Commission Act. Passed in 1938, it makes unfair trade practices and deceptive advertising illegal.

when issued In investment trading, a short form of "when, as and if issued." The term indicates a conditional transaction in a security authorized for issuance but not as yet actually issued. All "when issued" transactions are on an "if" basis, to be settled if and when the actual security is issued and the exchange or National Association of Securities Dealers rules the transactions are to be settled.   **2**

white-collar workers Workers in office and clerical jobs as distinguished from production workers and maintenance workers.

whole coverage Any form of insurance which provides for payment of all losses without any deductions.   **5**

wholesale price index A measure of the average change in the prices of 2,000 commodities at the primary market level (usually the level at which the commodity is first sold commercially in substantial volume).   **7**

wholesaler A merchant middleman who sells to retailers and other merchants and/or to industrial, institutional, and commercial users but who does not sell in significant amounts to ultimate consumers.   **13**

widow and orphan's risk A designation for a class of securities in which the investor is supposed to not be able to assume any important risk because of lack of business background and need for security. See "businessman's risk."

wildcat banking The period after 1836 under President Jackson in which many small banks were formed generally for the purpose of issuing bank notes which the wildcat banks tried not to redeem.

wildcat strike A strike called without the consent of the organized union, or in violation of a bargaining agreement "no strike" clause.   **12**

windfall profit An unexpected and unusually high profit.

wire house A member firm of the Stock Exchange with branch offices linked together by a communications network.   **2**

wire transfer An order to pay or to credit money transmitted by telegraph or cable. **25**

withdrawal Taking back, removing, getting out of. **38**

with exchange A designation on a check or draft of "payable with exchange" or "with exchange" indicates that any collection or exchange charges will be against the payer in the event it is a check, or the drawee in the event it is a draft.

withholding tax Making a deduction at the source of income for part of the wage earner's income-tax liability. **38**

without prejudice Part of an insurance policy nonwaiver agreement that holds that the insured who signs the agreement cannot legally construe certain actions, such as the determination of the value of a claim by the insurance company to be an admission of liability on their part. **5**

without recourse Words used in endorsing a note or bill to denote that the future holder is not to look to the endorser in case of nonpayment. **5**

working capital That portion of the capital of a business enterprise which is not invested in fixed assets but is kept liquid to care for day-to-day working needs. In an accounting sense, the excess of current assets over current liabilities. **34**

working-capital fund A fund established to finance activities, usually of a manufacturing or service nature, such as shops and garages, asphalt plants, and central purchases and stores departments. Sometimes called a revolving fund. **29**

working control Theoretically, ownership of 51 percent of a company's voting stock is necessary to exercise control. In practice—and this is particularly true in case of a large corporation—effective control sometimes can be exerted through ownership, individually or by a group acting in concert, of less than 50 percent. **2**

work-in-process inventory The asset value of the incompleted products which are in various stages of manufacture. **28**

Workmen's Compensation State laws under which workers or their relatives receive compensation for work-incurred illness, injury, or fatality.

work relief That type of employment which has as its immediate goal the provision of income to the workers, and the economic stimulation which such payments will have on a depressed economy. While projects may be completed such as roads, reforestation, and other public work projects, these are less directly of importance than the income-spending generated.

work-sharing Plan by which available work is distributed as evenly as possible among all workers when production slackens, or by which working time is generally reduced to prevent layoffs. **12**

work sheet In accounting, a working trial balance that includes columns for adjustments and for an adjusted trial balance. **16**

work unit The parts into which a job or operation is subdivided for cost accounting and other purposes. See "cost unit." **29**

World Bank Formerly the International Bank for Reconstruction and Development. Formed in 1945 for the purposes of helping finance the reconstruction of productive facilities destroyed during World War II and the development of member nations. It does not compete with regular commercial banks since the loans it makes are to governments, or to business firms which have the backing of their government, by the endorsement of their loan contract. The World Bank also will participate with commercial banks in making loans.

world-wide coverage An insurance policy clause in some policies that provides coverage in any place in the world. Jewelry, fur, personal effects, and personal property floaters may have this clause. **50**

writ An order of a court commanding that the will of the court be obeyed. **35**

write-down The reduction in the quotation of a thing or a ledger account to bring the present quotation in line with current values.

write-off An instrument or receivable account which has been determined to be uncollectable, since there are no known visible assets available with which the obligor can liquidate the obligation. Write-offs are charged as losses to either the surplus or the undivided profits account. **1**

write-up The increase in the quotation of a thing or of a ledger account to bring the present quotation in line with current values.

X

X-mark signature When a person is unable to sign his name because of illiteracy or injury, provision may be made for him to "sign" with an X. In these cases, his name is inserted by another, and the notation "his mark" is put next to the "X" and then witnessed by a person who, in addition, signs the instrument with the notation that he witnessed the "X."

Y

yardstick A schedule of fees, rates, or costs which may be used as a measurement of relationship by the one comparing his own performance with the yardstick.

yellow-dog contracts Agreements signed by workers as a condition of employment by which they promise not to join or remain in a union. The National Labor Relations Act, the Norris-LaGuardia Act, and the Railway Labor Act all prohibit them.   **12**

yield The annual rate of return from a security, expressed as a percentage of the amount invested.   **22**

yield test Measurement applied to bond investments. It is the relationship of the yield of bonds the holder has in his portfolio individually to the yield of fully taxable United States Government bonds of the same maturity. Yields of such corporate bonds of over 1½ percent higher than the United States Government bonds require that they be valued at market price rather than amortized value.   **5**

yield to maturity That rate of return expressed in a percentage that will be obtained on an investment if the investment is held to maturity. It takes into consideration that few investments are bought exactly at par, and thus have a capital gain or loss in addition to the rate of return stated on the face of the instrument.   **5**

York Antwerp Rules Body of regulations used by major maritime countries providing the procedure for settling a loss which involves a number of different interests; such as the owners of a ship, the owners of a cargo, the owners of related freight interests. A set of rules for the adjustment of general average loss. **51**

Z

zollverein German for customs union. See "customs union."

zone pricing Technique of charging all purchasers of material who are located within a stated geographical district the same delivered price for equal quantities of the material.

zoning The process of establishing by legislation certain restrictions upon the use to which property may be put. **33**

NUMERICAL LIST
OF
AUTHORITIES

The author gives special thanks to the following authorities or sources who have given permission to quote from their works.

1 National Cash Register Company, The (*Bank Terminology*)
2 New York Stock Exchange (*The Language of Investing—A Glossary*)
3 Wiesenberger & Company, Arthur (*Investment Companies*)
4 Federal Reserve Bank
5 Chamber of Commerce of the United States—Insurance Department
6 United States Department of Labor
7 Tax Foundation, Inc. (*Facts and Figures*)
8 Federal Reserve Bank of New York
9 Association of Commodity Commission Merchants, The
10 Clarke County Planning Commission
11 National Board of Fire Underwriters, The (*National Building Code*)
12 Commerce Clearing House, Inc. (*Labor Law Course, Copyrighted*)
13 American Marketing Association (*Report on Definitions*)
14 National Association of Investment Companies (*Glossary of Investment Company Terms*)
15 Society of Residential Appraisers (*Real Estate Appraisal Principles and Terminology*)
16 South Western Publishing Company (*Dictionary of Bookkeeping and Accounting Terminology*)
17 American Institute of Certified Public Accountants (*Terminology Bulletins*)
18 American Arbitration Association (*Labor Arbitration Procedures and Techniques*)
19 Association of American Railroads
20 Association of Consulting Management Engineers, Inc. (*Common Body of Knowledge Required by Management Consultants*)

21 Edison Electric Institute (*Glossary of Electric Terms, Financial and Technical*)
22 American Bankers Association, The (*Glossary of Fiduciary Terms*)
23 Burroughs Corporation—Marketing Division
24 United States Department of Commerce
25 American Institute of Banking
26 National Retail Credit Association (*Definition of Terms Used in Retail Credit and Collection Operations*)
27 Commerce Clearing House, Inc. (*Federal Tax Course, Copyrighted*)
28 National Cash Register Company, The (*Industrial Accounting Terminology, Copyrighted*)
29 Municipal Finance Officers Association (*Municipal Accounting Terminology*)
30 American Institute of Banking
31 American Savings and Loan Institute (*Handbook of Savings and Loans*)
32 Municipal Finance Officers Association (*Public Employee Retirement Terminology*)
33 American Institute of Banking
34 American Institute of Banking
35 Associated Credit Bureaus of America, Inc.
36 American Savings and Loan Institute
37 United States Department of Commerce—National Bureau of Standards
38 Cities Service Company—Business Research and Education Department
39 United States Post Office Department—Bureau of Operations (*Postal Terms Glossary*)
40 American Institute of Banking
41 United States Bureau of the Budget
42 Mutual of Omaha (*Glossary of Insurance Terms*)
43 Health Insurance Institute (*Source Book of Health Insurance Data*)
44 Cowan, Ron
45 New York Stock Exchange
46 Federal Reserve Bank of Philadelphia
47 Federal Reserve Bank of New York
48 Wall Street Journal
49 Federal Reserve Bank of Cleveland

50 Hartford Fire Insurance Company (*Glossary of Insurance Terms*)
51 Chamber of Commerce of the United States
52 Employers Mutual Liability Insurance Company of Wisconsin (*Dictionary of Insurance Terms*)
53 Institute of Life Insurance (*Life Insurance Fact Book*)
54 National Institute of Real Estate Brokers (*Real Estate Salesman's Handbook*)
55 Pacific Coast Stock Exchange (*Let's Look at Stocks and Bonds*)
56 Federal Reserve Bank of St. Louis
57 Lyons & Carnahan, Educational Publishers (*Burgess, Business Law*)
58 Macmillan Company, The (Mehr and Olson, *Modern Life Insurance, Copyrighted*)
59 National Foundation for Consumer Credit, Inc. (*Using Our Credit Intelligently*)
60 Small Business Administration
61 Dun & Bradstreet, Inc.
62 National Institute of Real Estate Brokers (*Exchange Systems and Procedures*)
63 Federal Communications Commission
64 Hogan, Ph.D., Ralph M.